Introduction to Argentina

*Para mi estimado amigo el Señor Don
Alexander ... ldell, Embajador
de los Estados ... idos de América.

Mayo de 1938.*

DOCTOR ROBERTO MARCELINO ORTIZ

Introduction to

ARGENTINA

BY

ALEXANDER WILBOURNE WEDDELL

Ambassador to Argentina

1933 to 1939

THE GREYSTONE PRESS

NEW YORK

Printed in the United States of America
THE WILLIAM BYRD PRESS, INC.
RICHMOND, VIRGINIA

To

The President of the
Argentine Republic

Doctor Roberto Marcelino Ortiz

APRIL 23, 1938.

MY DEAR FRIEND:

I take great pleasure in replying to your kind letter of the 19th instant.

I am deeply grateful that you intend to dedicate your book to me and I accept, as an honor, because I am convinced that you will produce a substantial and accurate work which will contribute to the greater reciprocal knowledge of our countries.

It will serve, also, to confirm the widespread feeling that you are the American Ambassador who has been closest to us, always a cordial friend, intelligent and comprehending, lending valuable collaboration in the maintenance of the ties between the two countries.

With cordial greetings from your friend,

R. M. ORTIZ.

The Honorable
    Alexander W. Weddell,
        Ambassador Extraordinary and Plenipotentiary
        of the United States of America.

(*Translation*)

La República Argentina ama la paz y el trabajo y, en el concierto de las naciones americanas, ha mantenido siempre una tradición de fraternidad continental, porque entiende que la unión definitiva de los nuevos países convertirá en una hermosa realidad el acercamiento de las sociedades, por influencia de su gravitación o de su espíritu.

(The Argentine Republic loves Peace and Labor, and, in the concert of American nations, it has always maintained a tradition of continental fraternity because it believes that the definitive union of the new countries will convert into a beautiful reality the drawing together of communities, through the power of their influence or of their spirit.)

From President Ortiz' Message of Greeting

to

The People of the United States

March 21, 1938

PAX

"Paz a la inmensa América. Paz en nombre de Dios.
Y pues aquí está el foco de una cultura nueva,
que sus principios lleve desde el Norte hasta el Sur,
hagamos la Unión viva que el nuevo triunfo lleva;
The Star Spangled Banner, con el blanco y azur."

From "Pax," poem pronounced by
Rubén Darío, at Columbia University
in the City of New York,
February 4, 1915.

Foreword

A strong motive animates me in offering to the public this friendly guide to Argentina: it is the conclusion, formed after a residence of over five years in the country, that although Americans who visit Argentina, and Argentines who visit the United States, return to their respective countries with something approaching a liking for the other, they begin their visits with a profound ignorance of what is before them. To many Americans Argentina calls up no vision beyond *tangos,* revolutions and *gauchos;* while in a kind of retaliation, there are many Argentines who think of us only as vulgar materialists, builders of fantastic skyscrapers, and as a people who nourish, in our social fabric, the gangster and the kidnaper. This mutual ignorance, this reciprocal misconception, I would in some degree remove, in so far as it exists among my own countrymen, and point out some of the outstanding characteristics and beauties of this "good neighbor" land, and of its friendly and courteous inhabitants, in order that they may seek to know it in increasing measure, and come to love it and its people as I do. To some friendly Argentine I leave the corresponding task of collaborating with me in my further endeavors, as my country's representative here, to enlighten his countrymen about the United States.

ALEXANDER WILBOURNE WEDDELL.

Buenos Aires, April 1, 1939.

[13]

Contents

XIII. NEARBY EXCURSIONS   148
       1. La Plata. 2. Luján. 3. Tigre.

XIV.   MAR DEL PLATA—ARGENTINE NEWPORT   159

XV.   RIVER TRIPS—IGUAZÚ, ASUNCIÓN, CONCORDIA   165

XVI.   SOUTHERN ARGENTINA—REGION OF LAKES
       AND MOUNTAINS   179

XVII. THE NORTHERN CENTRAL REGION   186
       1. Santa Fé. 2. Córdoba. 3. Tucumán. 4. Rosario de la
       Frontera. 5. Salta.

XVIII. MENDOZA—AN INLAND CALIFORNIA   208

XIX.   BIG GAME HUNTING, SHOOTING, FISHING   216

XX.   BIRDS, FLOWERS, TREES   229

XXI.   BY WAY OF BACKGROUND   248

       APPENDICES   257
       1. Air and Steamer Routes to Argentina. 2. Travel Agencies.
       3. "Personal Service". 4. Hotels. 5. Where to Lunch and
       Tea and Dine and Dance and Sup. 6. Antique Shops and
       Old Book Shops. 7. Notes on Fishing in Nahuel Huapí.
       8. Notes on Fishing in the Upper Paraná. 9. Map of Argen-
       tina (*Inside back cover*).

       ACKNOWLEDGMENTS   289

       INDEX   291

Illustrations

[17]

The illustrations are reproduced from the originals of Arthur Bauer, Fotaereas, La Nación, Foto Grete y Horacio Coppola, Edmund B. Besselievre, Torrero Hnos., E. T. Scott, The Jockey Club, Palau, Asociación Argentina de Polo, H. G. Olds, Dirección de Parques Nacionales, and La Prensa of Buenos Aires; Fortune Magazine of New York and the author.

Introduction to Argentina

CHAPTER I

Ways to Argentina

WERE I ASKED how to reach Buenos Aires, the ocean gateway of Argentina, I might reply somewhat as did Robert Louis Stevenson from Samoa, to an enquiring correspondent: "You take the steamer at New York, and my place is the second turn on the right!" But I must be more exact.

A little more than a decade ago, the traveler who desired to visit Argentina by the quickest route would take ship for Europe and proceed thence to Buenos Aires. He had the alternative of accepting the Spartan accommodations and inadequate service of an unimportant, if direct, steamer line, but this meant several more days of uncomfortable travel. Today the situation is changed and there is a wide choice. A traveler may now embark at New York at least weekly on vessels of the American Republics, or Furness Prince, or Grace Lines, and reach Buenos Aires within eighteen days. With the first two services mentioned he would continue in the Atlantic, steamers having to swerve well to the east in order to round the huge bulge of Northern Brazil, suggestive in its redundant outward thrust of the corsage of a dowager. His first South American port of call would be Rio de Janeiro—overwhelming in its languorous beauty as it "lies . . . all Danaë to the stars."

Should the traveler, however, elect to take the Grace Line, he would have the opportunity of seeing the Panama Canal, which is, as Bryce points out, "The greatest liberty man has ever taken with Nature"—perhaps his last huge affront to things as they are. Thence he would go down the often austere west coast of South America with a brief stop at Callao—Lima and on to Valparaiso, port for Santiago; from this capital over the Cordilleras and across Argentina by combination rail and motor, or by plane, until Buenos Aires was reached. Or he might continue by train from Valparaiso through Santiago, with a glimpse at that delightful capital, down to Osorno, in southern Chile, and from there by motor and launch through Andean passes and a marvelous lake region to San Carlos de Bariloche. From this little lake port, the train carries one in about thirty-eight hours to the capital and port of Buenos Aires, traversing a large extent of Argentine territory on the way.

But we are modern folk, and the desire to annihilate time and space is becoming stronger in each one of us. And so we may yield to the desire of sweeping "smoothly fleet, the long savannahs of the blue," and voyage in one of the wonderful air ships which now link Argentina and the United States in something under five days.

If flight is made from Miami in a glittering clipper, one may view from more than a mile in the air the mouth of the stupendous Amazon and also gain an overwhelming impression of the vast jungles and waterways of northern Brazil. By this route one sees towns like Bahía, for nearly two centuries the seat of a viceroyalty, with beautiful churches and convents. Even today, in its era of relative decline, it retains a subtle aroma of its past, when the representative of all the might and majesty of the great little kingdom of Portugal held his court there. Then comes the dazzling vision of Rio, as wonderful to approach by air as by sea.

But a flight via the east coast deprives one of the sight of the

Panama Canal from the air. In the alternative flight by the west coast one sees the Canal; one thrills to the vision of Peru, with its fadeless memories of Pizarro and his *conquistadores;* one has a view of snow-capped Andean peaks, Aconcagua and others, and the peaceful beauty of Santiago, in its setting of lofty mountains. Then follows the flight over the Cordilleras, past the Christ of the Andes, with its ceaseless call to Peace, through the Province of Mendoza, the California of Argentina, on to Córdoba, a centre of Argentine tradition, with a University founded in 1613, six years after our settlement at Jamestown, until finally Buenos Aires is reached.

But these routes do not exhaust the ways of approach; and I hope among my readers there may be found one or two possessing enough "high curiosity" to induce them to take the plane which flies from Rio, via São Paulo and Curityba over the dense jungles of the Paraná, circling over the stupendous falls of Iguazú, on to Asunción, capital of a plucky little nation, recently engaged in a hideous war, and thence down through Argentina to Buenos Aires. This would also afford constant glimpses of the vast river which empties into the estuary called el Rio de la Plata. Or, if our modern Icarus has elected the west coast, he may change planes at Arequipa, to spiral upwards through fleecy clouds until he is on a level with the Altiplano of Bolivia, to glide over this at approximately three miles above sea level, until he comes to earth at La Paz, whose airport hung aloft the city is 13,500 feet above the Pacific. From the Bolivian capital, he would fly over scenery gradually diminishing in severity and sublimity until he reached the calm spaces of Northern Argentina; thence to Buenos Aires. Each of the routes suggested has its special appeal and beauty.

CHAPTER II

When and How to Visit Argentina

〜〜〜〜〜〜〜〜〜〜〜〜〜〜〜〜〜〜〜〜〜〜〜〜〜〜〜

BROADLY SPEAKING, Argentina may be visited in comfort through-out the year; and this applies in special measure to the capital. Therefore, the visitor from the United States in planning his voyage will simply have to determine what he desires to escape and what he desires to see.

At present, the great majority of tourists arrive here in December, January or February; they thus avoid the northern winter, but plunge into the Argentine summer! A disadvantage of a visit in any of these three months is that a person who desires a taste of Argentine social life will find an empty capital. For smart Argentines have long since left town for their estancias, or for Mar del Plata, the Argentine Newport, or for the Lake and Mountain region of the south, the latter with a climate and scenery suggesting the Swiss mountains. Furthermore, the heat in these three months renders fascinating river trips such as those to the Falls of Iguazú, to Asunción, or by the Uruguay River to Concordia, rather less agreeable than if made earlier or later. The same drawback of heat would arise in travel to the interesting northern provinces. Also summer visitors miss the brilliant season of Opera and in general the delightful social life of the capital, best tasted in the months of June, July, and August.

However, in summer, visits may be made to nearby estancias, or to those lying south of the City, to Mar del Plata, and to the

Lakes. Temperatures in the capital itself are then not excessive as compared with New York or Washington, any heat wave being quickly lowered by the recurring cool wind known as the "pampero." On the other hand, in Argentina's early spring, in late autumn and especially in winter, a wider range of attractions beckons.

The necessity for adequate letters of introduction if one is to see anything of Argentine social life must be sharply emphasized. This would apply equally to a foreigner with social ambitions visiting New York or Washington or any European capital. However, the local necessity indicated becomes more apparent when it is recalled that in Argentina the industry of catering to the tourist is not so highly developed as in certain other countries; the visitor is consequently more restricted in his diversions, and time might occasionally drag were he without acquaintances.

But with appropriate introductions, the visitor will find himself warmly received into a social fabric of singularly high quality and beauty. Its dignity and simplicity, allied to elegance and luxury, is the natural flowering of the family life and background of a landed aristocracy, to which allusion is made throughout this volume.

The matter of hours observed in Buenos Aires, and in fact throughout the country, requires a special word here.

Luncheon, as in the United States, is usually served at one o'clock but guests do not linger long thereafter. So it is possible for the busy man to return to his office before three. In the case of bridge-luncheons, guests usually remain for afternoon tea. And tea is drunk at a later hour than with us because of the late dinner hour. Furthermore, room must be found in the evening for the innumerable cocktail parties which are as popular a form of entertainment here as elsewhere.

One is usually invited for dinner at nine o'clock although the hour is often fixed for nine-thirty. Guests are apt to wander in rather casually as the men have probably lingered late at the club, or, as have the women, attended afternoon parties, or been to "the Vermouth hour" at a cinema, or to one of the numerous lectures or concerts which usually begin at six o'clock. Bridge or music, but most usually conversation, fills up the remainder of the evening.

Perhaps due to an inheritance from Spanish forbears, guests generally arrive late for all functions. Apropos of this I am tempted to quote here from a witty volume of Julio Camba, *La Rana Viajera* in which, with delicious mockery, the author reproaches a compatriot for tardiness, indicating with inexorable logic that "an engagement is something that lies within frontiers not alone of time but of space." He then asks: "What would you say if, after having made an engagement for me to meet you at La Puerta del Sol, you learned that I was keeping the appointment in Los Cuatro Caminos?" But against these jibes we may place the biting observation of an oriental critic that a pedantic punctuality is one of the three great vices of our own country!

Clothing for Women

The Argentine woman is one of the smartest in the world. However, to a male observer there seems to be a conventionality in dress which at times almost suggests a uniform; the same chic hat tilted at the same angle, the same dress of black or other sombre color, cut to the same smart lines, suggests that the wearers are obeying an unwritten but positive rule! However, I am told by a woman friend that this taste for dark colors is changing, at Paris' mandate, and that all the colors of the rainbow are beginning to see the light.

But in daring to comment on women's clothes, there comes to mind the remark of the dying Newton: despite years of study the great ocean of Truth still lies undiscovered before me. My abysmal ignorance becomes the more apparent when I confess that I had passed the half-century mark before I realized that women do not dress to please or to captivate the male bird but to infuriate or provoke to envy members of their own sex! With this prefatory confession of ignorance and incompetence, I add a few paragraphs which have been furnished me by qualified feminine advisers concerning the clothes a woman visiting Argentina should bring with her:

"To a woman traveler proceeding to Argentina the type of clothing she will require and will wish to bring will depend entirely on the season in which she visits the country. In Argentina's winter season—June, July, August, September—she will need moderate-weight winter clothes, with an extra coat; a fur coat in this season is also useful. Since spring, summer and autumn here are normal for the respective seasons, what one would wear in Washington or Baltimore is required. Do not forget, however, that the seasons are reversed; that you may leave in New York's winter and require warm things for the first four or five days on the steamer, and arrive here in a summer for which you must be also prepared. In a word, two wardrobes are required for the visitor from the States to Argentina. And in any season you cross the Equator in coming, so at least ten days on shipboard require tropical attire. Remember too that in a plane a heavy coat is needed at times because of altitude, even over the Equator.

"The summer here is cooler than Washington or Chicago or New York, with cool breezes following days of heat.

"If one arrives in the gay winter season, as described above, the following would represent a minimum wardrobe: a suit; a morning dress; an afternoon dress, which can be worn for cocktails and simple dinners; a coat suitable to be worn with each; and evening dresses. The number and importance of evening dresses and wraps depends upon one's individual taste and the character of letters of introduction one may bring.

"When the opera season is at its height, in the winter, one would be happier wearing formal evening dress, especially on one of the fashionable nights or at gala performances. But on ordinary nights, street clothes may be worn.

"Riding and sport clothes here are the same as one would want in or near any large city in the United States or in Europe, either summer or winter.

"For a trip to the southern lakes warm clothes are needed. Around these lakes you will find salmon and trout fishing, riding, golf, motoring, and lake excursions; in winter the skiing fields are magnificent; the character of the diversions and sports named indicate sufficiently the clothing needed.

"There are excellent dressmaking establishments in Buenos Aires, one of these so good that the very chic wife of a member of the Embassy staff on the transfer of her husband to a post within five hundred miles of Paris, continued for several years to order her frocks from this city. There are good women's shoe-makers. However, ready-to-wear clothing, and shoes, are not as easy to find and satisfactory as those in the United States.

"To all this I would add that those who feel life to be dull, stale, flat and unprofitable without the services provided by beauty specialists will find plenty of them here."

Men's Clothes

In the height of the social season, evening dress at dinner or the Colón opera house (not at local theatres except on very special occasions) is as formal as in any city in the world. On the other hand, the morning coat and top hat, although *de rigueur* for weddings, receptions, certain days at the races, and many official ceremonies, is not so frequently worn as, for example, in London or New York. In dress for sports—riding, golfing, fishing, yachting in the myriad waterways of the Tigre and in the broad estuary of the Plata—the *appropriateness* of clothing, which after all is what gives smartness to sport clothes, is carefully observed.

With the foregoing in mind, I would suggest to the male visitor from my own country that, if he plans to be here during the Argentine winter, he bring a full dress suit; and, of course, a dinner jacket. This latter suggestion applies no matter when the visitor comes; it is unlikely that he will wear rigidly formal evening dress in the summer months. If it is planned to play golf or ride or go into the country or to make one of the river trips or a trip to the lakes or mountains, exactly similar clothing to that which would be worn in the States at corresponding places and seasons is recommended. And always remember that seasons in the two countries are reversed!

If one arrives in the Argentine summer and plans to visit the mountain or lake region, heavy tweeds and a sweater and windbreaker should be brought, together with a medium weight overcoat.

A most comfortable and practical sporting garb which is peculiar to Argentina is formed of loose baggy trousers, known as bombachas, which are worn with the bottom caught in soft riding boots, and a sports coat. This costume is especially adapted for the Argentine country-side, where briars and insects are encountered, and where one is constantly in the saddle. As there are excellent boot and shoe makers in Argentina, and good tailors, this costume is best ordered after arrival. It is essentially a country garment. However, your smartest riding togs will be quite correct in city or country.

A trip as far north as Iguazú, which in general is best visited in June, July or August, or a little earlier or later, brings you into a latitude and temperatures corresponding roughly to Palm Beach, although at times fairly cool weather may prevail, while the lake region, for special reason of location and height, suggests Southern Canada.

The Argentine man dresses extremely well and is meticulous in the choice of colors and materials, and in general the appearance of men in Argentine clubs or at the cinema or Opera or in smart hotels recalls Fifth Avenue or Savile Row.

How to Visit the Country

Although in general the tourist industry is not yet highly developed in Argentina, several good tourist agencies are to be found here—Villalonga, Exprinter, Cook, etc. In addition the National and several State Governments maintain bureaus which give the traveler valuable and extensive information concerning excursions to the North, South, and West. The names and addresses of these are given in Appendix II.

To the foregoing should be added the name of a unique organization here known as "Personal Service"—24-hour service, by the way—to which one may go as to a father confessor, propound the most fantastic questions, state the most bizarre needs, and expect and receive an answer and your needs supplied. The founder of this Personal Service, an American gentlewoman, with a wide knowledge of the world, gives a statement concerning her organization which is to be found in Appendix III.

CHAPTER III

Argentina of Today

THE NAME ARGENTINA is a happy transmutation into Latin of a part of the name of the loosely-knit political group which declared their independence from Spain in 1816—Las Provincias Unidas del *Rio* de la *Plata*—the United Provinces of the *Silver River*. But just here are two contradictions . . .: el Rio de la Plata is not a river but a vast estuary, and no silver is to be found in the region it washes! The error arose when Sebastian Cabot entered the broad gulf in 1526, and sent home rude silver ornaments taken from the Indians of fluvial tribes. Cabot leapt to the conclusion that here was doubtless a gateway to El Dorado and called the tawny flood "the silver river." This was five years before Pizarro's dazzling conquest of Perú. The news of Cabot's discovery was without question a powerful stimulus in promoting expeditions to the fabulous west in those spacious days when the New World, like a siren of old, beckoned men with promises of golden favors to be won by "desperate deeds of derring do."

(As an aside, and for the benefit of those who take a special interest in the origin of names, it may be mentioned that it is only in the Constitution of 1853 that the pleasantly mouth-filling word "Argentina" appears. It is not found in the solemn documents of similar character adopted in 1819 and 1826, which is the more surprising since the term in a geographical and racial sense was in common use long before that time; in fact, I have before me a reprint of a rather dull volume in *ottava rima* published in Lisbon, in 1602, which bears the following title: "Argentina y Conquista del Rio de la Plata con otros acaecimientos de los Reynos del Perú, Tucumán, y Estado del Brasil." In this work the author refers to "Argentinos" and "Argentinas," as well as to "Argentino." Its use in the Constitution of 1853 may have been due in part to the Argentine statesman, Alberdi, whose constructive work appeared at that time and set forth bases and points of departure for the political organization "de la República Argentina."

The political origins and growth of the new land are referred to in another chapter: just here we are only concerned with Argentina of today.

Take your compasses and mark out in the northern hemisphere the vast extent covered by this republic; you will find that in length it equals the wide expanse lying between Hudson Bay and the tip of Yucatan! In shape, it is like to a spear, with its blade in tropical forests and its point in Antarctic waters. Strictly speaking all Argentina, with the exception of a tiny area in the north, lies within the Temperate zone, with agricultural land as large in extent but far more fertile, than our great Mississippi Valley section; a black soil, more than a score of feet deep, which in all its years of cultivation has never needed any fertilizer. Further, there are no stones to be removed nor trees to be felled.

Argentina is a doubly happy land in that it has no color question and no race question. Its percentage of white population is far higher than our own and in the amalgam which is to make the Argentine of the future, the choice of emigrants thus far has been also more fortunate than with us. The hideous face of slavery was, practically speaking, never seen here, and in contradistinction to Great Britain which forced the slave trade on its

North American colonies, there was no practical reason to inspire the Spanish crown to similar action.

With regard to the Indians, of which nomadic tribes ranged the country, the Argentine method, both as colony and republic, was much like our own; first pushing the Indians westward and later practically exterminating them. The number of people in whose veins Indian blood courses is, according to an accepted authority, less than in any country of South America with the possible exception of Uruguay. Of the pure aborigenes a bare 50,000 are left. These latter nearly all live in the national territories of the North, Los Andes, Formosa, Chaco and Misiones; a few more linger in lower Patagonia. Three-fourths of the people are of European descent and the remaining fourth is almost entirely foreign born. Of our own countrymen there are in Buenos Aires perhaps two thousand, with a possible five hundred more scattered through the rest of the land.

To the foreigner who has never visited the country, the *pampa* and the *gaucho* are imagined to be the peculiar manifestations of Argentine life and setting. Certainly the "pampa grandiosa" will remain as a rich source of national health and wealth to "Buenos Aires, patria hermosa" but the true *gaucho* has almost disappeared from the landscape (as has our equally picturesque cowboy), yet lives today in the great epic *Martín Fierro,* in *Don Segundo Sombra,* and other similar works, as well as in the glowing historical canvases of an outstanding Argentine painter—Cesáreo Bernaldo de Quirós—whose work has won enthusiastic admiration in the United States. With a lively recollection of our own country, I had thought to find negroes in large numbers here, but it was a full month following my arrival before I saw even one, and he was in a museum—the doorkeeper!

Our own Government was among the first to recognize the political entity which is today represented by the Argentine Republic. This took place on January 27, 1823. In this the United States was only preceded by Portugal and Brazil; but it is not hypercritical to suggest that like France's recognition of the struggling North American colonies the action of the two latter named governments was prompted more by a desire to be offensive to the mother country than by any tender regard for the new-born nation.

But I am running ahead of my story, and those of my readers who may care to supplement what I have already written with something concerning the political birth and growth of Argentina will find this set forth in the chapter entitled "By Way of Background," which is placed at the back of this volume. Yet space should be found here to set forth in the best encyclopedic style that Argentina is a constitutional republic. The chief magistrate is the president, who is elected for six years by three hundred and seventy-six electors, appointed by the fourteen provinces and the capital; this number of electors is double the number of senators and deputies combined. Both the president and the vice-president must be Roman Catholics and Argentine by birth; and cannot be re-elected unless a period of six years intervenes. The national congress consists of a senate and chamber of deputies. The senate consists of thirty senators, two from the capital and two from each province, chosen by a special body of electors in the capital and by the legislatures in the provinces, for a period of nine years; one-third retiring every three years. The chamber of deputies now has one hundred and fifty-eight members elected directly by the people. Their term of office is four years, one-half retiring every two years. The two chambers meet annually from May to September. Doctor Roberto M. Ortiz entered upon his six-year term as president on February 20, 1938; the vice-president is Doctor Ramón S. Castillo.

The constitution of Argentina which, with certain small exceptions is almost the same as that of the United States, provides the best example to be found of the application of English law under Hispanic administration, of the grafting of a shoot from Anglo Saxon genius on a stock whose roots grew in Latin soil. To be borne in mind in this connection is the observation of a political philosopher that the Anglo-Saxon mentality is essentially legislative and the Latin mind essentially executive.

In such matters as affect the Government as a whole, control is in the hands of the central government. The governors of the various provinces, elected by the people, are invested with very extensive powers, and are independent of the central executive.

As stated elsewhere, Buenos Aires is governed by an intendente, or mayor, appointed by the president with the approval of the senate. He is assisted by a City Council of thirty, elected by the male inhabitants over eighteen years of age, including foreigners who comply with certain conditions. Voting is compulsory, under penalty of a fine. Other municipalities have constitutions similar in character to that of the federal district.

The area of the Argentine Republic is 2,797,113 square kilometres, in other words more than 200,000 square kilometres greater than the pre-war area of Belgium, Denmark, Germany, France, Holland, Norway, Portugal, Sweden, Switzerland and Spain, combined!

One further paragraph with regard to the economic aspects of Argentina. Its wealth arises from the tilling of the soil and the breeding of livestock. The capital of the country is a sublimated stock raising and farming center, as Mexico City is an exalted mining town. The three great agricultural products of the land are wheat, corn and linseed, of which Argentina is one of the foremost exporters. In the Provinces of Mendoza and San Juan and elsewhere the grape is cultivated, and wine, almost exclusively for domestic consumption, is made. There are large sugar refineries in the North and cotton is beginning to be grown in the Chaco. The number of cattle, sheep and horses within the national boundaries runs into many millions. Although the increase in this latter source of wealth has been large, the limitation of the pastoral area has not yet been reached. The export of meat was given a great stimulus when systems of cold storage and transport came into use, and much American and British capital is invested in this trade. Some thirty years ago Bryce, with a prophetic eye, wrote as follows:

"In this immense fertile and temperate country with hardly six people to a square mile, what limit can we set to the growth of wealth and population? Already the nation is larger than the Dutch or Portuguese or Swedish . . . It may one day be the most numerous among all the peoples that speak a tongue of Latin origin."

CHAPTER IV

The Argentine People

WHAT is the Argentine of today? In many respects he is a South American European, in blood and culture. In blood, Spain at the beginning, and Italy at a much later date, have been the principal contributors; yet, despite this fact, Argentine culture is essentially French, although other influences are beginning to be manifest, among which, it is gratifying to observe, some of those originating in our own country. This Gallic influence is perhaps explained, certainly in part, by the powerful repercussions of the French Revolution in all the Spanish possessions in the Americas; while both before and after that event the writings of French political philosophers were being widely read in the colonies. To this should be added the further fact that following the declarations of 1810 and 1816 looking toward Argentine independence, things Spanish were not popular here, and political leaders becoming further deeply versed in French political history were inevitably influenced thereby. This influence affected all the cultured and governing classes.

Other influences flow from British, Irish and German sources. The first two named are the older, and are perhaps more evident in the life of the country. Apart from Britain's invaluable economic contributions, its impulse in sports is apparent. The Irish element in the national life is a strong one, a community of faith having facilitated union through marriage, and generally furthered progress here. The Germans have also intermarried in great numbers, but their influence is not to be compared with the two latter named races.

However, even so superficial a survey as this of the ethnic elements making up the Argentine nation would be incomplete without emphasis on the contributions of the Basques, that remarkable race of whom so very little is known even to profound students. Not alone in the beginning but through the years, a substantial percentage of the Spaniards who came to Argentina were Basques, and these from the earliest times occupied a position and exercised an influence out of all proportion to their numbers. It is therefore no exaggeration to say that Argentine aristocracy in blood is in a certain measure Basque.

In my attempts to understand and appraise the Argentines sympathetically, there naturally arises a query as to what in the national character first or most deeply impresses the foreigner as a defect and what as the most attractive and impressive manifestation of the genius of the race. For the latter I would point unhesitatingly to the family tie—outstanding in its quality, strength and beauty.

The Argentine social fabric, it seems to me, is both patriarchal and matriarchal, and parental and filial devotions are as powerful as any to be found in the world. In saying this I recall the pessimistic remark of an Argentine friend that this family tie is being weakened. I did not and I do not agree. It is true that its outward manifestations are changing. And with the demolition or abandonment to other uses of huge old residences, families are being physically divided, many young folk beginning married life in apartment houses. Even then there is a tendency for relatives to lease quarters in the same building, or to build houses for joint occupancy. But the devotion uniting parent and child,

a vivifying stream which flows in both directions, remains un-
altered.

On the other hand, in praising what he calls the "jubilant
patriotism" of this people, Bryce remarks that an "acute and
friendly observer has said that patriotism among the Argentines
amounts to a mania;" he then proceeds to defend this manifestation of the national genius, to which various critics have alluded,
observing that "Such excess of sentiment is not only natural in a
young and growing nation, and innocent too (so long as it is not
aggressive) but is helpful in giving men something beyond their
own material enjoyments and vanities to think of and to work
for . . . if there is an excess, time will correct it."

Springing in large measure from the patriotism to which I
have alluded is a national pride which, if it has thus far avoided
the extravagances of chauvinism, manifests itself all too frequently
in an extreme sensitiveness to criticism. This is a national defect.
But it is equally a passing phase, and when I say passing I can
best illustrate my meaning by pointing out that in the United
States a number of years ago we were ourselves prone to resent
and to writhe under adverse comment by foreigners, especially if
these were English.

Nowadays the publication following a visit to our shores of the
adverse views of a modern Dickens or a Harriet Martineau or a
Mrs. Trollope, intended to "pour contempt on all our pride," if
they were not met with indifference, or at least partial acceptance
as being true (as in the case of works by Keyserling and Sieg-
fried), would provoke laughter and reflections on the critic's com-
petence. Argentina is rapidly arriving at the same attitude toward
her critics.

Argentina is Roman Catholic, very Roman Catholic, and any
attempt to picture the Argentine people must take into account

their strong religious convictions, a faith which runs like a golden thread through the fibre of national life. While there is no state religion, the Roman Catholic creed is supported by the State. However, all other faiths are tolerated, and freedom of conscience prevails. The freedom of conscience to which I refer is a very real thing, and such diverse religious elements as the Jews, the Seventh Day Adventists, Lutherans, Baptists, Methodists, and others, including the Salvation Army, carry on their activities in an atmosphere of entire tolerance.

Viscount Bryce was struck by the abstention of the Roman Church in Argentina from politics, and the extent to which freedom of religious worship is fully carried out and practised. "The happy detachment of the two spheres," (religion and politics) "which travellers observe and admire in North America," he feels deserves even more credit here.

A word concerning the Argentine priesthood: In nothing is the essential democracy of this great Church more clearly demonstrated than in the composition of its hierarchy here. For its "spiritual pastors and masters" the Church has reached into the very heart and substance of national life, without regard to the social or economic position of those to whom the vocation has come. The Cardinal-Archbishop, an apostolic figure with a strong building instinct which makes him active in the construction of new churches, is Argentine-born and bred, and this is generally true of the clergy, although there are a number of foreign priests and religious of a different language engaged in teaching here.

But what rather surprises an American is to notice how much the priest is a man apart. I remember the unconcealed amazement of various Argentine friends when I mentioned that the private chaplain of the saintly Archbishop Glennon of St. Louis, who was my house guest during the Eucharistic Congress, was no slouch when it came to playing golf. And I have never seen a priest at a theatrical performance in Argentina, no matter how grave the subject, nor have I ever encountered one in a club. Frankly, I like our customs better, where clergy of all creeds and denominations mingle easily in the social life. I would like to see the good, sincere, devoted men who make up the Argentine clergy in a closer daily-life contact with their male parishioners than is now the case.

And now, and partly by way of summary, I yield to the temptation to quote here a penetrating comment written by an Argentine now filling a high office in the Ministry of Foreign Affairs of his Government, Dr. Roberto Gache, in which in broad lines he traces the Argentine of today:

The Argentine people, considered from the social, the financial or the political standpoint, therefore have the qualities and the defects peculiar to anything that is new and improvised. No situation being definitive, each one is free to throw himself headlong into the struggle of appetites and ambitions. He does not limit his wishes to his present condition; he hopes always to improve it. The man tied hopelessly to his condition does not exist here.

CHAPTER V

Buenos Aires

"I used to call it 'Bewnus Airs'
Until a friend protested
That anyone who ever dares
Say that should be arrested.
I called it 'Bonus Iris' then,
But that provoked such laughter
I vowed I never would again
Pronounce the word thereafter.
But now, at last, no more disgrace!
I know just what to say.
I look the whole world in the face
And call it plain 'B.A.!' "

1. General Observations

BUENOS AIRES is Argentina in the same measure that London is England and Paris is France. It is the center of the social, political and economic life of the land; a land great in extent, in actualities and in potentialities.

The approach to the city is, for the sea-borne traveler, over the yellow waters of the wide arm of the ocean which is incorrectly called el *Rio* de la Plata; a name which has been worn down by sea-faring folk to "the River Plate."

The low-lying shores are crowned by numerous tall buildings, including a huge apartment house which is the last word in construction and is the loftiest reinforced concrete building in all South America. The series of docking basins is one of the most

AMERICAN CLIPPER PLANE OVER BUENOS AIRES

THE OLD PORT

The Plaza de Mayo, Parque Almirante Brown, and Casa Rosada

The Plaza San Martín

elaborate in the world, and is entirely artificial. Skillful and constant dredging operations keep the channel open and permit the entry and easy berthing of transatlantic steamers of large tonnage.

The section of the city where landings are made is delightfully clear and free of anything suggesting a slum section. For when these water spaces were created by the Government, care was taken to reserve the surrounding land for municipal purposes and so at any hour, day or night, passengers go to and fro in comfort, convenience and safety. The orientation of certain of the streets is such that one has pleasing vistas of huge vessels apparently lying at the end of various broad, well-paved thoroughfares, offering ready access to wharves and docks.

In a familiar chapter, Taine tells the reader that the critic is lost in Shakespeare as a traveler is lost in the streets of a huge city; a few buildings are pointed out and he is told to imagine the rest. I feel something of the difficulty which Taine indicated in attempting to describe Buenos Aires. For in extent alone it is one of the greatest cities in the world, covering approximately eighty square miles, in this respect being second only to London and Melbourne and surpassing Paris and Berlin. With nearly 2,400,000 inhabitants, it is the second largest of Latin cities in population.

The Federal Capital or Federal District (the two are identical) possesses a unicameral governmental body, and a mayor or intendente who is appointed by the President of the Republic. The situation is vaguely suggestive of Washington, save that instead of three commissioners there is one; added to this is the outstanding fact that the inhabitants, unlike those of the District of Columbia, have the right to vote in all elections. A compelling reason doubtless bringing about this latter situation lies in the fact that approximately a fifth of the population of the Republic is to be found in the Federal District.

Between the years 1932 and 1938 a far-reaching plan of municipal improvement was inaugurated. This included the laying down of a huge avenue, four hundred and eighty feet wide, with fountains, trees, garden spaces, etc., known as Nueve de Julio. This was made possible by the demolition of acres of built up property in the heart of the city. Underneath this vast thoroughfare, as thus far completed, parking space, normally lacking here, is provided for nearly a thousand motor cars, at once offering relief to traffic and a certain source of revenue to the city.

The stranger from an older civilization coming to Buenos Aires will be struck by its newness. A house dating from 1890 is considered fairly venerable here! And unfortunately the besom of reform and change, of which we have had evidence in so many cities in the United States, has been actively at work in Buenos Aires in destroying many lovely old residences and historic buildings, altering stately avenues, installing modernistic fountains, and so on.

Today perhaps the oldest, certainly the most historical structures left as witnesses of the past are a portion of an edifice where on a rainy day in May, 1810 a gathering of leading citizens took the first step toward ultimate independence; and the cathedral, which dates from the first third of the seventeenth century, wherein repose the remains of the national hero, San Martín.

To those of my readers who still retain, despite the easy habit of the motor car, the use of their lower limbs, it is suggested that much of interest and beauty in this capital is best seen on foot. The following short promenade is therefore suggested as a starter:

Begin at what is perhaps the most historic spot in Buenos Aires —La Casa Rosada (the Rose House)—which occupies approximately the site of the very first fort, built by Don Pedro de Mendoza in 1536.

La Casa Rosada has been in part recently demolished, but the principal façade and much of the principal structure still remains and is occupied by the President's office and several ministries. Two presidents have actually resided there, Roque Saenz Peña in 1910-1914, and General Uriburu in the months following the revolution of 1930. In it are to be found stately drawing and reception rooms, and offices, as well as an elegant chamber known as El Salón Blanco. Here retiring presidents formally hand over their symbol of office to their successors, here solemn international acts and treaties are frequently signed, here elaborate official dinners take place, and here the president receives from the hands of ambassadors and ministers their letters of credence. These latter documents, if an aside may be pardoned, are solemn requests to the persons in whose hands they are placed, in formal ceremonies, to give credence, to believe, what the bearers tell them; it requires no effort of the imagination to realize that such requests in the olden days of diplomacy presupposed inexhaustible stores of credulity on the part of the addressees. But here I dare to assert that, despite the contemptible times in which we live, the great art of human intercourse, which is diplomacy, is a truer, more happily realistic thing than at any time during the past. Methods, however, appear to have changed but little "with the process of the suns." The visit of the Queen of Sheba to Solomon was a commercial mission of the most practical order, despite the romantic implications which the present Ethiopian dynasty seeks to give it; and the fact that Alcibiades was the active Consul of Sparta in Athens goes to prove the unchanging quality of that alloy we call human nature. And the visits to Argentina of the former Prince of Wales and of the Crown Prince of Italy were not made to restore their health!

Following these visitors came a great figure whose purpose was

Peace! The arrival and sojourn of President Roosevelt in Buenos Aires were marked by scenes of delirious cordiality, in which this warm-hearted people gave vent to their emotions of hospitality and good feeling toward this herald of good will—spokesman for the good neighbor policy. A tablet on the great stairway of the American Embassy, placed by our Government on my initiative, records this visit. It bears the President's name, the dates of his stay, and a quotation from his fine speech delivered on December 1 in the Congressional Palace—"Democracy is still the hope of the world."

Echoes of this visit, agreeable or amusing or both, still reach my ear. One remark, made at the time, promises to attain a certain immortality; its author was a high functionary of the Foreign Office. Seeing the dense crowds gathered along the streets through which the President was passing, in which were hosts of beautiful women, hearing the enthusiastic shouts of the multitude, and seeing that unforgettable and conquering smile which the President was turning on, he exclaimed: "Ma foi, for the first time in my life I see sex-appeal being employed in international relations!"

But returning to our sightseers, who have perhaps erred and strayed in this interval, it should be remarked that the Buenos Aires of 1822, at the time of the first census, was a struggling town of perhaps 55,000 persons; in 1895 its population had grown to 663,854; in 1909 the inhabitants numbered 1,231,698. From this there was a further forward movement, and in 1936 the census revealed, as stated, a population of approximately 2,400,000.

Leaving the Casa Rosada behind, the pedestrian would do well to walk slowly up to the Avenida de Mayo. Within a hundred yards he will see in the center of a sunken garden a small obelisk, commemorating the *Cabildo Abierto*—the town meeting—of May 25, 1810, when the first steps toward independence were taken.

On his right is the cathedral to which reference has been made, and which should surely be visited. Here solemn Te Deums are chanted on festal days, and here acts of public mourning take place. On the first mentioned occasion, or whenever the President attends, there is set on a table immediately in front of his chair a roll, not unlike a cylindrical cotton bale enveloped in green and gold damask of finest quality. When seated for the first time with the diplomatic corps at a Te Deum, immediately opposite the President and his cabinet, my eyes fell on this object. Curiosity leapt to attention. Turning to the left to my German colleague I asked:

"What does that signify?"

"*Ich weiss nicht. Fragen sie den Italienen.*" Turning to the right, to the Italian Ambassador, who immediately outranked me in diplomatic precedence, I repeated my enquiry:

"*Non so; chiederó alla Francia,*" was the response. Above the organ's swell I caught the Frenchman's reply:

"*Fichtre! Je n'ai aucune idée, mais peut-être le Brésilien . . .*" I saw the Gaul nudge our Brazilian colleague. The latter had spent years in the United States, and prided himself on his acquaintance with *toute la finesse de la langue anglaise.* Back came his reply:

"Search me—never noticed it before. I'll dig it out of the Nuncio."

The ball of query was now on the five-yard line and headed straight for the representative of the Holy Father. To my surprise he, too, muffed it, with a grimace and a shrug. Curiosity had now become like to a voracious flea under knightly armor, but I had to support its bite until I cornered the Introducer of Ambassadors after the service.

The bale I had seen, this high official informed me, signifies

"El Patronato de la Iglesia,"—the power of the State in certain of its relations with the Roman Church. I later learned, and more specifically, that in form, if not in size, it symbolized the container, sometimes of lead, in which bulls issuing from the Holy See were sent to foreign rulers or powers. In this case it may be said to symbolize an assertion and an acceptance or ratification of the right of national patronage exercised by the President of Argentina in the presentation of names of bishops for sees or cathedrals.

Continuing up the avenue one is passing through an essential part of what is referred to, without sharply defined limits, as El Centro—the center of the city.

Soon after leaving the cathedral, in a brisk twenty-minutes' walk, the visitor has before him the monumental fountains in front of the Palacio Legislativo, or Capitol, a dignified structure completed in 1908 and suggesting in its general outlines our own Capitol which houses the upper and lower branches of the Congress.

The busy Avenida is intersected on either side at sharp angles by two important streets called diagonals. The Diagonal Norte, which is passed on the right soon after starting this promenade, bears as its true name the Avenida Roque Saenz Peña, after an Argentine statesman who was President from 1910 to 1914, and the other the Avenida Julio A. Roca, distinguished soldier, and president from 1898 to 1904. The effect of these Boulevards Haussmann, which were pierced at great cost, is to make of the Avenida de Mayo an arrow, driving from the House of Congress toward the great Rio de la Plata, the diagonals forming its barbs.

The former diagonal cuts across a famous thoroughfare, Florída, which requires special mention, because it is the street of streets, to the Porteño (inhabitant of the city) as to the visitor.

THE KAVANAGH BUILDING, TALLEST IN SOUTH AMERICA

AVENIDA NUEVE DE JULIO, WIDEST IN THE WORLD

La Florída

A street market, Buenos Aires

A bare ten blocks long and scarcely twenty feet wide between its narrow sidewalks, linking the Plaza San Martín with the Avenida de Mayo, it is a small thing beside its sisters Alvear, Nueve de Julio and Corrientes. Yet its history is the history of Buenos Aires.

Going back a long while to the time when it bore the name of Empedrado (the paved street)—doubtless because it was then the only thoroughfare in Buenos Aires which might be so designated —it later was renamed Unquera, honoring the memory of a brave sailor of the wars of independence; still later, with equally commemorative purpose, it received its present name, which is that of a tiny locality in Bolivia where, in 1817, Creole forces routed Spanish troops in the war of Independence, and by a happy coincidence, on May 25, the date of the famous Cabildo Abierto of 1810.

Florída—and let us recall here that it is pronounced "Flo-*ree*-da," and like Broadway or Piccadilly or Pall Mall, bears no connotative word—is to the Argentine and to the Porteño what Broadway of olden days was to the New Yorker and the boulevards to a hardened Parisian. It is the street which has for a full century been frequented by the creole aristocracy, and even in its present form it provides an objective vision of the Argentine of the past hundred years. For behind its brilliant lights, behind its smart shop windows, despite its outward sheathing of brick and marble and shining bronze, the traditional architecture of the city may yet be studied. And of all the streets of El Centro, it is the one that has suffered the least modification. Lift your eyes above the street signs, above the dazzling lights, and you will see the upper stories of residences of former days, façades on which time has deposited its unmistakable patina. A few folk still actually reside in this street! But the number is diminishing, and in only a few years business will have entirely enveloped and conquered the thoroughfare.

In days now gone beyond recall, Florída was a promenade for exclusive groups, beaux of the olden time cast glances intended to be devastating toward the precious cargo borne in the open carriages which thronged it. Now all is changed. The carriage is seen no more, and even a solitary horseman would provoke a riot. At certain hours, to accommodate the enormous number of folk who throng the street and completely fill it, it is strictly closed to wheeled traffic. This is usually between the hours of five and eight in the evening.

Florída is then at its best for purposes of study. In the pace of the promenaders one may almost discern the tension of the capital, political or otherwise. The tempo is accelerated by exciting news from abroad, while a heated debate in the Chamber of Deputies seems equally to find its repercussion in the active throng. A dull day, devoid of news, is marked by a sluggish pace of the promenaders.

HOTELS

The first thing to engage the attention of the traveler is, or should be, his hotel. In this respect Buenos Aires makes ample provision for all tastes and all purses.

If one arrives in the summer—December, January, February— care should be taken to make reservations well in advance as the influx of visitors then is considerable, and an eleventh hour arrival may find that there is no room in the inn which he may have chosen for his sojourn.

The leading hotel of the city, the Plaza, perhaps the smartest, and which has as its only serious rival the Alvear Palace, is situated near the business and official center. Nearby are the first-class

City and Continental Hotels. The Alvear Palace is a little remote from the center and is perhaps the farthest uptown; but it gains quiet and a certain elegance from this relatively slight withdrawal from the bustle of the downtown section.

On the main floor of the Plaza Hotel is a superb dining room with interesting murals by an Argentine artist depicting with fidelity scenes from gaucho life—a phase of Argentine growth which has just about disappeared except in remote districts. In this room are held the Fourth of July dinner dances of the American Society of the River Plate, when the colony gathers with its Argentine friends and representatives of the allies to dine and dance. Here, too, the American Legion gives its delightful annual fiesta, celebrating the anniversary of the Armistice; the annual dinner of the American Chamber of Commerce is also served here, on which occasion the President of the Chamber, a member of the Argentine cabinet, and the Ambassador speak on topics connected with the political and economic relations of the two countries; the members of the Rotary Club assemble here weekly, and an endless series of gatherings representing local or foreign activities is celebrated under this roof. Adjoining this dining room is an oval chamber which is becoming a favorite spot for bachelor dinner parties or for hosts whose hospitable impulses exceed the limits of their homes.

The City Hotel is one of the best in the capital and maintains an excellent restaurant with a well known dance orchestra, both of which are patronized not only by its large clientele, but by outsiders.

The Continental Hotel, on the corner of the "Diagonal Norte" and Maipú, has a comfortable "American Bar" downstairs and an air-conditioned restaurant, on the street level, that is famous for its food. Lovers of sea-food go on Thursday evenings to dine on lobster received that afternoon from Chile by plane. Its wine list is also to be recommended.

Following the hotels named, but more moderate in price are those listed in Appendix IV.

WHERE TO LUNCH AND TEA AND DINE AND DANCE AND SUP

A word remains to be said before naming some of the better-known restaurants: it is that, as in the case of the hotels, the list does not pretend to be complete; the places indicated are those which have been actually tested by competent critics and found interesting and satisfactory.

In what it offers to the experienced traveler who has learned in his wanderings to be something of a gourmet, Argentina is verily a promised land. Blessed with a soil of incomparable richness, which has been and is being tilled with skill and science, possessing live-stock of all kinds whose pure blood is being constantly replenished by prize-winners from the greatest breeding farms of the world, it is inevitable that in all that contributes to the nourishment of man the country should be supreme.

Having in mind that important passage of food from field and meadow and farm-yard to the table, it will be discovered soon after leaving Buenos Aires that the general standard of cooking outside the capital is not as high, for example, as in rural France. On the other hand, in the restaurants of Buenos Aires, where the cuisine follows the Gallic tradition, if affected in various pleasing degrees by secrets of the art having their birth in Italy or Spain, the standard is a high one, while the quality of the products served is in many ways the best in the world.

Joshua, of old, sent out his spies to tell him of the goodly land he was soon to occupy. By proxy, I am going to play the rôle of spy for you, in matters culinary in Buenos Aires. I say by proxy, for in order to do justice to this important subject I enlisted the services of a charming young friend, Ted Maffitt, whom I know now, from the effortless ease and authority with which he writes, to be of distinctly nocturnal habits. This collaborator returns with much information concerning places where one may lunch or sup or tea or dine to his satisfaction, as well as dance, while in Buenos Aires. The report omits the various clubs, since these are described in another chapter; and of course, as suggested, it does not attempt to exhaust the subject. It is, however, a fairly comprehensive statement; and besides, the visitor who lingers long enough to explore the various places mentioned will ere then have begun to make his own list. This valuable culinary and Terpsichorean information will be found in Appendix IV.

Doctors, Surgeons, Oculists, Dentists

As pointed out elsewhere, Argentina lies almost entirely in the temperate zone. Local maladies are therefore limited to those usually to be found in this climatic range. It possesses a public health service of high efficiency and epidemics are as rare as in the United States; added to this there is to be found in the capital a body of notably progressive scientists in the medical and surgical professions, including oculists and dentists of the first order; many of these speak English fluently, and add to their scientific attainments up-to-date equipment. The intending traveler may therefore set sail for Argentina in the confident belief that in case of illness or accident his needs will be met.

2. *Architecture; Streets*

The new arrival in Buenos Aires will be at once struck by an animation suggestive of New York, and a physical exterior reminiscent of Paris, yet with a kind of Latin grace lending suavity to the deep rhythmic pulse of what one feels to be a great city.

The width and beauty of many streets and avenues, the generous provision of parks and open spaces, together with the representative architecture of many public buildings, provoke respect.

The fringes of the city however are, in general, unattractive, with large numbers of single story and rather mean houses facing unpaved streets. Furthermore, because of the low-lying character of much of the land, the drainage problem, now actively engaging the attention of the municipal authorities, is a difficult one, and as a result a torrential downpour floods many streets, especially in the poorer and in the outlying parts of the city.

The parks of Buenos Aires should arouse the pride of every Argentine. The city has fully a hundred parks and squares, embracing perhaps three thousand acres. The largest of these is the Parque 3 de Febrero, its name recalling the day in 1852 when General Justo José de Urquiza crushed the forces of the dictator Rosas at Caseros, ending the latter's tyranny of eighteen years.

Visitors should note the Argentine habit of choosing historic dates for names of streets. To those of us who actually pretend to a modicum of culture, and yet can remember but few year dates, save 1066 and all that, or 1492, or 1776, it would be at once a spur to patriotism and an aid to memory if we had streets named Fourth of July and October 19, and April 19, and so on. Here, in Argentina, not only the schoolboy, who might be supposed to know, but the mature man or woman can give you, without hesitation, at least the day and month of the earliest cry of independence here in the capital, at least partly because of his daily walk carrying him to La Avenida de Mayo, or down the street called 25 de Mayo. Or he may have parked his car underneath the vast avenue, perhaps the widest in the world, known as 9 de Julio, to which he need add only the year date, 1816, to recall Argentina's declaration of independence. I commend this fashion to our fed-

eral and city fathers, whose imagination in naming streets seems
not to run beyond the patronymics of a few Revolutionary soldiers or energetic real estate agents of the moment.

Equally to be admired is the good taste that gives to other streets
names which call up further historical events, not to mention those
bearing the patronymics of outstanding figures of former days.
Illustrative of such street names, a full list of which would tax my
space and perhaps your patience, may be mentioned thoroughfares
recalling San Martín, Rivadavia, Belgrano, Mitre, Uriburu, Alem,
Dorrego, Irigoyen, Pellegrini, Campillo, Nazar, Anchorena, Castex, Alzaga, Casares, Ortiz, Basualdo, Pueyrredon, Moreno, Saave-
dra and Paz, to name but a few. In certain cases care is taken that
no mistake shall be made in the individual on whom the distinction is bestowed,—for example, Calle Presidente José E. Uriburu;
and as regards dates for street names, 15 de Noviembre, 1889, may
be mentioned for exactness of designation.

In the former case—the commemoration of historical events by
street names—Defensa, Victoria, and Reconquista, recall the two
disastrous expeditions sent by England against Buenos Aires at
the beginning of the nineteenth century. The second expedition
was under the command of Lieutenant General John Whitelocke
and resulted in his complete overthrow.

Apropos of this latter humiliating defeat there comes to mind a
story told me by my delightful British colleague in Buenos Aires,
Sir Esmond Ovey. It concerns a young and embryonic diplomatist
who was undergoing the written examination for the service some
years ago. He progressed well with his answers until he landed
with a sickening thud on the following: "Tell what you know of
Whitelocke's expedition to Buenos Aires." Turning his memory
upside down and inside out the young aspirant found it to be
completely blank on this particular historical event. Quick think-

ing was necessary, and while the future Metternich was not strong on certain facts of history, he possessed without doubt an excellent knowledge of the psychology of his own countrymen and of their ways of doing things. His first reaction was that if the expedition had been a British victory a knowledge of it would have been *caned* into him at an early date. Furthermore, with a parliament in which to ask questions and the *Times* to which to address letters, he felt that these channels would have been utilized by Whitelocke's friends in any controversy, so, after some mastication of the end of his pen holder, he wrote approximately as follows:

"This expedition to the great city which is now the capital of the flourishing Argentine Republic, reflected but little glory on British arms. It was the subject matter of lively debate in Parliament, where questions were propounded to the Government by the Opposition, there was acrimonious correspondence in the *Times,* and a military court of inquiry to determine the guilt of the officer or officers concerned."

The candidate later learned that this brilliant piece of divination was considered satisfactory by the examiners!

A further and final reference to the streets of Buenos Aires before passing on: A French traveler and author of former days has praised the loveliness of the names chosen for thoroughfares, citing among others Esmeralda, Cerrito, Arenales. I would like to expand his list by adding at least the following: Acevedo, Balcarce, Ballivián, Calderón, Flores, Iraola, Lanús, Madero, Novaro, Pirovano, Tuyú, Sarmiento. (And here tucked away in a paragraph which probably no one will read I would like to whisper to myself, diplomatist and all, that there is a street called Monroe, named after a fellow-Virginian, who propounded the doctrine, the unilateral doctrine, with which his name is associated!)

It is particularly in architecture that French influence is appa-

THE AMERICAN EMBASSY, BUENOS AIRES, FROM THE UPPER GARDEN

TABLET IN THE AMERICAN EMBASSY, COMMEMORATING THE VISIT
OF PRESIDENT ROOSEVELT

rent in physical things in Buenos Aires. This is natural, for in addition to the cultural forces mentioned elsewhere which have been at work for many years is the further fact that many outstanding architects have studied in Paris, and this has left its natural and pleasing impression. As a logical result much of the architecture is French Renaissance.

Especially noteworthy, either for charm or historic interest, or both, are the Palacio Legislativo; the Palacio de Justicia; El Concejo Deliberante; the Colón Opera House; the General Post-Office Building; the Jockey Club; La Casa Rosada or Casa de Gobierno; various national and foreign bank buildings, including the Bank of Boston and the National City Bank; el Ministerio de Obras Públicas, el Colegio Nacional de Buenos Aires; the edifice of the Yacimientos Petrolíferos Fiscales (Government Oil Fields); those of various oil and electric companies, etc.

Of less interest, save as an indication of certain trends, are the number of modern and modernistic residences and apartment houses, notably the Edificio Kavanagh, best viewed from the water, the Mihanovich Building, and others. The impressive structure formerly occupied by several de Anchorena families, now the Ministry for Foreign Affairs, and known as el Palacio San Martín, in the square of the same name; the mansions of the Paz, Ortiz Basualdo, Uribelarrea, and Errazuriz families—the latter now housing the Museo Nacional de Arte Decorativo; the American Embassy, built by Doctor Ernesto Bosch from plans by Sergent, probably the finest residence in the city; and Doctor Bosch's present charming house in Calle Montevideo may all be studied with interest and profit in any consideration of Buenos Aires structures. Buildings usually carry the names of the architects; a pleasing idea. Authors sign their books and painters their canvases. Why should architects be forgotten?

In past years the municipality has made an annual award for the most attractively designed business and residence structures. This of itself is a decided stimulus to good work.

Street Scenes and Characters

It is to be regretted that although the aquarelles and lithographs of Emeric Vidal and César Bacle and Carlos Morel preserve some of the charm and interest of the Buenos Aires of a century or more ago, there seems no one of their caliber now who is concerned to preserve for posterity in graphic form the various types which give an added cachet to the city.

I have in mind especially the chimney sweeps who, however, as compared with others I shall name, are new comers, and of Teutonic origin. These gentry, it will be recalled, occupied in the London of former days a certain fixed position, as representing an extreme in the social scale. Here in the Buenos Aires of today, they are to be encountered moving about "on their lawful occasions," and wearing a garb suggestive of diplomatic representatives of some African kingdom—a morning coat, and dark trousers. With top hats crowning grimy faces, they are usually seen astride bicycles, with the implements of their calling hung from the handle bars; super-sweeps run to motorcycles. Alas, it is easy to foresee the time when our besmudged friends will have been air-conditioned out of existence.

> *Golden lads and girls all must,*
> *As chimney sweepers, come to dust.*

Another type doomed to extinction by "eversharp" blades and by electrical appliances for lifting the fungi from the masculine countenance is the knife and scissors grinder, a character given a kind of immortality in the Muse's Heaven by Canning's witty verses. I think I shall never forget the plaintive note which he sounds on a penny whistle to proclaim his presence to vigilant housewives—now high, now low, with a plaintive and appealing middle note.

Air conditioning will also be the death of my friend Manuel, with whom I occasionally stop to chat, and who, with his parents and younger brothers, manufactures in a tiny back room the household brushes of excellent quality he sells along the streets.

Not to be overlooked, because of his primitive roaster and his somewhat sketchy garb, is *el manicero* (the peanut vendor) whose appeal and methods, if they find expression in a different language, are yet not unlike those to be seen at home.

There is also *el barquillero,* who sells from a metal cylinder a thin rolled wafer called *barquillo,* the edible contents of which are often displaced by a prize of little value, making of the cylinder a kind of ambulatory grab bag, with a special appeal to children. The *barquillero* announces his arrival by measured strokes on a metal triangle, whose familiar sound is at once an intimation and an invitation to the little folk to try their luck. And who that has arrived by train has failed to notice "Mateo," the cabby, a cognomen as sacredly reserved for his tribe as "George" for our Pullman porters. He too is passing rapidly. Here might be recalled a local saying to the effect that Buenos Aires is the horses' cemetery (*el cementerio de los caballos*), the tremendous distances proving fatal in many cases.

All these types to which I have referred, figures happily familiar in former days, are slowly disappearing from the principal streets, and now are more often found in thoroughfares remote from the center, anticipating, perhaps, their final disappearance from the scene.

I had hoped for a certain longevity, if not immortality for a bewhiskered worthy who used to haunt La Costanera, the great avenue which skirts the river, and the broad plaza in front of La Casa Rosada. It was he, I believe, who colored the huge flock of pigeons which, as if he were a modern St. Francis of Assisi, would descend in a fluttering eddy about his shoulders when he called them. Perhaps, too, it was he who dyed a large number of pigeons red and blue which, with other uncolored snowy-white brethren, he drew in a mad swirl of vari-colored pinions over the street through which President Roosevelt was passing at the time of his visit in December, 1936. But he has recently died, and is doubtless succeeded by some young fellow who wears store clothes and uses hair oil.

With these street characters I would link, although in a quite different category, the children of the national schools who throng the streets at certain hours each wearing a long white blouse. The custom to me is charming and practical; it saves wear on clothes and, better than this, tends to eliminate economic differences which would be apparent in ordinary dress.

MUSEUMS

Anyone wishing to make something more than a superficial study of things Argentine would do well to begin with a visit to some of the museums of the capital.

First of all he should go to the Museo Histórico Nacional, in Calle Defensa 1600, set in a lovely park where he will find a helpful and informative collection of paintings, maps, portraits, and other material relating to colonial days and especially of the long period of the war of independence. This should be supple-

The Palace of Justice, Buenos Aires

The Casa Rosada

EL BARQUILLERO

mented by a visit to the Museo Fernandez Blanco, Victoria 1420, and to the small Museo Colonial, Calle Suipacha 1422 (it is necessary to arrange this through the office of the intendente).

In this latter will be found much of interest to the student of the period of "The Tyranny," to which reference is made in "Background" Chapter XXI: scarfs worn by adherents of Rosas, crimson in color as a tribute to this sinister figure; numerous pictures of the tyrant, demonstrating at least his unusual physical beauty; souvenirs of his lovely daughter who possessed all the devotion, graces and high qualities of an Antigone; engravings depicting the execution of the poor Camila O'Gorman and her equally unfortunate young lover; etc. This latter reference brings to memory one of the most heart-rending and tragic stories of the Rosas régime, if not of all Argentine history, and depicts in unfading colors the sanguinary character of this ruthless tyrant. At the risk of a long aside the story of this passion should be told. In its poignancy, it is comparable to the stark tragedy of Paolo and Francesca, or of Abélard and Eloïse.

The year was 1848. Camila O'Gorman, a girl of rare beauty, of highest social position, and an intimate of Manuelita Rosas, the daughter of the Tyrant, went one day to the church of El Socorro. The preacher was a young priest, Gutierrez, the sound of whose voice caused a storm in the heart of the young girl of twenty. It is not known how out of this encounter romance grew, but it did, and one winter morning, these two passionate pilgrims fled from Buenos Aires, disappearing as completely as if the ground had swallowed them up. When told of their flight, the Tyrant grew livid with anger, not so much because of the pain which such a scandal caused to pious folk, but rather because of a prompt realization that the incident would be seized upon by his enemies, notably in Montevideo, for a fresh outburst of attacks against him and his administration. Orders were sent in all directions to seek the young lovers and return them to Buenos Aires, "the theatre of their horrible crime."

Months passed by before a chance meeting of Gutierrez with a brother priest in a dim street of an obscure town in Corrientes, brought about their arrest. Camila and Gutierrez were hurried down to Buenos Aires, and there by order of the Tyrant thrown into the common jail, loaded with irons on hands and feet. It is to the credit of the callous jailer that he made an effort to find manacles of lightest weight to be worn by Camila, and wrapped these with cloths that her delicate hands and feet should not suffer unduly. But the iron had long since entered into her heart.

The day following their arrival in the capital, without trial, without warrant of law, in pursuit of a ruthless and inexorable policy which had drenched his country in blood, Rosas gave orders for their execution the next morning. The officer charged with this hideous duty protested to Rosas, adding as a final appeal that Camila was soon to become a mother. He was brutally repulsed with the threat that he might also lose his life should he hesitate in carrying out the orders given him. The pleas of Manuelita with her father were equally unavailing, and plans for the execution were hurried forward. On August 18, 1848, tightly bound in chairs, and with bandaged eyes, the two culprits were placed in front of the firing squad. Turning her bandaged head in the direction of her lover, Camila asked in broken tones if he were there. "I am here, Camila," he replied, in a firm voice; and after the very slightest pause, added "We shall soon be together in heaven." A moment later, a ragged volley seemed to end it all; but not so. The clothing of the unhappy Camila, the expectant mother, was ignited by the wadding of the rifles and she fell forward enveloped in flames and screaming with anguish until a more merciful volley ended her suffering and silenced her cries.

These hideous facts are taken from the writings of Argentine historians. And yet there is a movement on foot to erect a monument to Juan Manuel de Rosas; as one who deserves well of his country. Should this be done, it could only be when this tragic story of two "who loved not wisely but too well," with the Tyrant's other brutalities and crimes, has been forgotten.

Any serious student of Argentine and South American history will wish to consult the valuable historical material brought together in the Museo Mitre, Calle San Martín 336. Here, in the family home of Bartolomé Mitre, general and president, poet and historian, brilliant commentator of Dante, and founder of "La Nación," is a library of first importance in all that relates to Latin American history.

In El Museo Nacional de Bellas Artes, Avenida Alvear 2273, temporary expositions are held from time to time of works of artistic appeal illustrating the old or new world. There is also a permanent exposition of paintings of value and interest.

Under the Department of Bellas Artes is also the Museo de Arte Decorativo, which is housed in the magnificent Errazuriz palace, Avenida Alvear 2802. This sumptuous private residence with most of its furniture and works of art including superb tapestries, was acquired by the Federal Government in 1937. Its architect, Sergent, also designed the American Embassy.

Through many years wealthy Argentines have with taste and discrimination purchased Old World art treasures and brought them home. And perhaps the real artistic treasures of Argentina are to be found in various private residences and private museums of the capital. For example, there are exquisite frescoes by Sert, in the Pereda Palace, a residence occupied by President Vargas of Brazil when he visited Argentina in 1936; while the Llobet,

Guerrico and Gonzales Garaño collections make a strong appeal to every art-lover. These treasures, however, are for the most part behind closed doors and only personal friends or those with appropriate letters have the privilege of enjoying them. But in increasing measure public museums are being enriched through the generosity of patriotic citizens, and with the passage of time these should become collections accessible to the general public.

In addition to the public museums already mentioned it is probable that the Museo Argentino de Ciencias Naturales, Peru 208; the Museo Etnográfico, Moreno 350; the Museo de Farmacología, Córdoba 2182; the Museo Social Argentino, Viamonte 1455; may make their appeal to visitors especially interested in the directions indicated.

To this list should be added the name of the Museo Etnológico of La Plata, rich in objects brought back after searches made in the Patagonian region.

ANTIQUES

Emily Dickinson in one of her incisive poems remarks that she never heard "the word 'escape' without a quicker blood." I confess that "my heart leaps up when I behold" the word "antiques" over a door.

Unfortunately, to those of my readers who may suffer from the malady to which I confess, an infirmity which makes one bolt into strange shops wherein objects which bear the alleged patina of age are for sale, I must hasten to point out that the number of such places in Buenos Aires is not great; furthermore, Argentina being like our own, a young country, there is little here of an artistic nature of local origin possessing at the same time the virtue of antiquity. But bearing in mind the great wealth of Argentina and the Old World treasures which have been brought here from abroad, and which on occasion come into the market, one's interest is kept constantly alive and the chase sometimes rewarded.

A list of antique shops appears as Appendix V. In these, as is suggested, occasional bargains are found. Such finds would embrace furniture, mirrors, old Spanish paintings, ecclesiastical vestments, fragments of ruby velvet; candlesticks, and other things having a foreign origin.

On the other hand, less difficulty is encountered in finding old silver stirrups, bowls and pitchers; maté bowls and bombillas, in the same metal; a variety of objects in leather; vicuña rugs,— delightfully light, warm and comfortable, ideal for bed covers or motor robes; boleadores of yesterday's manufacture, and occasionally old ones; riding whips (here called rebenques); and belts in leather or in bright colored wool. In addition, Pardo has from time to time interesting Inca funerary jars and feather robes from Inca tombs. Also to be found, provided one is patient, are the lovely tortoise-shell combs which the belles of Argentina affected a century or more ago. These combs are sometimes over 24 inches wide, and the embarrassment which their dimensions occasionally caused their wearers or bystanders is mocked in the contemporary caricatures of Bacle and in the satirical literature of the times.

Occasionally a big flag bearing the word "Remate" (Auction) is to be seen flying over some old house doomed to demolition. This represents a heaven-sent opportunity to the case-hardened antique hunter, which should not be lost. To bid successfully, however, one should be accompanied by some one with a good knowledge of Spanish.

In addition to the places which offer antiques, there are many old book shops in the capital, wherein one may pass delightful hours browsing. Some of these are also listed in Appendix V.

Naturally books in Spanish are most frequently found, and liturgical works from early Spanish or Italian presses are not unusual, together with French political and historical works and *belles lettres*. But real bargains go only to the persistent searcher. Fortunately I do not have to remind the really *endurci bouquineur* that in his search for Elzevirs and Plantins and Aldines, it is "the rapture of pursuing" that is the best part of the hunt, and too often its only reward.

CHURCHES

"La Ciudad de la Santísima Trinidad y Puerto de Santa María de los Buenos Aires" (The City of the Most Holy Trinity and Port of Saint Mary of the Good Airs) is the designation of the capital of Argentina in ecclesiastical documents. And to this lofty title King Philip V of Spain added in 1716 "muy noble y leal" (very noble and loyal). The patron since 1580 has been San Martín of Tours; however, following the reconquest of the city from the British in 1807, Santa Clara was named minor patron.

The Diocese of Buenos Aires was created in 1620, a full thirteen years after the foundation of the first permanent English settlement within the boundaries of the present United States, at Jamestown, Virginia, and the same year which saw the founding of Plymouth Colony. This creation was carved from the ancient Diocese of Paraguay. In 1865 the Archbishopric of Buenos Aires was created. Ten Bishoprics depended from this, until 1933, when the Argentine Congress created additional Sees, and elevated to Archdioceses several existing dioceses. In 1936 the Pope conferred the red hat on the head of the Church in Argentina, so that the ecclesiastical organization of the Roman Church in the Republic now has as its chief a Cardinal-Archbishop, of Buenos Aires, Doctor Santiago Luis Copello, who is assisted by six other Archbishops and fourteen Bishops.

Because of its relative newness as a great metropolis Buenos Aires can offer for the visitors' delectation no such historic and magnificent ecclesiastical structures as are to be found in the old world. But there are various churches here which merit attention and which the visitor is urged to see.

The first of these is Nuestra Señora del Pilar which adjoins the cemetery of La Recoleta, referred to elsewhere.

This pleasant and highly characteristic colonial edifice was commenced in 1716 and inaugurated sixteen years later. The Recoletos, a branch of the Franciscan order, ruled over this until 1822. At that time reforms carried out by Rivadavia caused the convent to be converted into a barracks and the adjoining land into a cemetery.

The bricks used in the construction of the church are said to be among the earliest made in Buenos Aires. The windows are fitted with extremely thin translucent sheets of stone. Particularly to be remarked are the figures of the Christ and of San Pedro de Alcántara, both the work of the great Spanish sculptor Alonso Cano and said to have been presented by Philip III of Spain. In the sacristy are superb wardrobes and chests of drawers in which are kept the rich vestments belonging to the church.

An even earlier church is La Basílica de Nuestra Señora de la Merced, at the corner of Reconquista and Cangallo (Basílica, it will be recalled, is the title now given by the Pope to privileged churches remarkable for antiquity or historical associations; they are either major or minor).

La Merced was originally constructed in 1604, reconstructed by General José Ruiz de Arellano in 1732 and practically made over in 1889. Preserving in all its harmony the colonial tint that makes it stand out from other similar structures here, it is one of the loveliest churches of the capital. In the tympanum is seen in high relief General Belgrano in the act of delivering his staff of office to La Virgen de la Merced.

Worthy of notice is an antique statue of the Christ of Humility and Patience over the first altar at the right on entering; this is said to be the work of an Indian convert of more than two centuries ago. The handsome communion rail, the gift of La Condesa Pombo de Devoto, should also be examined. The archives of La Merced are particularly rich, having been begun in 1601, and are thus the oldest in Buenos Aires. This church in its inception was a monastery of the Order of the Mercedarios.

Nuestra Señora de la Piedad is at the corner of Bartolomé mitre and Paraná. The Parish itself dates from 1769; the beautiful temple is the work of the architect Canale with later alterations by J. Bucchiazzo. In the opinion of many critics La Piedad is the most praiseworthy of all the churches of Buenos Aires. Within its walls is venerated a miraculous image of the Saviour which dates however only from the close of the last century.

The Cathedral, the mother church of Buenos Aires, was founded in the first third of the seventeenth century. The labor of construction was a prime care to various Bishops over a long series of years, so much so that there remains a saying among porteños when a great and interminable work is in progress that it "es la obra de la catedral" (it is the erection of the cathedral). Only in the time of Rivadavia, in the first half of the nineteenth century, was the façade given its present form. The tympanum of the façade of the cathedral represents the meeting of Joseph with his father and brothers in Egypt.

The architecture of the cathedral is Romanesque, with tall columns supporting the portico. The central nave measures 75 meters and the crossing 49 meters. The sacristies of the canons and of the clergy merit a visit. The woodwork here is entirely of the jacarandá tree, elaborately and beautifully carved. Here are pre-served beautiful manuscripts, superb chalices and other antique objects of art. Also two pictures attributed to Rubens.

In the vaults of the cathedral are the remains of the liberator, Don José de San Martín, who in a certain moral grandeur, quite apart from his military achievements, ranks with our Washing-ton; of General Gregorio Las Heras; General Bruno Mauricio de Zabala (1682-1736), founder of Montevideo, and other distin-guished dead.

The church of San Juan Bautista at the corner of Alsina and Piedras is under the direction of the Fathers of the Order of Jesus de Betharam, and embraces also a convent of Capuchin nuns of the Order of Nuestra Señora del Pilar. This ancient sub-parish of the native Indians was erected in 1753; within its vaults are the remains of an early Viceroy, Melo. Worthy of notice is a painting on linen representing the adoration of the Christ Child by the Magi; this is seen on the choir screen near the high altar. The story of this work is interesting. It was ordered by Francis I of France from the artist Bathou. When received it was sent by Francis to the Sovereigns of Spain who in turn sent it to the Philippine Islands. During the course of the voyage, the vessel bearing it was captured by an Argentine corsair near the Canary Islands. It was then brought to Buenos Aires by one of the pirates and placed on sale. A certain canon Vidal seeing it and realizing its artistic value, apart from its sacred portrayal, purchased it for fifteen ounces, and placed it in the church.

El Convento de las Monjas Dominicanas, or of Santa Catalina de Siena, at the corner of San Martín and Viamonte, is probably closed to the public, but should be mentioned because of its rela-tive antiquity. On Christmas day 1745, the pious nuns began to occupy this convent, having come from Córdoba. On July 5, 1807 the convent was sacked by the British Army and on the altar of the nuns may yet be seen traces of the invaders' disastrous entry. This date, called by the nuns "La Entrada de los Ingleses," is commemorated annually with a solemn Te Deum, "The Divine Providence having that day delivered them from great evils."

La Basílica del Santísimo Rosario Santo Domingo, at the corner of Defensa and Belgrano, commonly called La Iglesia del Santo Domingo, and its convent, known as El Convento de San Pedro González Telmo, is more intimately connected with the history of the city than any other building in Buenos Aires; "every brick," says an enthusiastic historian, "recalls a glorious deed of our history." The cornerstone was laid on June 29, 1756 and in 1783 it was consecrated to Nuestra Señora del Rosario; in 1909 the Holy Father designated it a minor basilica.

In the portico of the temple on the left as one enters is a superb monument by Martin Casals to the great Dominican Bishop of Cuyo, Fray Marcelino del Carmelo Benavente. During the British invasions the church was repeatedly struck by cannon balls; reproductions of projectiles on the left tower recall these attacks.

In front of the church is the tomb of General Manuel Belgrano (1770-1820), initiator of and leader in the Wars of Independence, to whom the nation owes the design of the national standard.

In a chapel on the left of the high altar are a number of British flags captured during the invasion of 1807, and presented, with other trophies from the same source, by General Liniers. Also preserved in this church are Spanish flags wrested from the enemy at the Battle of Tucumán and deposited in the convent by General Belgrano. Distinguished Argentines whose remains rest within the church are General Matías Zapiola and General Antonio González Balcarce.

CEMETERIES

The reference to doctors and surgeons concluding the previous section leads one's thoughts in a logical sequence to a consideration of the cemeteries of this capital! There are many, but only three which are likely to be of interest to the traveler—el Cementerio del Norte, better known as La Recoleta; el Cementerio del Oeste, or Chacarita; and el Cementerio de los Disidentes, or the British Cemetery.

La Recoleta occupies a large plot of ground about three hundred yards north of the Alvear Palace Hotel. Strictly speaking, the name derives from Recoleto, which means a member of the order once occupying the adjoining monastery. These Recoletos formed a branch of the Franciscan Order, and the founders aimed at a detachment from earthly things and a recollection in God. And considering its meaning, what a beautiful name for a cemetery.

The public use of this Campo Santo dates from perhaps less than a century ago, but to call the names of those interred within its limits is not merely to cite the names of national heroes, but at once to read the Golden Book of Argentines, in political, social, economic, intellectual and commercial life.

In design the cemetery is a checker-board, the narrow streets crossing each other at right angles. Entrance is through a monumental gateway, where there is a mortuary chapel, and administrative offices. La Recoleta is to me, as I believe it will prove to most visitors, one of the most interesting cities of the dead in the world. It is, so far as I know, unique among cemeteries in the New World. This arises in part from the fact that the ground-space being extremely circumscribed, it has been necessary to limit the size of memorials above ground, and to go well below the surface to obtain sufficient space in family vaults; and the result has been that literally every square inch of surface not necessary for passageways is covered with tiny chapels built immediately above vaults. In these chapels masses can be said and on the altars fresh flowers may be placed and candles lighted.

As for myself, I cannot visit the Recoleta without being moved when reading the names graven over the tombs. It is the Argentine of the past which speaks to me in this national pantheon. It is furthermore a spot already grown sacred to me, and making its personal appeal; for even in my brief stay in Argentina its gates have opened to receive the remains of men and women who honored me with their friendship and whose families I count among my intimates.

The British Cemetery was in the past possessed of what might be called an ambulatory character! Originally it was located in Calle Juncal, in a now densely populated residential section, but as early as 1833 the encroachment of dwellings and the growth of the city made a move necessary. Accordingly, the remains of early Britons and Americans and a number of other nationalities, not of the Roman Catholic faith, were removed to a site in Calle Victoria. But again the growth of the city made a change advisable, and in 1892 a large tract of ground was acquired adjoining the Cementerio del Oeste, or Charcarita. The site formerly occupied has been converted into an attractive park, Plaza 1° de Mayo.

Somewhere in one of the three cemeteries, in an unmarked grave, lie the remains of the first American minister to this country, Caesar Augustus Rodney (1772-1824), lawyer, statesman and diplomat. He was the nephew of Caesar Rodney, a signer of

Scott

Monument to Caesar Augustus Rodney, first United States
Minister to Argentina

THE CEMETERY OF THE RECOLETA, BUENOS AIRES

Fort

THE COLON THEATRE

Besseli

the Declaration of Independence, who assisted in his education, and generously remembered him in his will.

Caesar Augustus pursued politics actively and successfully, and attached himself to Mr. Jefferson, fighting some of his battles in the House of Representatives, especially in the matter of the Louisiana purchase and the Twelfth Amendment to the Federal Constitution. He was rewarded in 1807 by being named Jefferson's Attorney General, in which rôle he took an active part in the prosecution of Aaron Burr. He had an honorable record in the War of 1812, and in 1817 was appointed by President Monroe a member of a special commission to visit South America for the purpose of ascertaining the political status of various newly-established republics. His fellow-commissioners were Theodorick Bland of Virginia and John Graham. The commission spent some time in Buenos Aires in 1818. After a term in the Senate, Rodney resigned to accept appointment by Mr. Monroe as first Minister Plenipotentiary from the United States to what is now the Argentine Republic, for which his experience and knowledge fitted him. He presented his credentials on December 27, 1823, illness having somewhat delayed his reception. His commission is dated exactly eleven months earlier.

Rodney never recovered his health in Buenos Aires and died on June 10, 1824, seven months following his arrival. On the day of his death the Argentine Congress proclaimed public mourning and the newspapers carried black borders. His funeral oration was pronounced by General Rivadavia, a former president of the country, and contemporary accounts, which the cold judgment of later days confirms, rank this oration with some of Bossuet's great utterances over distinguished dead. There stands today in the Anglican pro-cathedral of St. John in Buenos Aires a cenotaph erected in his memory by the Buenos Aires Government.

It is interesting to recall here that Rodney's daughter married a Presbyterian clergyman named Parvin and was the first Evangelical missionary to give her life to Latin America. She and her husband were also buried in this first Protestant Cemetery, but no trace of their resting place is to be found.

This has been a long digression, and I hasten now in conclusion to tell my impatient reader that the present British cemetery has a vague suggestion of the leafy, floral, garden-like quality, which is the peculiar characteristic of cemeteries at home, and especially of those in England.

In addition to the naturally preponderant British names, many names of men and women prominent in the American colony in Argentina in past years are to be seen on the tombstones, as well as those of early sea captains and other seafaring folk, who engaged in the brisk trade maintained between the United States and Argentina in the early part of the nineteenth century.

A tablet sent down from the United States, and placed in the first cemetery in Calle Juncal to John M. Forbes, of "Florida," but really of the well-known Massachusetts family, was successively transferred and is now to be seen on the present cemetery wall. Forbes, who was Rodney's Secretary of Legation, served as Chargé d'Affaires after his death for seven years, until his own demise.

As indicated, the extensive Chacarita cemetery is the neighbor of the British cemetery. This is the largest and most crowded of all the burial places in Buenos Aires. The approach is through impressive monumental gateways from which one proceeds by broad avenues to its various sections. To be remarked are the number and substantial quality of the family vaults. Also the various chapel-mausoleums belonging to communities, associations or societies, in which provision is made for religious services, with innumerable shelves above and below ground in which interments may be made.

In the center of the cemetery is a huge crematorium, for although the Roman Church does not favor cremation, the policy of the Municipality is in a contrary sense and bodies are cremated on request without charge in the case of families too poor to pay. However, in a special section of the crematorium, provision is made for the disposal of bodies at an established fee.

Such solemn days as All Saints' and All Souls' are observed throughout the country with all the tenderness and fervor and deeply-rooted faith characterizing a people so essentially Roman Catholic as the Argentines. All Saints' Day offers a particularly impressive and moving sight, when relatives and friends of those who are buried therein gather in the various cemeteries and with tender hands place fresh flowers and "fair linen cloths" on the graves and on the altars in the tombs.

3. *The American Colony in Buenos Aires*

The American Colony in Buenos Aires is one of which our compatriots may be proud. Its distinguishing marks are its high quality and its homogeneity. Furthermore, the fact that its members, in a certain measure, belong to the same economic class, represented by heads of enterprises, facilitates easy intercourse with each other and with other foreign and Argentine groups.

The colony is relatively small, yet exercises an influence out of all proportion to its numbers. This influence is seen and felt in a variety of ways, but is most manifest through the operation of various organizations such as *The American Club, The American Chamber of Commerce, The American Society of the River Plate, The American Legion, Spencer Ely Post, No. 1, and The American Women's Club.*

Our Government is represented in Argentina by an Ambassador, who is assisted by a Counselor and several Secretaries. The Embassy staff also includes a Military, a Naval, a Commercial and an Agricultural Attaché.

There is also a Consul General, two Consuls and seven Vice-Consuls, who carry out many important duties.

THE ARGENTINE NORTH AMERICAN CULTURAL INSTITUTE

Allied to activities of the American colony in this country is an organization which I would like particularly to bring to the notice of every compatriot who visits Argentina. I refer to the Instituto Cultural Argentino Norteamericano, or Argentine North American Cultural Institute, familiarly known as the ICANA, whose activities are best described by the following text which appears on its letter heads:

The Instituto Cultural Argentino-Norteamericano, organized by Argentine citizens, is a private association and, as indicated by its name, exclusively for promoting mutual cultural understanding, with entire avoidance of commercial or political matters. It carries out its purpose by teaching English, exchanging professors, establishing scholarships, holding of art exhibitions and lectures, circulating books, etc. It is closely connected with the most important intellectual centres of the United States, and enjoys the individual and collective cooperation of the American organizations in Argentina. It believes finally, that this loyal and friendly collaboration must be beneficial to both democracies, whose ideals, which are parallel notwithstanding racial differences, may together work for a still higher level of civilization.

The outstanding Argentines who make up the governing body of the Institute, together with our compatriots who cooperate with them, are giving "without money and without price" valuable thought and time in laudable effort in directions which the extract quoted sets forth. It is an organization in which my predecessor and I have taken and take the deepest interest, and I am happy to place on record my gratitude and thanks to its managers for their useful work.

British and American Benevolent Society

An organization in which members of the American Colony in Buenos Aires take an effective and continued interest is the British and American Benevolent Society, senior organization in the two communities of those which exist for the relief of distress among our less fortunate countrymen here.

The Annual Cattle Show

Happy the traveler whose visit to Buenos Aires occurs toward the end of August. For then he has the opportunity of witnessing what is one of the most interesting ceremonies and sights of all modern Argentina, the inauguration of the great cattle show— La Exposición Nacional de Ganadería—held annually under the auspices of La Sociedad Rural Argentina.

The solemn opening, which is always attended by the President of the Republic, foreign diplomatists, members of the Argentine Cabinet, Argentines outstanding in the breeding of cattle, in agricultural and pastoral pursuits, and in finance and commerce, has already assumed a traditional character as more than fifty years have elapsed since these expositions were inaugurated. Each year places in evidence in the exhibits the results of individual and collective efforts of breeders and the high quality of the principal source of wealth of the country. When it is recalled that more than ninety-five percent of the value of Argentine exports arises from products of field and farm and breeding ground, the occasion to which I refer is seen to be a manifestation of the most vital interests of the land.

On the day of the inauguration and during the course of the exposition the very finest examples of live stock are on display; bulls of various classes—Shorthorns, Aberdeen Angus, Herefords, Holland-Argentine—all of first quality. They are led in solemn procession, bearing on their heads the distinctive mark of their triumph, and later are seen in their stalls, each skillfully bedded down to emphasize a physical appearance which would appear to mark him out from his fellows.

Magnificent rams after being paraded are to be seen lying or standing in their little pens, with a coat of wool beautifully cleaned and combed and of magnificent depth, length and quality —Lincolns, Romney Marshes, Corriedales, Argentine Merinos, Oxford and Hampshires and South Downs (with what promises of thick juicy chops!) and Karakules.

The displays of swine and poultry and canines are interesting but, of course, best of all are the horses: polo ponies, perfect in their clean lines; chargers, fitted for hard campaigns; thoroughbreds; tractable saddle horses; artillery horses; Clydesdales, wearing muffs around their feet; Percherons, etc.

Such an exposition is a natural opportunity for the manufacturers of agricultural machinery and products to bring their wares to the attention of an interested public, and once interest is surfeited in viewing the animals, there are the various exhibits of the character indicated to attract.

The exposition of 1937 began on August 21 and lasted for some ten days. This would seem to be the normal length of the show, during the course of which an unbroken stream of visitors flows through the gates. In the last days most of the animals are auctioned off, and one of these sales is worth attending. The enthusiastic auctioneer often makes a speech over a particularly fine animal, reciting his pedigree as if he were a Garter King-at-Arms speaking of royalty; in a word, the contrast is striking between such sales and those, for example, in Scotland, where the dour salesman is apt, to use the stock phrase, to "cut the cackle" and bring his hammer down in a very short time.

BOOKS AND MAGAZINES

The interested reader is informed that he may buy American books in the small but up to date shop of the Instituto Cultural Argentino-Norteamericano, Maipú 686, referred to in the preceding Chapter.

Books in English as well as magazines may be found at Harrods, Florída 877, at Mitchell's English Book Store in Calle Cangallo 580 and at Mackern's, in the Retiro and Constitution railway stations. The latest issues of magazines and newspapers will be found at Harrods, and at Rodriguez, 277 Maipú; magazines in various languages are to be seen at the "Librería Sarmiento," Libertad 1224.

French books may be bought in El Palacio del Libro, Librería Hachette, S.A. in Calle Maipú 49, and at Viau's, Florída 530.

For those who have the courage to look a stock-broker in the face a visit may be made to an American bank through whom quotations from the New York and other exchanges can be obtained.

CHAPTER VI

Argentine Society

ARGENTINE SOCIETY is, to employ a phrase familiar to my countrymen, "a closed shop;" a Frenchman would say it was "très fermée!" Furthermore, comparable to conditions prevailing in London and in Paris, and in contradiction to those existing in the United States, when one speaks of Argentine society one means the society of the federal capital. It is true that in cities like Córdoba, Salta, Tucumán, Mendoza, and others, there exists a flavor of tradition and an indefinable quality of conservatism that stem from colonial and to viceregal days; yet these cities are too remote and too essentially local in quality to alter seriously what I have just said.

An acute observer of Argentine life, Jules Huret, writing a quarter of a century ago, confirms my belief that this society of which I speak is one which in its customs, in its outward seeming, is one of the most correct in the world; and in this correctness is seen the conserving and powerful influence of the Church.

Since there is no divorce law, divorce may be said to be unknown locally and persons obtaining a separation in nearby Uruguay or elsewhere are frowned upon.

About two hundred families make up the Argentine social fabric, but these are interwoven to an astonishing degree, and with their ramifications in the political, social and intellectual life of the country form an all powerful group.

I suggested above that the society of Buenos Aires is a closed one. It would ill become me, who have enjoyed a lavish hospitality and warmth of welcome here to which I find no parallel in any previous experience, to criticize this; I do not; *je constate.* Seeking, however, a reason for this aloofness and exclusiveness I seem to find it in certain measure in the closeness of the family tie, which makes an Argentine household, particularly one of the old régime, sufficient unto itself. For in this family life, parents, uncles, aunts, cousins, nieces, etc., are in such close and constant contact that not a great deal of time is left for the outsider! This Argentine reserve is especially to be remarked in relations with foreigners. A measure of necessary self-protection is, perhaps, inevitable in a country and society which has had to stand what can only be called the shocks of successive waves of immigration, and one whose reputedly fabulous wealth attracted too often men whose aims were entirely mercenary. Again, the Argentine is by nature slow to give his friendship; like a certain type of shy Englishman, he must be "stalked;" but once that friendship is given, it persists, "through good and through evil report." To all this should be added the almost cloistered position occupied by women for centuries in countries like Spain, something that persisted in the colonies, and the slow wearing down of the attitude of their natural protectors toward strangers.

The great majority of our own compatriots come to Argentina to reside with the idea of returning home in a few years; it often happens therefore that at least the feminine members of the family make no real effort to learn the rich idiom of the country, with all the flattering implications to the Argentine of such an attempt, and thus a barrier of language persists even where the Argentine speaks English with ease.

A discouragement to the study of Spanish, however, is found in the fact that Argentines are excellent linguists, if an unwarranted and persistent shyness makes them often conceal it. Apropos of this latter I recall an occasion when at an official dinner a charming *caballero* was seated next my wife, who speaks her own special brand of Spanish. After twenty minutes of difficult talk in the tongue of Cervantes, her dinner companion turned and said in an English impeccable from the standpoint of accent and grammar: "Now let *me* work a little while!"

And so, my advice to my compatriots who come to this country for even a brief sojourn is: study Spanish!

As in old civilizations, Argentine society reaches its fullest expression in the formal dinner, where foregather men of a high standard of physical beauty, hard-muscled and fit through participation in various sports, and women of marked loveliness, wearing "des costumes qui sont pour les yeux une ivresse." The tactful guest sends flowers the morning before a dinner to which he is invited.

Also, in the case of weddings, where the friendship is not quite close enough to warrant a present, flowers may be appropriately sent to carry good wishes, to the house in which the reception is to be held.

To these finishing-school remarks should be added a word concerning the great importance to the visitor of leaving cards— promptly on arrival, and immediately after being entertained, and especially in case of family bereavements. And do not fail to indicate your local address. I say this despite the fact that a young matron from "the Sticks" who was caressingly chided by my wife for this omission, remarked that "it was no longer smart!" Oh, shame, Oh, pity, Oh, *Hell!* No longer smart—perhaps not *necessary* for the Duke of Wellington or 'Gene Tunney, but "not smart!" Perish the thought! and save a distracted secretary the necessity of telephoning hotels, the consulate, or possibly mutual friends, to

learn where to return them. The social leaders are in large measure the descendants of early inhabitants of Buenos Aires and the
outlying district—government officials, merchants, landowners—
who around the turn of the nineteenth century began to interest
themselves in political life and eventually became the leaders of
the independence movement. These men and their descendants
may be said to be the aristocrats of Argentina, and certain names
persist up to the present, their bearers being the outstanding
figures in the political, social, economic, professional and diplomatic life of the Republic. A French observer goes so far as to
say that "during more than a century the entire life of the country
has been dominated by what is commonly called 'society.'" But
duplicating what has occurred in every country in the world,
especially following periods of political upheaval, later comers,
acquirers of wealth, whose sons and daughters were favored with
all the advantages that wealth gives, have intermarried with
descendants of these "Founding Fathers," and thus names relatively modern are interwoven with those of men who played their
part in the Cabildo movement of Buenos Aires of 1810, or who
six years later signed the great Declaration of Argentine Independence. We have then a social fabric whose roots are deeply
grounded in tradition and which in essentials is marked by a
strong conservatism. But this same society is in a sense being
attacked on all sides and from within by modern trends. Its own
members, some of whom have spent the greater part of their
years abroad, return with many contributions of positive value
and some others of doubtful consequence. In addition there is the
steady to and fro movement of foreigners, many of these men and
women of distinction, each of whom in his way leaves an impress
on the structure of Argentine life.

Contrary to the rule in many civilizations, particularly old ones, the large family is common in the highest classes rather than in the proletariat, despite the implications of the latter word. Early marriages are also encouraged, with a happy companionship resulting between parent and child as the latter reaches maturity. I recall a delightful instance in a prominent family where a charming matron is the mother of an adorable baby who is younger than one of her own grandchildren! In a word, Argentina is breeding from the top, not, as we, from the bottom. However, a well informed Argentine friend insists that my remarks are less true of the present generation, at least in the cities, where the young folk prefer flats to patriarchal dwellings.

Women in Argentina do not have the freedom of their sisters in England, in the Scandinavian countries, or in the United States. Nor has the Argentine woman yet been granted the vote; furthermore, she seems indifferent to it, and to the power its possession confers.

This latter statement, however, requires clarifying, for I am not unmindful that in political and in other affairs the Argentine woman does play, certainly in individual cases, a powerful part.

Illustrative of this there comes to mind a salon maintained over many years by a woman of unusual gifts, Señora Susana Torres de Castex. However, when I refer to her merely as Doña Susana, I identify her at once for every man and woman of prominence in Buenos Aires, if not in the Republic. In another age she would have been one of those rare women who frequented the Hôtel de Rambouillet. Possessing in unusual measure a love for and a natural understanding of politics, she drew around her the real rulers of Argentina, not alone of the group for the moment in power, but also of the Opposition; and on the neutral ground of her drawing-room political passions seemed repressed, if not forgotten.

In addition to her political gifts, Doña Susana possessed that rare jewel, a perfect chef, whom she inspired, so that a meal at her table was something no gourmet would ever forget.

In the sprightly pages of my colleague Hugh Wilson's recent book, "The Education of a Diplomat," is a lively portrait of this delightful woman as he knew her some twenty years ago, including a tribute to her versatility as displayed in her intense love of music and kindred arts.

Doña Susana's death some two years ago was a very personal loss both to me and to my wife. She was our friend. If it were a question of meeting this or that member of the Government in a natural, easy, unconstrained way, it was she who could arrange it; if it was desired to have a suggestion whispered to a prominent member of the Senate or of the Chamber of Deputies, it could be safely entrusted to her.

But more than these things was the gift to her friends of her own vigorous and arresting personality.

Then there was the Señorita María de Baudrix, who died quite recently. She was of a great family and resided in one of the oldest houses in Buenos Aires. To her evenings at home and Thursday luncheons she was wont to draw every person of consequence living in or visiting this country. Politics were her passion and in the conversation around her one felt the force of Freeman's remark that history is the politics of yesterday and politics are the history of today. For some time she was uncompromisingly in the Opposition, but her politics never affected her rather sardonic sense of humor or the depth of her interest in contemporary affairs. She seemed a modern Princesse de Lieven—with her wings clipped. She, too, realized the sweet, seducing charm of good food, and I recall telling her that if I were king I should insist on decorating her chef, to be told in reply that he already had the Palms!

Speaking generally of the position of women here, it may be pointed out that the great advance in sports and in the pursuit of outdoor activities is slowly changing appearance of things. As yet, however, unmarried girls never receive male visitors except in company, and this is equally true of matrons.

Since its founding more than a century ago, an organization which is now a powerful and continuing influence for good throughout this Republic, la Sociedad de Beneficencia, may be said by its acts to have merited the slogan "It's smart to be charitable."

This really amazing organization, with its years of tradition and service behind it, its official relationship to the Government under the Ministry for Foreign Affairs and Worship (from which it receives subsidies equalling 12,000,000 pesos a year), assuring its officers a distinguished precedence at official functions, its important trust funds, administered with probity and skill, its immense physical structure, manifest in hospitals, orphan asylums, homes for the aged and poor, clinics, popular kitchens, and other services, is a factor of powerful significance in this Republic. A former diplomatist told me some years ago of an incident which illustrates the influence of this organization. He reached Buenos Aires at a moment when relations between his own country and Argentina were distinctly frigid, and he was being allowed to cool his heels for weeks with no indication from the Chief Executive as to when he would be permitted to present his letters of credence. Meeting the President of the Beneficencia he half confided to her his opinion that international relations were hardly improved by the lack of consideration being shown him. Within twenty-four hours he was informed of the date on which the Chief Magistrate would receive him!

The work of the Beneficencia is carried on by women who are

the very flower of Argentine society, and I am able to testify from personal knowledge to the self-denial and the self-abnegation which this gallant band of women display. There is a double motive inspiring them: their underlying humanity which their deep faith nourishes, and the realization that they are carrying on a great tradition. There are women in the Beneficencia Society actively assisting in its diverse charities whose mothers and grandmothers and great-grandmothers were officers or directors. Election to its Executive Council is a kind of patent of nobility, but with all the implications of *noblesse oblige* in the labor and self-denial required.

The extent and diversity of the activities of the Beneficencia are too great to permit of aught save passing mention. But space must be found for a word relating to its admirable Instituto de Maternidad.

In this Maternidad, expectant mothers from all over the Republic are received; 6,500 births within its walls represent an annual average, of which three-fourths are emergency cases, arriving at all hours of the day and night.

A complete clinic exists, with extensive activities reaching beyond the walls, such as prenatal and post-natal consultations, with social prophylaxis, etc. An additional aspect of its labors is the training offered, ranging from elementary courses to post-graduate instruction. Into its well-equipped laboratories converges everything of a scientific character. The character of the Instituto is one of social service, receiving indigent expectant mothers, caring for those recently confined, giving them additional help including education in the care and feeding of their offspring, and it is active in other phases of humanitarian work.

Ranking with the Beneficencia in the character and quality of the charitable work achieved is the association known as Las

Cantinas Maternales. This organization, although lacking the age of the Beneficencia, has already nearly a quarter century of fruitful existence. Its founder and active head and guiding spirit, Señora de Martinez de Hoz, is the gracious châtelaine of the beautiful property near Mar del Plata to which reference is made in Chapter XII.

This association may be said to find its inspiration and raison d'être in the words of Pasteur: "I do not ask of an unfortunate: of what country and religion are you; I say to him: You suffer, that is enough; I will help you."

In fulfillment of this ideal, fourteen branches of Las Cantinas Maternales are now actively at work in the capital and in the provinces from which the expectant or nursing mother, infants and children of tender years, and school children, may receive daily food, material help, and counsel. Furthermore, medical care is also given, mothers are taught how to care for their children, and clothing is distributed where needed. In carrying on this work the founder-president is assisted by a group of women representing highest Argentine tradition. The organization has been adopted by the National Council of Education which gratefully uses its services to provide school buffets (cantinas escolares).

If I seem to stress unduly the work of the Beneficencia and of Las Cantinas Maternales, it is because in no city with which I am familiar is charitable work of equal quality and value carried on to the same extent and by the same component elements as these.

The Argentine woman then is seen to be a devoted mother, a tireless laborer in the task of ameliorating human suffering, yet charmingly mundane. Also she is very beautiful. Perhaps her eyes are her most distinctive feature. Their brilliance is best suggested by a phrase in one of Ellen Fowler's witty novels, wherein her heroine is described as having "eyes quite too showy to be worn except with evening dress!" These are almost invariably shadowed by eyelashes so long as to frequently provoke the belief that they are artificial; in at least one case, and under proper chaperonage, I was allowed to disprove my conviction by actually pulling them!

Argentine society is amazingly inter-related; in fact a person who loves to indulge in gossip finds his style somewhat cramped in this country because he is liable to make his remarks to a brother, sister, aunt or uncle of the person concerned.

Identifications, however, are greatly helped by the fact that a woman may be said to retain her Christian and family name after marriage, and she is commonly referred to as Señora Maria Thus and So, wife of Señor This and That. And for one who like myself is interested in genealogy and has often run into a stone wall in tracing family origins in wills and other documents giving only the baptismal name of a spouse or married daughter, it is very helpful to know that Señora So and So was the daughter of Such a Couple and to learn in turn from his card the name of the mother of the man who has just been presented.

Some years ago there appeared in an American magazine an article entitled "The Commercial Value of the Social Column." The facts it set forth could doubtless be duplicated here. And certainly the development of the social column in Argentina is as marked as in the United States. I do not make this observation by way of felicitation; I only note the fact. As often happens with us, those charged with preparing the social notes are gentlewomen; at large functions they are usually found seated near the door in order to write down the names of all who attend. Practically all the newspapers publish copious social notes, but it is indicative of the customs of the people that in the Argentine summer the local social column almost ceases to appear and is replaced by one covering activities at Mar del Plata, with occasional reference to other resorts. Furthermore, local radio stations announce social functions, often with lists of guests, and other minutiae, which would indicate a vigorous interest in other people's affairs.

In these social notes it is frequently stated that Señora X has given or is about to give a dinner or a reception or a ball or what not, "en retribución de atenciones recibidas"—literally, in retribution of attentions received. Let not a compatriot who may read this sentence raise an eyebrow or permit a smile to plant wrinkles in his face. The word "retribución" is not to be thought of as the equivalent of our word "retribution," with its suggestion of punishment. The phrase quoted is really a frank recognition by Argentines of the fact that acceptance of hospitality implies an obligation which must be met: assent to this principle facilitates human intercourse in many ways, and even if we agree today in the truth of Byron's familiar lines, that:

> *Society is now one polished horde,*
> *Formed of two mighty tribes, the Bores and Bored,*

we cannot disregard the fact that man is a social animal, seeking the companionship of his fellows, and equally anxious to be sought out.

A pleasing custom prevailing in Buenos Aires and in other cities in the Republic, which I have never remarked, certainly not in like measure, elsewhere in my wanderings, is the farewell party given by persons about to depart on a foreign journey; a somewhat similar function is offered by those returning after travel to countries beyond the seas. These gatherings afford a pleasing opportunity to speed or to welcome friends. However, despite greetings exchanged on the former occasions one is not absolved from going to the steamer or the train or air port the following day again to register grief or veil the rapture felt at the departure of bosom friends; as a result a popular figure draws a crowd at station or dock comparable in its density and animation to a small section of Broadway on a New Year's Eve.

Another local custom—one which I frankly like—is the "homenaje" or homage, being constantly paid to others by friends, social, professional, or commercial. These take the form of a dinner, or reception, or presentation of a parchment; on this latter are set forth the virtues of the person honored, while at the social gatherings at least a dozen orators tell the world and the honored guest what a marvelous fellow he is. People participate cheerfully in these functions because each one cherishes the idea that it may be his turn next.

June, July and August see the social whirl in its most active form. By the end of September or soon after spirits are flagging a bit and formal dinners and receptions diminish in number. Men appear in the evenings more and more in dinner jackets or lounge suits, and there is an added dash of informality in women's dresses. Newspaper columns begin to be filled by lists of departures of social luminaries either for Europe or, too rarely, for the United States, or for *el campo,* the countryside, or open country; (Americans and English adopting this latter term talk of the rural parts of Argentine as "the camp," an expression which at first puzzles the visitor).

Just here is as good a place as any to point out that the people of Buenos Aires divide the inhabitants of the country into two classes: themselves, who are called the Porteños (men of the Port); and all the rest! There is nothing invidious in this ethnico-geographical division. And I recall a negro preacher in my town who declared, with a commendable state pride, that the races of man fall properly into four categories—the Huguenots and the Hottentots, the Abyssinians and the Virginians!

CHAPTER VII

The Theatre and the Opera

∽∽∽∽∽∽∽∽∽∽∽∽∽∽∽∽∽∽∽∽∽∽∽∽∽∽

THE PASSION TO ACT in the theatre and the passion to go to the theatre are elemental desires in mankind. And certainly it is in the very genius of the Argentine people to love a good spectacle. It inevitably follows that from an early time there have been in this country theatrical diversions of various kinds, in which folk gave vent, if vicariously, to their emotions and to the expression of that make-believe which is in each one of us in varying measure.

One of the first of the local places of amusement in which such diversions took place was not really a theatre but an attempt to create a place of outdoor entertainment in which spectacles of various kinds would form but a part. This was known as El Jardin Argentino and came into being in the time of Rivadavia, in the first quarter of the last century. It was designed along the lines and sometimes called by the name of "Vauxhall," a London resort which, it will be recalled, was frequented by Mr. Arthur Pendennis in certain critical years. However, the first of the play-houses was probably "El Argentino" erected on a site later occupied by "El Colón," the predecessor in tradition but not in locality of the present superb organization and structure to which reference is made later. Also to be mentioned was the informal and noisy "Alcázar"—*El Teatrillo de la gente alegre*—as remarks a chronicler of the old city, a phrase which might be fairly translated as "the Little Theatre of the Village Cut-ups."

It was in the original Colón structure that La Ristori and Salvini were first seen and heard, in both instances to the accompaniment of the delirious applause of the public. However, it would be difficult to say, generally speaking, that these outlets of emotions did anything toward advancing the intellectual life of the country or developing budding creative or imitative theatrical talent in individuals. Furthermore, there were other elements to militate against growth of anything like a national drama and a national theatre in Argentina. Among the first of these may be pointed out the essentially rural character of the Republic, and the further fact that Buenos Aires itself remained for long years a comparatively small town; so that there was the resulting absence of a public to respond to and to support dramatic talent; in a country so devoutly Roman Catholic as this, the traditional attitude of the Church toward the play-actor may have survived through the centuries from the time when actors were largely excluded from bourgeois society, denied burial in consecrated ground and wandered about in troupes, like gypsies, as Gautier has pictured in the fascinating pages of "Le Capitaine Fracasse." But doubtless more than these reasons, if conspiring with them, is the fact that the years which saw the beginnings of Argentine wealth and culture, saw also the decline in the dramatic art, in actor and playwright, in Spain, to which country because of the heritage from it of "a tongue understanded of the people" Argentina would have naturally looked first for guidance.

In any event, nothing like a local school of playwrights or of players of marked originality has as yet arisen. However, the foregoing remarks must be qualified, as regards the actual artist, for the popular theatre of Argentina has for years past been a very vivid thing, smacking absolutely of the soil in which it has flourished, and, within certain limits, training a school of men and women making peculiar appeal to their compatriots. (A reference to this popular theatre appears in another chapter).

Just here a special word must be said concerning the recent coming into existence in Buenos Aires of El Teatro del Pueblo (the People's Theatre). The ideal of this theatre is to experiment, to develop, and to disseminate throughout the Republic sound knowledge of the stage, classical and modern, naturally conserving what is indigenous to the country, to the end that this latter may be given back to the people strengthened, purified, and renewed. It is in the advance guard of national culture.

This People's Theatre has been in existence, as suggested, but a few years. It began in a modest way under the direction of Leonidas Barletta, and after working in what might be called its laboratory, initiated its first cycle by a series of performances in the suburbs and in towns near the capital. Finally, the Municipality granted it the use of one of the large theatres in Buenos Aires, where it recently performed Gogol's "Inspector" and "L'Ecole des Maris" of Molière. The People's Theatre has been able thus far, without subvention, and with resulting independence, to offer more than two thousand performances against a charge of the equivalent of only five cents. It is inaugurating what is practically the new theatre of Argentina.

An added impulse in this general direction is being given by the National Institute of Musical Studies, created by the National Cultural Commission, which has organized and carried through, in recent years, cycles of conferences on matters relating to the stage.

Furthermore, this same Cultural Commission has organized El Teatro Nacional de Comedia, whose first season was inaugurated in 1936. Performances were given in the Cervantes Theatre, one of the very best in Buenos Aires, and tours throughout the country were also carried out, fulfilling the ends contemplated by the Government in founding the Commission, which were nothing less than the creation of a stage and a seat of culture, as the name implies.

Perhaps because Argentines are so deeply musical, the task of presenting opera, certainly in recent years, has not been so difficult as the presentation of plays. This is hardly the place to go into the beginnings of either drama or opera, but since the latter, in the "Colón," is one of the peculiar glories of Argentina of today, its efforts and triumphs of the past quarter century must be emphasized.

The present great home of the Colón Theatre, after some eight years of building, was opened for its first season on May 25, 1908. The opera chosen was Verdi's "Aida." The date corresponds to the anniversary of the initial movement for independence in this city, and to the lofty emotions provoked by the music was added the solemn pride of remembrance of the historical associations of the day; the public filling the huge edifice were thus doubly moved, and this by subtle sensory channels was communicated to conductor and orchestra and vocalists, so that those who recall that night testify that the occasion was one of breathtaking emotion and beauty.

Described in bald statistical form it may be pointed out that the Colón, possessing a capacity for 3500 spectators is in this respect ahead of any opera house in Europe or the Americas, and perhaps of any in the world, if we except El Liceo of Barcelona, which is said to accommodate 3600 spectators.

The Colón occupies a huge city block, and in area, with the exception of such houses in Paris and Vienna, is not exceeded elsewhere. Its stage is also unequalled in length and breadth, receiving at times as many as 600 performers. To the foregoing should be added the imposing architecture of the building itself, both externally and internally, and the ample and noble salons, stairways and foyers which easily take care of the teeming public during the course of the long entr'actes which make of these occasions outstanding social functions in Argentina.

There can be no doubt that in that section of Vanity Fair to be found in Buenos Aires the Colón presents during the season a scene of rare loveliness. Performances usually begin at nine-thirty, and while boxholders who may have lingered over peacocks' tongues and Falernian, may slip into their places even if they arrive late, the general public must wait until the conclusion of an act before entering. As a result, this is one place where people are usually on time and in their seats before the tap of the director's bâton relieves what is sometimes to the music-lover an almost painful tension of expectation.

The attention of the visitor is sure to be called to the heavy bronze grills on either side of the pit and under the first row of boxes. These barriers, suggesting the screens found in oriental palaces, conceal boxes in which Argentine men, and especially women, who are in mourning, or who, for any other reason—a boil on the nose for example—desire to hear "music's golden tongue," and yet be hidden, may go nightly in the season and, reversing the rôle so glibly assigned to little children, hear and not be seen.

A gala night at the Colón Opera, especially on the dates of May 25 and July 9, is an impressive sight. The attendance of the President insures that the mounted grenadiers of San Martín in their blue and red uniforms of the style of over a century ago, with towering shakos and unsheathed sabres, shall form an aisle from the street, up the stairway of honor, and on to the presidential box. This same aisle is also maintained to the first floor for boxholders, and down its length pass the wealth and beauty and power of the Republic—women in exquisite toilettes, ambassadors and ministers in gorgeous uniforms, wearing every decoration under the sun, high officials of the army and navy in the gala uniform of their rank, all uniting to form an unforgettable sight. The singing of the national anthem which inaugurates official performances is executed by the chorus of the Opera itself and is a moving thing. With the conclusion of each act there is a rapid flow of the brilliant public in all directions through the vast salons and foyers, its elements seeing, and taking care to be seen, until the warning bell signals the time for the return to boxes and seats.

Among the various directors who have conducted in the Colón in the past quarter century must be mentioned one who is particularly dear to the Argentine public, not alone for his brilliant qualifications, but because he is a "native son," a porteño. I refer to Hector Panizza who was born in Buenos Aires in 1875. In the course of his studies and career he has conducted in La Scala of Milan, together with Toscanini, in Turin and other European centers. Recently he has won success in Vienna, while within the past twelve months he has conducted in New York, obtaining a brilliant success at the Metropolitan Opera House.

It need hardly be indicated that the Colón Opera is a subsidized one—funds coming from the authorities of the Municipality. The amount of this, in the past year was approximately $550,000, but I incline to think that it is an item in the budget which causes the general public the least concern. In which respect we are unfortunately behind the Argentines. Imagine a politician in the United States who would dare include in a budget a subsidy for opera or drama.

In the summer months, with the opera house long since closed, many of its artists are to be heard in open air performances given in el Parque 3 de Febrero in Palermo. Here for the equivalent of fifteen cents (or for sixty cents, if you don't care how you spend your money and wish a box), one may witness good ballets and hear good opera or attend excellent concerts. This summer opera is something that should especially appeal to the visitor who comes in January and February.

Needless to say, during the course of the year in Buenos Aires, excluding the summer months, the greatest artists of the world are to be heard and seen—dancers, pianists, violinists, etc., so that the dweller in this capital and the stranger within the gates are peculiarly blest in these cultural privileges.

CHAPTER VIII

The Argentine Press

∽∽∽∽∽∽∽∽∽∽∽∽∽∽∽∽∽∽∽∽∽∽∽∽∽∽∽

THE PRESENT-DAY NEWSPAPERS in Argentina had their beginnings after the overthrow of Rosas in 1852. Under this despot free thought and freedom of expression were suppressed and the development of truly great, free newspapers was consequently impossible. With the throwing off of this incubus and the gradual ending of the disorders and confusions thereafter the ground was prepared for the establishment of two of the present morning papers.

The first of these, "La Prensa," was founded in 1869 by José C. Paz, father of the present owner and publisher, and from the beginning has been an organ of complete independence. Today it circulates widely throughout Argentina and neighboring countries and is considered a powerful instrument in moulding public opinion, in promoting public welfare, and in contributing to cultural development.

In 1870 came the birth of "La Nación," which was established by Bartolomé Mitre—statesman, soldier and historian—shortly after retiring from the presidency of the Republic. Since that time "La Nación" has steadily grown into an important morning paper of wide circulation and influence, making admirable contributions to the cultural advancement of the country and living up to its founder's ideal that it should be "a tribune of doctrine."

"El Diario" is also an old established journal having been

founded in 1881 by Manuel Lainez, a distinguished journalist and legislator. An important present day morning paper in Buenos Aires is "El Mundo," founded only recently—May 14, 1928. It is a tabloid-size paper, patterned somewhat after the New York "Daily News," very progressive, and keenly alert to the rapidly changing methods of newspaper production and presentation.

In the afternoon field the city of Buenos Aires has four important papers. One of the largest of these, from the standpoint of circulation as well as popular appeal is "Crítica," established in 1913. The oldest of the afternoon papers is "La Razón," founded in 1904. It circulates widely through the upper economic classes and enjoys a corresponding prestige. The third is "Noticias Gráficas," founded by Jorge Mitre, grandson of the founder of "La Nación." A fourth afternoon paper "Pregón," began publication on May 12, 1938.

Besides these leading newspapers in the nation's capital, every important provincial city, such as Rosario, Santa Fé, Córdoba, Mendoza, La Plata and Bahía Blanca has its own paper, or papers, many of commendable caliber, although the larger papers of Buenos Aires naturally overshadow them in national and world importance.

Publishers of newspapers throughout the Republic have been quick to recognize that there is an insatiable hunger in Argentina for knowledge not only of European matters, but also of those relating to North America, other parts of South America, Asia and the rest of the globe. Through the great world news agencies, these papers furnish their readers with what is perhaps the largest and most thorough picture of international events to be found anywhere.

In the opinion of one of my distinguished predecessors, "Argentine newspapers, with hardly any exception save in New York, are on a higher intellectual level than ours." If my own national pride prevents me from entirely sharing my colleague's view, I can certainly bear testimony to the lofty quality of thought and the marked literary flavor of the editorials appearing in the leading Argentine journals. And it can be asserted without fear of contradiction that in naming the five or six great newspapers of the world today at least two Argentine journals, with a long record of vigor and success behind them, must be included in the group.

There can be no doubt that one of the most important factors in the enviable position which the press of Argentina holds today is the provision in the nation's constitution establishing the freedom of the press. This safeguard has contributed not alone to the independence of the newspapers to criticize, praise, build up or destroy, in accordance with the viewpoint of the paper, but has been of inestimable value in the development of Argentina as a nation.

Another favorable factor in the creation of a great press has been the constant insistence of publisher and public on supplying the very best that the journalistic world produces. Aside from a complete foreign and local news service, the leading papers present their readers with the works of well-known commentators and writers, such as André Maurois, David Lloyd George, Winston Churchill, Gèneviève Tabouis, André Geraud (Pertinax), Ernest Hemingway, Webb Miller, J. W. T. Mason and others.

The publishers of the principal papers are as aware of the entertainment value of their publications as their colleagues in Europe and the United States, and the best feature articles, comics, photographs and cartoons that can be found in the world are part of their daily publications.

It follows from what I have said that the Argentine public is proud of its great newspapers and supports them well, praising their achievements and quickly reacting to any weaknesses. The Argentine himself will, and with reason, tell you that his newspapers are as good as any in the world. And he looks to them as a continued vital factor in the further progress of his nation, realizing, as do the responsible publishers, that the Argentine press still has a great task to perform.

There are two good English-language papers that arrive at breakfast time, the Buenos Aires *Herald* and the *Standard*. While these latter make their special appeal to the resident American and British colonies, they are a gift from heaven to the traveler who does not read Spanish. Other publications in a score or more of other languages supply the news-cravings of respective colonies.

In conclusion I am tempted to allude to a pungent illustration of the freedom of speech existing in this country to be found in the performances of some of the smaller and popular playhouses. The mocking wit in the dialogue is in its swiftness too much like a machine gun for me to grasp; and some of the language is too much the argot of the moment for me to understand even if I caught the words. But what is inescapable is the amiable malice and biting satire which the actors display in treating of political matters. "Mr. Dooley" whose pitiless comments on men and events in the United States some thirty years ago made him famous, and Will Rogers, equally remembered for his wise and humorous observations, find their counterpart in types like the monologist of the Maipo Theater. Very daring, very penetrating, generally irreverent, the Argentine artists are not a whit behind their brothers in the United States and are treated with the same wise tolerance by municipal, state and federal authorities as in my own country.

CHAPTER IX

Clubs

THE AVERAGE ARGENTINE is, to employ Doctor Johnson's familiar phrase, "a clubbable man." This is evidenced by the number and variety of clubs to be found in the capital and elsewhere throughout the land.

I have been a happy guest in many Argentine clubs, and I would like to bear testimony to the cordiality and friendliness to be found in these, but more especially in that fortress of conservatism, the Círculo de Armas, in Calle Corrientes, where the atmosphere of geniality equals that of any club I have ever known. In extraordinary measure the members are friends, and warm friends. After more than fifty years of existence, a mellowness has come with the years. This club is at its best between seven and half past nine in the evening. In this brief period good fellowship, good talk, healthy gossip of politics, economics and social life, prevail. The bar, which measures perhaps six feet across, does not actually open until 8 o'clock when it begins to be favored with a choice clientele! This vital adjunct to good fellowship is best described in the language of the gifted Doctor Bagby of my native state who, referring to a similar altar of Bacchus, remarked that "the bar was small, but vigorous and healthy!"

But tribute should be paid to the moderation of Argentines. To this graceful and restrained people, alcohol in its protean forms is merely an agreeable accessory to the fine art of living and is rarely abused. In my five years of life here I could count on one hand the number of intoxicated people that I have seen, and none of these was, I think, of the country. And one of my predecessors, Stimson, resident here for seven years, states in his "My United States," a delightful volume: "I have never seen an Argentine gentleman drunk." It flows from this that I have never had to adopt the plan resorted to by an English diplomat of the eighteenth century, Sir William Temple, as reported by Dr. Johnson, who had one or more secretaries "to do my drinking for me"—as he declared!

In Florída is the headquarters of the outstanding organization known as the Jockey Club, a huge pile housing rare books and pictures, vintage wines worthy to be mentioned with these fruits of the spirit, added to a rich cuisine, which makes it a mecca for the stranger within the gates. A visitor should make every effort to have a meal there and, if in summer, either on the terrace or else in the air-conditioned dining room. To the visitor who wishes to pursue some line of reading, and who has the leisure, the rich shelves of this club's library are open and may be unhesitatingly recommended. At the Jockey Club, there is an all-day-long come and go of outstanding figures in the national and resident-foreigner life. Here too a great deal of official entertaining is done by diplomats, especially if they are bachelors; here farewell to freedom is celebrated with gusto by prospective benedicts; here out-of-town visitors are brought for entertainment and to be impressed; and here, in a sense, may be said to center the vast and important interests of the country which cluster around the breeding of horses, the raising of livestock and the tilling of the soil. At the Jockey Club, one feels strongly the essentially pastoral and agricultural character of the country, as well as the cultural adjuncts I have indicated.

The Jockey Club maintains wonderful race courses in Palermo

and in San Isidro; every Saturday and Sunday and holiday throughout the year one or the other of these is thronged by smartly dressed folk who go to witness the first-class flat racing which prevails. Every care is taken of the diminutive jockeys and their families, and within a few yards of the Palermo course is a hospital, as well as schools for the children of the jockeys and an equine museum. The magnificent San Isidro course is forty minutes further out and next to it are superb golf courses maintained by the Jockey Club. To the golfer Buenos Aires offers a large number and a fair variety of courses. In Palermo itself, and close to the race course of that name, are the excellent links of the Argentine Golf Club. Mention must be also made of the delightful course at Olivos, and at San Andrés; the last named being particularly frequented by Americans and Scots, and the course at the Hurlingham Club, the latter a bit of old England dropped in the lap of the pampa. In addition, the Swift meat-packing company has a good course in La Plata, and there are various other clubs which may be used to avoid monotony.

Over many of these golf courses to which I have referred I have wielded a powerful if inefficient club, and from a first-hand knowledge of them I would urge my compatriots to be sure to include their golf clubs in their baggage even if they are to spend only a few days here.

A club which appeals to me in particular is the Gimnasia y Esgrima, unique in conception and operation, and offering to an incredibly large number of persons, and for very moderate fees, every advantage to be found within the portals of its aristocratic brothers of Corrientes and Florída. Doctor Ricardo Aldao may be said to be the creator and patron saint of the club named. It was he, I am told, who conceived the idea of securing the passage of an act of Congress which gave to the organization the uncollected winning tickets in the lottery, a sum which had been accumulating for many years. With this in hand it was possible to lay out grounds and erect large and handsome buildings; as a result the young Argentine man or woman of moderate means may play tennis or basketball or take riding lessons or swim or dance for very moderate dues. It would be difficult to overestimate the spiritual advantage flowing to the youth of the country from such an organization as this.

The call of the sea is strong in many Argentines and the creation of yacht and boat clubs is a natural expression of this. There are many of these associations in Buenos Aires and its neighborhood, but within city limits the outstanding one is the Yacht Club Argentino, situated in an attractive building at the entrance into the Dársena Norte from the Canal Norte, which latter leads out to the broad spaces of the Plata.

A delightful and tranquil spot on summer evenings, even for those who do not leave the pier, it becomes an active, bustling place when one of the frequent yacht races is taking place. Various types of sailing craft are to be seen and in addition swift power boats, launches and luxurious ocean-going craft make their home nearby.

The club is a pleasant place at which to dine and chat of things dear to sailormen, who speak the same spiritual language the world over.

Aquatic clubs, in addition to those to be found at Tigre (principally for folk interested in rowing), are el Club Náutico Olivos, el Yacht Club Buenos Aires, el Yacht Club San Isídro.

One must include in any mention of the good things of life a unique organization now nearly twenty years old, composed in very large measure of my compatriots and known as the *Gormandizers' Club*. Happy is the man who is bidden to attend one of its weekly luncheons; only death should make you excuse yourself, and even then you should arrange to be represented by your executor.

The guiding spirit of this interesting organization will be identified by his many friends under the initials "J. B." Gifted with a natural instinct for good food, which would have made him a boon companion of Brillat-Savarin had he lived about a century earlier, J. B. is up betimes, on Thursday mornings looking through La Plata market, at the hour when sea food and other delicacies begin to arrive from Mar del Plata or the countryside. Choice of foods is then made, and everything is ready for the midday meal which is served, in "Los Patitos," in Calle Carabelas, in a private room adorned with amusing caricatures of present or former Gormandizers. On entering, one sees J. B. looking like an alchemist of old, bending over vials and retorts and such things, which on further examination are seen to be containers for the makings of a marvelous cocktail whose secret is locked in J. B.'s head. These stimuli to good digestion having been consumed, seats are taken without regard to protocol or precedent and the matter in hand attacked with a will. The group is made up of the leaders of the American colony, but their prominence in the community is forgotten and all business cares laid aside in the flow and inter-play of good feeling and good fellowship. May the shadow of no Gormandizer grow less! And it will not, as long as he continues his present delightful habit.

Cultural Trends; University Life

1. *Cultural Trends*

AN OBSERVER and critic of something less than a century ago, viewing the course of events in the River Plate region, would have remarked that its inhabitants appeared to be emerging from civil strife and revolutions following their separation from Spain, that they seemed to be free from external danger or even menace, to have left behind them a cruel period of domestic tyranny, to be exempt from potential domestic conflicts which might arise through mixtures of race or color, with no sundering religious question to vex them, and possessed of a land whose wealth seemed to be of fabulous character.

Such an observer might well have asked himself: in what measure and in what directions the intellectual life of the Argentine of tomorrow would arise and manifest itself? And further, would the artistic and literary genius of the racial elements in principal measure composing it—Spanish and Basque (and, by a kind of adoption, French)—flower in their transplanted state? (I make no mention of Italian elements since these have come in appreciable numbers only recently.)

These hypothetical questions, after the lapse of some four score years, I now set myself to answer—also to make a prophecy. But first let us examine the situation today:

[108]

With the passage of years Argentine wealth has continued to grow; the present character of the country is largely rural, and only in very slight degree industrial; the temper of the people seems inclined to peace. Bearing these facts in mind a student of affairs today, if coming from the United States, is further helped to an understanding of Argentina and its people by recalling the many and close analogies to be remarked in the history of the two republics.

In both cases, in the beginning, we see a limited population established on the fringes of a country of vast potential wealth; these elements suffer oppression by short-sighted statesmen; there is a wilderness to be won and Indian tribes to subjugate—or annihilate; and internal strife to be overcome, in order to fuse conflicting parties into a united people. Here analogies begin to fade. For there are today great differences between the two countries, arising from the fact that Argentina continues, as suggested, essentially pastoral and agricultural, and with a very limited population, having in mind its vast extent, while the United States is both agricultural and industrial, and with a population of such magnitude that we have already reached what might be called our economic frontiers.

In any general survey of the cultural scene a point which should not be overlooked is that at the moment when Argentina was achieving its independence the sun of Spanish glory was entering its long period of eclipse, and those beneficent beams which in an earlier period and with circumstances favoring might have kindled a flame of Iberian genius on these far-off shores were fading.

It was natural, therefore, that men whose intelligence and genius were to guide and develop the young country should turn to the nearest Latin sister, France, as a source of inspiration and guidance. And so, as I have suggested in various chapters, French political thought and history profoundly affected these early nation-builders.

But just here it may be fairly questioned (in view of this Gallic influence and prestige, which continues in literary and artistic ways to be seen and felt in the Argentina of today, if in declining measure), why Argentina turned to the United States in selecting a political framework, taking over the constitution of 1789 almost bodily? This query is perhaps partly answered by pointing out that the internal strife marking the many years between the declaration of freedom and the adoption in 1853 of the constitution (which, with changes in 1860, is Argentina's Magna Charta) had revealed the intensity of local loyalties and the apparent impossibility of welding a nation after the pattern of France out of provinces intensely proud and conscious of their quasi-independence, of inducing them to accept the relatively humble political status of departments under prefects linking them to a strong central government.

Other and what might be called centrifugal forces were also at work, forces having historical and geographical origins—the memory of old allegiances to vanished viceroyalties, with persisting business and social ties which the very immensity of the country fostered, and the obstacles to rapid and easy inter-provincial contacts arising from this same vast national area.

Argentina's constitutional structure of today may therefore be said to represent a measure of compromise between Anglo-Saxon and Gallic political ideologies, for it possesses an executive more powerful than exists in the United States, and provinces with lesser powers than those retained by our respective states.

The familiar saying that "the blood of the martyrs is the seed of the Church" seems to have a certain application when one considers the intellectual life of this country. Much of its literature, certainly in its early manifestations, may be said to be a literature of revolt—the work of men who were being cruelly persecuted. And in extraordinary measure the newspaper has been the field in which this has flourished. Glancing quickly over the history of the years preceding and following the attainment of freedom, and the period of tyranny, it is plain that some of the choicest intellects of the country were in exile, and while in this banishment naturally engaged in polemical writing. This was notably the case with Sarmiento, who, from across the Chilean border, made his voice heard in every remote hamlet despite the vigilance of Rosas' lieutenants.

A characteristic of the writers of prominence of today is a tendency to pursue historical and social studies, rather than to produce works purely of the imagination. I make this remark having in mind the various societies consecrated to historical studies in the capital, in Mendoza, in Córdoba, and elsewhere, which are producing a quantity of historical material of first quality. Especially to be singled out from these is *La Junta de Historia y Numismática,* which under the Presidency of Dr. Ricardo Levene, had charge of the Second International Congress of the History of America, which assembled in Buenos Aires in July, 1937. This tendency toward historical studies may be said to arise in a natural and spontaneous way from a race whose primary concern has been the conquest and formation of their country. Illustrative of this is the fact that the great men of Argentina have been men of action, men of the tented field, even if some of these have shown marked versatility in addition to gifts of leadership.

A further consideration of Argentina's intellectual trends requires an examination of the internal and external forces which are evident at present, or that may be anticipated in the future, which will affect the growth of the cultural life of the country.

In the first place, it should be pointed out that there are no internal problems of race or color or religion to affect this: for there are no negroes, the Indians are in a tiny minority, and the country is, largely speaking, of a common faith. One might suppose that influences originating in Paris, in view of what has been previously said, would continue to be potent. But this is no longer the case, for if special reasons favored this influence in the past, these no longer exist, and, as a brilliant and scholarly Argentine, Sir Guillermo L. remarked to me recently, the Argentine is "waterproof," or is certainly becoming so, as regards alien influence.

Here I am impelled to add a very brief but most pregnant paragraph, which qualifies every prediction or forecast I may make herein: it is to point out that the success or failure of Argentina in solving her vital problems, in building her intellectual life of the future, will depend on how she selects her immigrants in years to come.

Artistic impulse and expression in Argentina, as manifest in its music, painting and sculpture, not to mention other fruits of the spirit, are not below what might be expected from a country whose people are animated by such ancient and artistic racial and cultural strains; and in these manifestations there is a frank and vigorous national quality which frequently finds its base and inspiration in folklore or in themes suggested by the rich historic pre-colonial and early-colonial periods, yet does not depart in its best examples from classical canons tested and tried and approved by the centuries. Where there is divergence into so-called modernistic channels, critics in general consider these tendencies as worthy of respect, since they express in greater or less measure the spontaneity of sentiment which animates their creators.

We see the modern Argentine, therefore, master of a new and immensely wealthy country, perhaps somewhat too preoccupied by "the cares and riches of this world," yet manifesting a vigorous and a healthy intellectual life whose highest development is the creation of newspapers which are second to none in the world.

Having all the foregoing in mind, I dare to predict that with the passage of time Argentina will manifest a cultural and intellectual life distinct, fresh, individualistic—in which outside influences, if observed, will be seen as merely guideposts, *points de repère*—marked by a breadth and sweep suggestive of its wide pampas and an elevation comparable to its great Andean heights.

It is not meant to suggest by the foregoing that Argentine intellectuals will close their ears, as if to siren and deceptive notes, to what may come to them from other countries. Far from that; for as we learn from Bryce, the Argentine mentality is a tolerant one, and certainly there is every indication on the part of Argentine intellectuals of a desire for close co-operation and collaboration with men of like minds wherever they may be found. The truth of what I say is happily illustrated by eloquent words addressed by the President of the P. E. N. Club of Buenos Aires, Doctor Carlos Ibarguren, to the assembled delegates to the 14th International Congress of that club, held in Buenos Aires in September, 1936.

It is soothing and encouraging in times of misery, hatreds and social struggles, to witness this cordial meeting of writers of the most varied tendencies and doctrines, who have come from all parts of the world to discuss subjects relating to literature. And for the Argentine Republic—a quiet corner of the earth—it means a singular honor to welcome the eminent representatives of universal intelligence. We are proud to have as our guests such illustrious personalities. But in a still greater degree does it exalt us to know that in this hall are gathered the exponents of cultures that represent the highest expression of many peoples, and to behold this Congress, now opening, as a symbolic manifestation of the human mind risen above the bustle of a mechanical civilization, of economic and political materialism, and of the inflamed passions that are agitating mankind at this transcendental moment of History.

2. *Phases of University Life*

And in what surroundings will the exponent, the type, of this intellectual life of the future be nourished? He will not be, I am sure, a product of foreign universities, he will not have sat at the feet of foreign Gamaliels; he will be, on the contrary, a man in very essence of his country, to whom Argentina will give as did England to Rupert Brooke,—

> . . . *her flowers to love, her ways to roam,* . . .
> *Her sights and sounds; dreams happy as her day;*

Doubtless there existed in Argentina of earlier days, perhaps as an inheritance from Spain, a belief which was manifest in Virginia as a colony, that education was a privilege reserved to a special class. If so, it has entirely disappeared. And it was Sarmiento, he who called himself "the schoolmaster President," who most completely grasped the need, the necessity, of popular education to maintain the real prosperity of the country.

Sarmiento had studied the school systems of the United States, and following this founded training schools for teachers in the Republic with instructors whom he brought from our country. The need was great, for in 1869, at the time of the first national census, illiteracy was general; but in the half century following, the strides made in eliminating this were enormous, and today illiteracy among voters in the federal capital has dwindled to 2.6 per cent.

Free primary education in Argentina is provided by the general and provincial governments, and there are secondary national and provincial schools throughout the country.

There are five leading universities—at Córdoba, founded in 1613, at Buenos Aires, dating from 1821, and at La Plata, opened in 1897, all of which are referred to elsewhere. There is also a small university at Tucumán, and another, the National University of the Litoral, in Santa Fé, with branches in Rosario and Corrientes.

The influence exercised by the University of Córdoba under its Jesuit founders over a long period has been already pointed out; it was more than two hundred years old when its brother at Buenos Aires, which has now outgrown it, came into being, and these two remain at the forefront as seats of Argentine culture.

In the opinion of competent Argentine critics, the University of Buenos Aires is the center of university instruction for all South America. To its halls come sons of well-to-do families of other Latin American countries to obtain a finished education. And if from various European countries young men are sent to England or France or Germany to pursue University courses, in less and less degree, save perhaps in the direction of the United States (and in limited numbers there), are Argentines seeking cultural advantages beyond their own frontiers. And this is as it should be.

Medical students in Argentina pursue courses during seven years, and in law, engineering, and other professions, six years; it is therefore seen that starting with primary studies a young man will have to give a total of some twenty-one years in order to fit himself for the practice of one of these professions.

What strikes a stranger most sharply in considering Argentine university life is the comparative absence therefrom of what we know in our country as campus life and activities. Perhaps to an Argentine the difference is more apparent than real, but certainly a visitor from the United States gains the impression that the

Argentine university is primarily a place in which to acquire the type of education obtained from books and by contacts with fellow students, and that social activities of the kind which play so large a part in universities and colleges and high schools at home are non-existent here. For example, there are no Greek-letter organizations, and consequently no fraternity dances, and no "rushing" of candidates; again, the variety of student organizations which are so often a plague to our college authorities, if present here, are in limited number, and consequently the many engrossing struggles for offices with their consequent distraction of students' thoughts do not arise locally; nor are there junior proms or senior balls. It is true, however, that student organizations sometimes organize dances, and banquets are constantly held, the latter marked by an ebullient gaiety which is not without charm.

While what I have said in a preceding paragraph concerning the practical absence of political struggles for office in purely student organizations in Argentine universities is true, a certain phase of interior political life to which reference is made later must be emphasized here. These center around the election of officers of university centers and around the election of student delegates to the Board of Directors of the various faculties; and inevitably the political complexion in national politics of electors and candidates is manifest in these struggles. In these bitterly contested elections all the methods familiar to municipal, state and national elections in the United States are evident—newspaper publicity, campaign speeches in person or by radio, individual canvases, correspondence, etc.

In the matter of sports a difference at least in degree between universities in Argentina and in the United States is also evident. The average Argentine student must either find an outlet for his exuberant youth through the facilities provided by some university club or else by membership in a non-collegiate organization; he may also engage in some phase of the annual competitions, national or international (organized in the case of the University in the capital by the Federación Universitaria de Deportes, which itself depends upon the Federación Universitaria de Buenos Aires).

But broadly speaking, interest in athletics in Argentine universities is not intense; and it is doubtless due to this as well as to the absence of intra-mural activities in social and political matters, as understood in the United States, that the thoughts of the student are turned to outside things, especially as these have a repercussion on interior affairs. Hence to be observed in university life is the intensity of interest with which students follow political events, domestic and foreign, and the extent and manner of its manifestation.

If the student of today is essentially democratic in his ideologies, he represents at the same time every shade of political thought!

One of the student groups which is frankly "rightist" and embraces a minority in the entire student body, has as its stronghold the Faculty of Law and Social Sciences, where it overwhelmingly outnumbers the democratic or "reform" student. (This latter term is applied to partisans of further reform of the university structure, a movement begun and carried out in 1914, under President Irigoyen, seeking to permit the participation of the student body in the government of the several faculties through the election of representatives to the Board of Directors, to implant the practice of allowing students to have a voice in the choice of professors and, in a word, to impose, as they assert, the principle of the triumph of the best and most intelligent.)

This democratic element is made up of many groups, including radicals and socialists, and these latter are strongly entrenched in the medical faculties. It is inevitable that there should be students with communist leanings; these, however, usually endeavor to work through extremists in democratic groups. But their number is extremely limited, and they are in general anathema to both rightists and others.

From this brief outline of certain aspects of university life it is seen that it lends itself easily to participation in the political life of the nation, in which, and to repeat, students take keen interest and in which they often play an active part.

It is apposite to remark that when it is desired to insure the success of a political movement in Argentina, an attempt is usually made by party leaders to interest and mobilize university students. This support once obtained, its manifestations are carefully taken into account by the general public, by the newspapers, and by the Government, since at times it constitutes a determining factor in the fate of important issues.

Student action is often manifested through pronouncements by student bodies of the various schools—law, medicine, engineering—or by the federation of each university, which represents the union of various groups. In the capital, this is known as the University Federation of Buenos Aires. In matters of prime importance the Argentine University Federation, in which is concentrated the federated groups of all the universities of the country, may be brought into action.

When the result desired by one of these entities is not attained, one of three things may occur: first, if the matter is not important, the particular body contents itself with registering a protest; second, a newspaper campaign may be carried on, together with lectures, meetings, etc.; and third, if a question of principle or of fundamental interest is involved, a strike may be called, which may be partial, affecting only a determined group; or general, embracing a single university; or even national, if the student bodies of the five universities existing in Argentina leave the classroom.

Within each of the political parties, from extreme left to extreme right, students form a special nucleus whose sympathy and aid is constantly sought by political leaders. And it is not too much to say that these students are the shock troops used to open the attack in many undertakings of a political character, and that leaders of political parties place them in their first line of trenches.

CHAPTER XI

Sports

Racing, Polo, Football, and Tennis

~~~~~~

Racing

SPENDING as he does a portion of the year in the country, and growing up in equine surroundings or atmosphere, the wealthy Argentine has always ridden well; his apprenticeship beginning in his babyhood. It follows logically that with the advance in regulated and controlled racing coincident with the creation of the Jockey Club in Buenos Aires and pale copies of it elsewhere, together with the number of polo clubs formed throughout the Republic, the upper economic class in Argentina have given themselves wholeheartedly to these two sports. In the first, racing, in the usual somewhat vicarious manner, since, at least in Buenos Aires, there are practically no gentlemen jockeys, and in the second named, polo, as active participants as members of the various polo teams.

However my observation regarding gentlemen riders in races requires modification, for there comes to mind a pleasing book by Captain Macnie entitled "Work and Play in the Argentine," in which he describes some of the good racing of former years at Venado Tuerto, in which horses were ridden by owners. This author also tells a master story about that altogether charming Argentine sportsman, Jack Nelson, whose comrades most foolishly, and quite unnecessarily, since they knew the mettle of their opponent, "waited for Jack," with the inevitable result! But you must buy the book and read the story for yourself.

In the opinion of many competent judges the Argentines are the outstanding riders of the world. Most of them start to ride bareback or with a sheepskin only. And they sit well down in their saddles, with that perfect balance which regards the stirrup as a support and not as an aid. However, in various parts of the world there may be superior cross-country riders, men who can negotiate such a Galway stone wall as Lever describes, or a five-barred gate, better than an Argentine, owing to differences in early training, but by and large my statement of Argentine outstanding equestrian skill stands.

As for the man of the camp—"The gauchos are well known to be perfect riders," wrote Darwin a full century ago. In fact the riding of the gaucho was something that constantly filled the young scientist with amazement. He records that watching a rider as he galloped along at a rapid pace he saw an ostrich spring from its nest directly beneath the horse's nose. "The young colt bounded on one side like a stag; but as for the man, all that could be said was that he started and took fright *with* his horse." Bryce remarks that the true gaucho never dismounted from his animal "except to sleep beside it!"

In view of what I have said, it is superfluous to remark that every Argentine of a certain economic class rides, and since horses are relatively cheap, the opportunity to study equitation is within the reach of persons with even moderate purses. The parks and suburbs of the capital are filled with riders in the early morning; while on Sundays and holidays one may encounter many far better and as many inferior riders as in Central Park on similar days. Of course, a part of every sojourn in the country, no matter how short, is spent on horseback.

When one considers the profound influence on the economic life of the country of the existence of this cheap means of locomotion over vast expanses and the vital importance of the horse in the running of cattle, with the natural resulting repercussion upon the daily social life of the people, it is remarkable that forms of sport not involving riding, which are touched on elsewhere, have been able to gain a foothold and eventually to entrench themselves firmly in the country.

Turning now to racing, it may be observed that the man who loves to watch the horses in swift flow around a track may indulge this amiable weakness on Saturdays and Sundays and holidays throughout the year in Buenos Aires, and on many days during the twelve months in La Plata, two hours distant by train or motor.

Races at the hippodrome in the beautiful section of Palermo begin promptly, the first contest commencing at, say, 1:15, followed at half-hour intervals by seven others. The last race is usually run at 5:20 (the opening and closing hours noted may be advanced or retarded, according to the season).

The traveler of standing will have no difficulty in securing through a member a card to the members' stand where delightful luncheons and afternoon teas are served. Ladies escorted by members or by persons holding guest cards enter without tickets and without payment of an entrance fee.

What has been said above applies in essentials to the races which are being held from time to time and in increasing number in the new hippodrome of the Jockey Club at San Isidro, about twenty-five minutes by motor from the center of the City. At this latter course races are run on grass; at Palermo there are dirt tracks.

There are six more important weight for age and sex races during the season; they correspond to certain well known races in England: 1000 Guineas, 2000 Guineas, Newmarket Stakes, Gold Cup, Derby, Saint Léger and are as follows:

1.—Run on the first Sunday of August:

GRAN POLLA DE POTRANCAS (corresponding to the 1000 Guineas in England) for three-year-old fillies.

Distance 1600 meters.

    1st Prize......8000 pesos or 70% of entrance fees.

    2nd Prize......1200 pesos or 20% of entrance fees.

    3rd Prize...... 600 pesos or 10% of entrance fees.

    and a 2000 peso premium to the breeder of the winner.

(In 1937 the prize in money turned out to be for the

    Gran Polla de Potrancas   1st Prize......20,647 pesos

                               2nd Prize...... 5,085 pesos

                               3rd Prize...... 2,542 pesos

and 2000 pesos to the breeder.)

2.—Run on the second Sunday of August:

GRAN POLLA DE POTRILLOS (corresponding to the 2000 Guineas) for three-year-old colts.

Distance 1600 meters.

    1st Prize......8000 pesos or 70% of entrance fees.

    2nd Prize......1200 pesos or 20% of entrance fees.

    3rd Prize...... 600 pesos or 10% of entrance fees.

    and a 2000 peso premium to the breeder of the winner.

(In 1937 the prize in money turned out to be for the

    Gran Polla de Potrillos   1st Prize......23,430 pesos

                                2nd Prize...... 5,880 pesos

                               3rd Prize...... 2,940 pesos

and 2000 pesos to the breeder.)

3.—Run on the first Sunday in September:

GRAN PREMIO JOCKEY CLUB (corresponding to the Newmarket Stakes) for three-year-olds, both sexes.

Distance 2000 meters. This year the winner will be awarded

1st Prize......40,000 pesos

2nd Prize...... 8,000 pesos

3rd Prize...... 4,000 pesos

and a 2000 peso premium to the breeder of the winner.

4.—Run on a Sunday about the middle of September:

GRAN PREMIO DE HONOR or *COPA DE ORO* (corresponding to the Ascot Gold Cup) for horses any age.

Distance 3500 meters. In former years a gold cup was awarded. Now the winner gets a trophy, besides the established prize in money.

1st Prize......40,000 pesos

2nd Prize...... 8,000 pesos

3rd Prize...... 4,000 pesos

and a 2000 peso premium to the breeder of the winner.

5.—Run on the first Sunday of October:

GRAN PREMIO NACIONAL (corresponding to the Epsom Derby Stakes) for three-year-old colts and fillies. This is the most important race of the year because the "crack" of the year is confirmed as such on this occasion.

Distance 2500 meters.

1st Prize......100,000 pesos

2nd Prize...... 15,000 pesos

3rd Prize...... 7,000 pesos

and a 5000 peso premium to the breeder.

6.—Run on the first Sunday in November:

GRAN PREMIO CARLOS PELLEGRINI (corresponding to the Doncaster Saint Léger) when older horses can run as well as three-year-olds. This race is very important because it is the occasion on which the best colt and fillies of the year are faced with those of the preceding years.

Distance 3000 meters.

> 1st Prize......50,000 pesos
> 2nd Prize......10,000 pesos
> 3rd Prize...... 5,000 pesos

No premium to the breeder.

On a sunny day, especially in the autumn, when there is the faintest suggestion of coolness in the air, when the eucalyptus trees seem at their very best, when the leaves of the silver cotton woods are turning golden, the drive out to the course at Palermo, or better still to San Isidro, is a pleasing revelation of the porteños in their leisure hours. Every taxi seems crowded, every private motor filled with men and women in their Sunday best. Except on high feast days, however, the occasions are quite informal. But the day of the Gran Premio Nacional is an impressive thing; the President attends in state, driving down the course in a carriage drawn by four horses, preceded and followed by the Mounted Grenadiers of San Martín in their picturesque uniform of the War of Independence, mounted on superb horses. Arriving opposite the members' stand the Chief Magistrate is met by the President and Directors of the Jockey Club and escorted to the official stand where are gathered to receive him the diplomatic corps, the members of the Cabinet, high officials and leaders of the social life of the capital. The stranger within the gates must not fail to attend the races on such a day as this.

The crowds attending the races in Buenos Aires are not unlike those elsewhere in the world, save that the roar that goes up as the horses come well into sight, and the frenzied applause that greets the winner, has an added touch of fervor.

A word about the Jockey Club itself is appropriate here. In the chapter on "Clubs," reference is made to the elaborate building occupied by the institution in Florída. This was erected in 1897, but the organization which it houses dates back to 1881, when a group of outstanding Argentines met and took steps looking to the creation of what is now a great organization of social and national representative character. In the fifty-seven years which have elapsed since this creative work was undertaken the broad progressive lines then traced for its conduct have been followed in undeviating fashion by the successors of the founders. To scan the list of founder members and of the men who have been chosen in successive years to guide the destinies of the Jockey Club is to read the Golden Book of Argentine aristocracy.

The outstanding figure in the creation of the Jockey Club is Carlos Pellegrini (President of the Republic from 1890 to 1892) who guided its destinies at various times until his death in 1906. Son of a French father and an English (Argentine-born) mother, Pellegrini was yet a thorough Argentine, representative of the cosmopolitan elements which have so powerfully affected the character of the Argentine nation. Called on to face the terrific financial international crisis of the early 1890's, which began to be felt in Argentina in 1889, he met this with brilliance and vigor. In his titanic task of forwarding recovery he was aided, an Argentine historian remarks, by two potent allies—the railway and the plow!—the creation of railway lines having an accelerated movement about this time while the economic effect of the immigration of agricultural laborers, which began around 1870, was beginning to be observed in these years of stress.

An important labor carried out by the Jockey Club is the maintenance of the Argentine Stud Book, created at the time the Club was founded. The Stud Book is a work which a great English sportsman, Lord Derby, pointed out, is to the equine race of pure blood what the Civil Register is to human beings.

In the Argentine Stud Book were registered at the time of its creation all pure blooded animals in the country, and subsequently all introduced from Europe. This priceless record is watched over by a special committee of seven members of the Club.

Nothing is more admirable than the manner and the extent to which the Jockey Club has responded to charitable appeals. These benefactions have not been limited to cases of need arising within the Republic, for international disasters of great extent have equally been ameliorated by this organization, and within a period of less than forty years following its founding, the Club gave of its funds approximately nine million pesos! There have been other and characteristic manifestations of the generous and charitable instincts of those controlling this truly national body, a complete list of which would occupy too much space.

For a full forty years past there has existed in the Jockey Club a school of fencing under accomplished masters, and assaults-at-arms held under its auspices bring out a rare display of talent in the use of the foil, the sword and the saber.

It was Rusiñol I believe who once remarked that a house without books was like a garden without flowers. The Jockey Club is particularly rich in its really excellent library, perhaps one of the best club libraries to be found in the world. It now possesses some 40,000 volumes well arranged and catalogued. Non-club members, under certain conditions, may also be given access to these treasures.

To the riches of the mind represented by its library should be added the valuable art collection of the Club, which embraces canvasses by such painters as Van Loo, Roybet, Sorolla, Goya, Fantin Latour, Isabey, Fromentin, L'Hermite, Troyon, Besnard, Corot, Reynolds, and David.

Polo

The Spaniards imported the first horses into what is now Argentina in 1536, when Mendoza founded Buenos Aires. These were of Barb strain, with a cross of Arab and Andalusian blood. Following the wiping out of this first Colony these progenitors ran wild and grew in numbers on the pampas for hundreds of years (the first thoroughbred strains were not introduced until about the middle of the last century). Thus the first requisite of polo, a large supply of relatively cheap horses, was assured.

Polo in Argentina dates back as far as 1875; it is therefore evident that it has been played here almost as long as in England or the United States.

The development of polo was greatly facilitated by the natural advantages of the country: first, the flatness of the plains, making good and cheap polo-grounds possible; second, the type of cattle pony used on the estancias, which make excellent polo mounts; third, the fact elsewhere noted that almost without exception the average camp-man is the best of natural horsemen. As a result of these three facts, together with certain economic considerations, Argentina ranks today as one of the leading polo-playing countries of the world.

The local pioneers were a handful of Britons who, living up to their sporting tradition, started playing in the year named on their

THE STANDS AT THE JOCKEY CLUB COURSE, SAN ISIDRO, BUENOS AIRES

RACE TRACK AND POLO GROUNDS, PALERMO, BUENOS AIRES

The Argentine-American polo matches for the "Americas Cup"

Polo match, Buenos Aires

Asociación Argentina de

estancias in the Provinces of Buenos Aires, Santa Fé and Entre Rios.

Five years later, in 1880, polo was played in the then suburbs of Buenos Aires; starting in Caballito on what is now the property of the Western Railway Athletic Club, it became so popular, that later clubs were founded in Belgrano, Buenos Aires and Quilmes.

In the early days, as far back as 1890, the mounts were mainly the rough "criollo" ponies (descendants of the 76 Barbs imported by Mendoza and previously referred to). From that period until 1914 half-breeds were mainly in demand. Then came the greatest development of all when breeders with highly commendable foresight and enthusiasm began to acquire the best sires available in England. It is interesting to note that the fame of the Argentine pony is now world-wide, and in recent times easily fifty percent of the mounts used in international contests have been Argentine bred. Furthermore, for many years there has been a continuous exportation of polo mounts from this country.

From the time of its inception here the governing body of polo was the River Plate Polo Association, an organization which continued to function until 1923, when the Argentine Polo Association was founded.

There are now ninety-one clubs established in various parts of the Republic all affiliated with this Association, having one hundred and fifty playing fields, and controlling between them a huge list of over twenty-two hundred handicapped players.

Polo in Argentina goes on all the year round, principally in the country during the summer months, which is a great advantage for players wishing to train themselves and their ponies for the more serious events of the actual polo season.

From May onward the game is played in and around the capital where the more important clubs flourish, foremost among which is the Hurlingham Club. It offers facilities for every kind of sport, with polo-fields and stabling for three hundred ponies, golf-links, tennis, rackets and bat five courts, cricket fields, swimming pools, etc., and with a first-rate members' club house. The other leading clubs are Tortugas and Los Indios.

Opposite the Jockey Club race course at Palermo, in a truly unique situation, only a few minutes drive from the center of the city, is the Campo Argentino de Polo, where the most important matches are staged. The Finals, the Open Championship and International matches offer a colorful spectacle, amid wonderful surroundings. And as polo is an increasingly popular game, the stands, which can seat 20,000 are always filled to capacity whenever these contests take place.

Although individual and brilliant Argentine players early began to be seen on fields abroad, it was not until 1922 that an all-Argentine team—men and mounts—went on a tour of the United States and Europe. This Argentine Expeditionary Force was made up of Luis Lacey, a grand figure of international polo, who retired from the game last year, Jack D. Nelson, Prince Rupert of this great game, and the Miles brothers. Thus for the first time Argentine players and ponies, *as a team,* entered the world arena, in which they have continued to play so important a part. And what a spectacular entry it was! For this team won the open championship in England and in the United States, the only matches lost being against the United States' "Big Four"—but only after the open championship had been won!

In 1924 an Argentine team won the Olympic Open Championship in Paris (twelve years elapsed before this competition was held again, in Berlin, when the Argentines again won!)

Following this Paris triumph, and in 1928, the Argentines sent a team to compete in the series of games held in the United States for the Championship of the Americas, ceding the title to the American team, however, after losing two out of three games.

But in 1930 the Santa Paula team, made up of the sturdy veteran Andrada, Gazzotti, and the Reynal brothers, went north and captured the previously lost prize.

In 1932 an American team of unusual strength and distinction visited Argentina and won the Championship of the Americas in a series of brilliant matches.

However, in 1936 an Argentine team, in which were Jack D. Nelson (Captain), Andrada, Gazzotti, Cavanagh, and Duggan, went north and avenged the defeat of 1932. (It was this same team which, as noted above, won the Olympic Open Championship at Berlin in the same year.)

Football

There can be no doubt that despite its foreign origin and relatively recent arrival, Association Football is the national game, the baseball, of Argentina. During 1937 some two million spectators enjoyed this exciting sport in the various stadia of Buenos Aires, entry to which was possible at prices ranging from the equivalent of 15 to 30 cents. And there were no ticket speculators!

Professional football is under the direction and control of the Association named, with which forty-nine clubs are affiliated, practically all in the federal capital. In addition there exists a Federal Football Council, which although of recent creation, is accomplishing much in drawing closer together the 125 football leagues scattered throughout the country from Mendoza in the west to Formosa and Rio Negro in the far north and south.

Of the forty-nine clubs which make up the Argentine Football Association, sixteen possess their own stadia. These have a combined seating capacity of 625,000! The largest of these bowls is that of the Club Atlético del River Plate, known popularly as "los millionarios," whose new Monumental Stadium on the noble avenue leading from the city toward Tigre will hold 125,000 spectators. El Club Atlético Boca Juniors ("Geneises") is soon to have a stadium to seat 100,000; this latter will also contain a huge swimming pool, bowling alleys, basketball courts, etc. The erection of both these stadia was made possible through loans from the federal Government; an indication of the interest which the authorities are taking in this popular sport.

It is unnecessary to point out that the word football in their titles does not exhaust the activities of the various clubs, especially the larger ones; the River Plate, for example, embraces also in its activities basketball, swimming, tennis, wrestling, boxing, fencing, cycling and even pingpong and chess, the latter sport for hardening the arteries if not the muscles.

Departing now from the pedantry of statistics it is interesting to point out the real passion that seems to possess Argentine youth to play football. In vacant lots and too often in the streets, boys and young men are seen kicking or dribbling the ball, and this street education often turns out students who become professionals.

Apart from these redoubtable professionals, the Argentine amateur is a high class player. The truth of this statement was recently demonstrated by the playing of an amateur team formed under the auspices of the Argentine Football Association which went up to the Pan-American games held in Dallas in 1937. There in the "Cotton Bowl" they cleaned up in overwhelming fashion teams from the United States and from Canada.

As a result of these activities which may be noticed throughout the nation, and which the federal as well as provincial authorities are doing so much to promote, the generation of Argentines now coming to maturity suggest in many ways our young folk at home—bright-eyed and slim waisted, speaking often in their own soft tongue of the advantage of "keeping fit."

The football season in Buenos Aires runs for approximately nine months, from April to December, and a visitor must not fail to take in at least one game while here. The intense excitement of the crowd, the outstanding brilliancy of the players, the huge stadium loaded to the gunwales with enthusiasts, the vociferous applause, the violence of the reactions of the crowd to unpopular decisions, all provide a real thrill of emotion for the spectator.

Tennis

It was Charles II, I believe, who remarked that England was the country in which one could take exercise in comfort more days in the year than anywhere else in the world. The gay King's geographical knowledge was not faulty, it was limited: he knew nothing of California or of Argentina. Certain it is that barring occasional rainy periods, lovers of tennis may daily demonstrate, as Shakespeare reminds us, "The faith they have in tennis and tall stockings"—except that the stockings have gone. But the pulchritude revealed locally by young folk in their modern tennis garb is equal to any in the world, and makes me yearn to be young with them again—say about fifty! Again it must be remarked that tennis in Argentina is the game of a limited few, and hardly a popular form of exercise. However, there are excellent courts in Buenos Aires and a few others are to be found in some of the cities and resorts; but it must be kept in mind that an Argentine in the country is drawn to a horse as to a magnet, and tennis courts, even after being provided, are often neglected. The Argentine loves diversions marked by speed and quick movement, but in general he prefers the motive power to be external.

CHAPTER XII

The Argentine Countryside

1. Stock Raising and Farming

IF THE BRAIN OF ARGENTINA is to be found in its great capital, Buenos Aires, its soul, its essential character, must be sought in the country. In the metropolis, where one finds more than a fifth of the entire population of the republic, is located the seat of government; and its financial, economic, intellectual and social life hold sway there. Yet my opening statement remains true; the real Argentina lies beyond city limits. For after all Buenos Aires is the least Argentine of Argentine cities; linguistically, for example, it is a Tower of Babel. I can best illustrate this latter statement by pointing to the six different nationalities to be found among the servants in my own house!

As it is, Buenos Aires, chief seaport and gateway of the country, sits at this entrance, like St. Matthew at the customs' gate and levies tribute on all who enter or depart.

A little more than a century ago, at the time of the Declaration of Independence, the vast territory which we now know as Argentina held a population of perhaps a half million, of whom the majority were native-born, including a number of Indians and negro-and-Indian half breeds. These latter elements which made no essential contribution to national life or character, have tended for one reason or another to disappear, or else to be found in limited numbers in remote districts.

The life of the new nation therefore began with various great creative forces at work, in a country of almost unparalleled actual or potential wealth, with a very limited number of inhabitants, yet possessing a political and racial organism adapted to receive into its institutions and its own civilization great numbers of the white race. In addition to these factors livestock of various kinds introduced in the earliest colonial period were to be found in many sections and being practically unutilized were naturally increasing by leaps and bounds.

It is well to recall the observation of the well-known Argentine economist, Doctor Alejandro E. Bunge, in one of his scholarly studies of the economy of the republic, that at the time of the conquest this far-flung territory was largely uninhabited either by man or by domestic animals. The few wandering Indian tribes were low in the scale of civilization, did not cultivate the soil, and had only the guanaco and the South American ostrich on which to feed. And since the chase furnished but little food to these nomads, their numbers remained practically stationary. The new-comer, therefore, entered into a vast patrimony which constituted a geographic-economic unity. Little by little the immense territory was brought into subjection. Great areas were fenced off so that cattle might not stray; still later, and within the past half-century, the exportation of chilled beef and mutton began, greatly adding to national wealth. This followed, after long years, a period when hides and other by-products were a staple, when cattle were slaughtered for these by-products, and the carcasses thrown away! However, it was the vast current of immigration, largely Italian, setting in after 1870, which was so profoundly to affect national life, and bring into being a new source of riches.

Let us consider for a moment the situation in the year just

named: Argentina was then a country so essentially given to the breeding of cattle, so entirely unagricultural, that it imported from Chile, from the United States, and perhaps other countries, the flour needed for daily bread. As suggested, the coming of the Italian farmer-laborer radically altered all this and farming began.

And now I venture a prophecy: That some of my readers will live to see the time when the United States will send missions, like that of Joseph's brethren, down into Argentina to buy wheat and also meat!

What manner of country is the area in which Argentina breeds cattle and grows its grain? It is a vast zone, rectangular in shape, and extending nearly six hundred miles north and south, with a width of 360 miles east and west, and which takes in practically all the provinces (please look at the map again) of Entre Rios, Santa Fé, Córdoba, Buenos Aires, and a small part of the territory of La Pampa. Its area equals approximately that of the combined territory of the three states of Illinois, Iowa, and Missouri. This immense extent of land on which there were no trees to fell, no stones to remove, and over which movement in every direction is easy, is the Pampa—a land "so kind that just tickle her with a hoe and she laughs with a harvest."

Practically the entire zone is as flat as a spatula, although from time to time are to be seen small, low hills, with an occasional clump of forest, usually not indigenous, called a monte; and these serve as landmarks in an otherwise trackless steppe. However, trees and wood lots are confined to parks and lanes, near houses; and there are often rows of trees along boundary lines which have been set out by the respective owners. Except for small areas of wet and swampy lands almost the whole of the huge territory is tillable and it would be perhaps difficult to find anywhere in the world an area of similar extent with such a small percentage of waste land. The physical setting I have described, and the difficulties overcome in the beginning in catching wild horses and cattle and in herding these when tamed, produced a type of plainsman, suggesting our cowboy, called the gaucho—said to mean "stranger"—around whom clings the romance of the pampa. He is a vanishing type but the tradition which he represented survived and had a marked influence in political development for many years. He has been immortalized by the Argentine poet José Hernandez who in 1872 published "El Gaucho Martín Fierro."

Although fictitious the poem is intensely realistic. In broad lines it tells the story of a man of the country who had been pressed into an infantry battalion on the frontier. Under atrocious treatment by his commanding officer he deserts and becomes a sort of Ishmael. Defeating the squad of police sent to take him, he lives for a time among the Indians, suffers the "misfortune" of killing in fair fight two local ruffians and bullies, and becomes distinguished as a troubadour—a "payador" in creole patois— improvising couplets and singing them to the accompaniment of a guitar.

Equally worthy of the reader's interest, as depicting much the same type as "Martín Fierro" is Rafael Obligado's stirring poem of "Santos Vega, el payador, Aquel de larga fama," who died with a love-song on his lips.

Despite the possibly extravagant terms I have used in referring to this region which is the cereal and cattle zone of the Republic, it must be remembered that it yet embraces less than a fourth of the entire area of Argentina; and that there are vast areas of comparatively undeveloped or else arid land included within the national boundaries, the latter only awaiting water's magic kiss to wake it to productivity.

However this relatively restricted zone referred to is the leading source of the livestock and crop production of the country, and its greatest source of wealth. Of the two, livestock raising is the senior in age, for, as I have attempted to point out, the gifts of various kinds which nature so lavished on the new land tended to channel the activities of the Argentine landholder into the running of cattle, something that could be performed largely on horseback and with a relatively limited number of employees.

Furthermore, it should be borne in mind that the Argentine is by nature a conservative, averse to change. And even if the tide of immigration which began some sixty years ago had not risen to a point where agriculture could be profitably pursued, the fact that livestock raising has been the traditional source of wealth in the Argentine, with a certain social and economic status linked to it, would have tended to keep him to this form of exploitation of the country.

The estancias, as the great farm estates are called, are institutions reflecting wealth and a manner of living, with an agricultural aristocracy as a logical product. A certain parallel to this might have been observed prior to 1860 in the United States, on the large cotton plantations of the South, which disappeared with slavery; the end of a hideous institution, but also the death of the fairest social system which we have yet developed in the United States.

Again the estanciero, or gentleman farmer, has been quick to recognize that the abandonment of cattle raising and the adoption of grain farming inevitably means the end of personal control and direction of extensive herds and flocks; in thus ceasing to direct actual operations he becomes concerned in the handling of from scores to hundreds of tenants, each offering his peculiar difficulties.

Much of the pasture land in all these zones, however, is equally cereal land and its utilization as pasture is influenced greatly by the prevailing situation of large land holdings and (given sufficient capital) the ease with which these tracts are operated as cattle and sheep estancias. These capital requirements are considerable in respect to the investment on land, fences and cattle, but the estancias represent without doubt the simplest means of administering large holdings. They are the only means by which owners can personally direct and manage operations on such large tracts, of which the minimum size is about 5,000 acres. The income from cattle and sheep is, moreover, more constant and dependable than from crops, and it is stated that in the five-year period prior to the last year or two of high grain prices, the returns from livestock or from estancias have been uniformly better than from crops.

But most observers recognize that substantial amounts of the present grazing land of the Argentine are being very inadequately and poorly utilized and that only the wealth of some of the old land owning families and their income from large tracts has enabled them to carry on as they have, remaining insensitive to low financial returns, if not losses. Rising land values before the depression enabled many to persist in a tradition and to postpone changes and adjustments inherent in low returns and poor management, but the depression and the liquidation of estates are bringing about the breaking up of holdings and better utilization of properties. This emphasis upon better returns is opening up grazing tracts—many of them poorly managed—to tenant grain farmers. It is in consequence of these broad developments that grain farming is gaining ground.

We see, therefore, Argentina of today rather at the crossroads, with a tendency toward increasing agricultural production, especially as the number of small tenant farmers or small proprietors increases and as immigration begins to make itself felt within the country.

But I began these observations less with a view to analysing the pastoral and agricultural actualities and possibilities, than to speak of the gracious civilization which exists among the landed folk of this country. With a full realization of the perils of generalizing, I want to sketch in brief strokes, as in a measure typical, life on one of the estancias which I recently visited.

2. Glimpses of Estancia Life

In the late afternoon of a limpid day in the early fall we started, my wife and I, for a visit to "Miraflores" the country home of our friends Señor and Señora Angel Sanchez Elía. The train carried us in four hours to a station whence we drove by motor in about fifty minutes to our haven. We were accompanied on our journey by our host, his son and the latter's fiancée.

It was approaching midnight when we neared the house, which lay several miles within the entrance gates to the property. (It was, I believe, Dr. Bagby, in his inimitable "Old Virginia Gentleman" who prescribed five miles from the front gate as the proper limit for a gentleman's estate; no looking over fences and destroying one's privacy in that case!) Our hostess was waiting to receive us and with her "a rosebud garden of girls" and young folk, who were also house guests and whose laughter we heard as we drew up at the front door.

After an exchange of greetings we were shown to our rooms and slept soundly until the singing of innumerable birds awakened us about 9 o'clock the next morning.

My first activity after breakfast was to take a look at the house and its setting, something that I could not do the night before in the darkness. What I saw was a delightful, ample and informal piece of construction, with the date of its erection "1887" (which is ancient for a building in Argentina), set in the plaster work of the upper story. The house is of two stories, with terraces elevated a single step above the surrounding lawn, and running around three sides; French windows give on this, and permit ready access to every room. Clambering up the veranda pillars and overflowing on the terrace above were masses of jessamine and clematis in full bloom, in and out of which darted belated humming birds, in lightning-like raids on the honey in the flowers. Various out-buildings are much older than the house, while the property itself has been in the same family since 1816.

The morning was spent in pleasant chatter and in walks in the beautiful gardens, splashing in the swimming pool, and in examining and admiring some of the especially magnificent trees on the lawns, including several fine English oaks.

In the afternoon we drove with our host in a roomy victoria over a portion of the property, he acting as coachman, and I beside him on the box. We passed various dependencies, the ample stables, the fronton court, the manager's attractive cottage, the huge barns. A well-defined road led toward the bed of the river, which at the moment was almost dry; but as a matter of fact the horses' heads could be turned in any direction because of the flatness of the plain, for we were in the center of the pampa.

As we drew nearer to the river-bed flocks of flamingoes soared in rose-colored spirals in the still air and were silhouetted against the blue of the sky. Gulls, too, were seen, daring an inland voyage. The only sounds were those which came from feathered throats— doves in soft complaint, the hoarse note of the chajas (a species of wild turkey), the chatter of parrots, the crows of Argentina in their destructiveness, and the shrill cry of the teru-tero, a bird which according to Darwin, "appears to hate mankind."

We continued to drive slowly, letting the peace of the plain enter into our city-jaded brains and bodies. After a late tea we drove again until it was time to return for the evening meal.

The next day we set out by motor, and for the first time I had borne in on me the immensity and wonder and beauty of the pampa. But for clumps of trees which dotted the landscape in several directions and marked the location of houses, one had the sensation of being on a trackless sea, only there was rich soil under foot. At sunset the feeling produced was that this gorgeous spectacle was taking place on the very property on which we stood. In viewing all this a sensation of solitude, of immense, immeasureable distances, came over me, and with these emotions was united that strangeness allied to beauty which is said to constitute romance.

During the course of this motor drive, and as the road simply faded out beneath us, I saw the eyes of my host searching the wide expanse for a landmark, for in its immensity the pampa offers facilities for losing one's self! And perhaps it was something like a sixth sense, developed by a birth in and lifelong contact with these plains rather than by anything he actually saw that finally led us in the desired direction—to an estancia known as "Kakel" held today by descendants of the original owner, Máximo Elía. It was in the dim past a frontier fort against the Indians, and an old piece of cannon mounted on the terrace at the rear of the house, where magnificent trees were growing, through which came the last rays of the setting sun, recalled former days. A descendant of the builder of the time-stained house told of his great-grandfather employing in his dealings with the Indians

A VIEW OF "ACELAIN"   THE CHAPEL AT "ACELAIN"

TYPICAL FARM LABORERS, WEARING BOMBACHAS

The Pereda family's "Villa María"

Stacking hay in the camp

Penn-like methods which insured him their continuing affection and confidence.

On our return journey my host drove with entire surety of touch, although to me the road soon became invisible, and even the blue velvet sky overhead later grew dim as rain began to threaten.

As we drove along we felt the deep enchantment, the infinity, the weird calm of the boundless moorland, an expanse which we all knew extended on the west to the first rises signalling the approach to the Andes, and on the east to where the Atlantic washed the shores. It was the steppe of Russia, the African veldt, the savanna of Brazil, mingled into one, and yet with its own distinctive and haunting qualities.

As we neared "Miraflores" a throbbing murmur came from the trees in the park surrounding the house. It was not a series of cries, it was not the multitudinous chattering of rooks or swallows going to rest, it was simply the plaintive and appealing note of hundreds of wood-pigeons in the oak and beechen glooms.

Another year, in early autumn, found us as happy guests in a country of low hills and valleys, near Tandil, at "Azucena." The beautiful modern house, built in the Spanish style, is set in the midst of a park which is reached from the gate of the estancia by an avenue formed of poplars (alamos canadiensis) over six miles long!

We were taken on charming drives to visit various neighbors, on one of these lunching at "Acelain" with Argentina's great novelist, Señor Enrique Larreta, (author of that really outstanding work "La Gloria de Don Ramiro"), his gracious wife, and delightful family. Here was another house in the Spanish tradition, a great house, furnished with old world treasures, with chapel, cloister, guest-wing, and beautiful Spanish gardens, whose long pools and cool greens vied with the blaze of color of the other and flower-planted gardens.

Near enough to Buenos Aires to make it conveniently accessible is the estate known as "Villa María," seat of the Pereda family, and, like their town house, with its Sert frescoes and old world treasures, an abode of beauty and charm. Because of its accessibility and the markedly hospitable impulses of its owners our visiting compatriots know it perhaps better than other properties.

The gracious, rambling house, with deep verandas, is set in an extensive park with fine trees. I remember stately processions of pedigreed bulls being led across the foot of the lawn for inspection by the guests, the great animals with gentle eyes waddling on their peg-like legs, seemingly quite aware of their perfection.

There is a form of local entertainment known as an *asado* (literally, roasted), which is so characteristic of the country, so redolent of the soil, as to merit a special word. An asado is an al fresco meal served alike as a sophisticated picnic in an estancia garden, or as the rude meal of gauchos in the vast expanse of the pampa. One served in our honor, typical of many, will long linger in memory. It took place under one of the glorious trees on an estate, not far from the house, so that missing salt or mustard or even sliced cucumbers presented no problem, as picnics so often do. At this repast we were stayed with flagons of red wine to wash down the juicy cuts from the lamb which was served; and afterwards, like surfeited boa constrictors, we lolled about and sympathized with that Roman emperor who yearned for a palate and gullet of abnormal length that he might the longer taste his food!

But not every *asado* is alike. It may, and generally does, at least in the neighborhood of Buenos Aires, consist of a lamb as the pièce de résistance, one whose ancestry is a guarantee that the meat will be succulent. But in certain regions an ox roasted whole is served, the scene recalling an old-fashioned barbecue in the South in my boyhood days, when the issues of elections were followed with burning interest, and folk journeyed great distances to hear political speakers and to eat and drink heavily.

A word may be said here as to the method of preparing a lamb *asado*. The carcass is impaled on two flat steel rods whose ends are stuck deep into the ground and at an angle permitting the slow fire over which the carcass is thus inclined to accomplish its beneficent work. The roasting usually consumes several hours and a skillful *asadero* or cook is necessary to ensure a satisfactory result. Everything is informal. You may sit in the shade and watch the slow process of cooking, and have the ears tickled by the gentle hiss of the roasting flesh, or else study the bronzed features of the asadero and his picturesque garb. He of course wears boots and the baggy trousers known as bombachas; these latter are held up by a broad leather belt studded with silver coins and tiny decorative chains in the same metal; a bright colored shirt, a scarf carelessly knotted around the throat, and a broad brimmed low crowned hat, complete the costume—or almost so, for there is also a wicked looking knife, of the type associated with the name of Colonel Bowie of Alamo fame, stuck in the belt at the back. At the proper time this is drawn with a flourish and utilized to cut rich slices or spear the kidneys in response to the appeals of delicate palates. The men folk first bring appropriate morsels to the ladies, and their needs being met, they proceed with appetites calculated to alarm one not "to the manner born" to meet their own needs. As suggested, red wine is a proper drink with this, but the bombilla of maté is often passed around; the chemical elements of this drink are similar to a salad, and make possible the meat diet which still forms the staple food of country folk. However at estancias delicious salads and vegetables accompany the asado.

Of the food of Argentina in general, a distinguished predecessor, Mr. Stimson, has written with authority and charm, and I quote him here:

Argentine cooking resembles ours in the South, but sublimated. For instance, they have fifty-odd ways of cooking and serving corn-mais—we but two; almost as many for squash, including delicious soups; and are quite as fond as we are of mince pies— empanadas—while Irish stew—puchero—is the common family entrée—with every species of bean, many varieties we do not have, but the baked bean a standard as in New England. But they always begin with *fiambres,* which are hardly hors d'oeuvres, for they consist of huge slices of ham, beef or turkey; but never, except in Buenos Aires, soup. Only after an Argentine has taken the edge off his appetite with fiambres, squash soup and a plate of puchero does the real repast begin: turkey, stuffed with truffles (never partridge or quail, they are thought too common), asado (barbecued beef), lamb chops, fresh cut—but long before this a North American is done.

My reference to the pampa and to its peculiar product the gaucho, demand a brief word concerning his steed—el caballo criollo.

Even today, despite the network of railways laid over parts of the country, despite the increasing number of highways and the motor cars which speed over them, the creole horse, so moderate in his needs in the way of food and water, and with such extraordinary powers of endurance, remains to the pampa what the camel is to the desert; and certainly between the two beasts, having in mind the vital rôles they play, there is a relative comparison.

The vanishing gaucho and the humble workman of the camp trust blindly in their mount. Armed only with a ferocious knife called a *facon,* with a poncho strapped to the saddle bow for sole protection against rain and cold, together with the requisites for preparing maté, (thus taking with them practically all that they possess, including a guitar, the playing of which provides an outlet for the romantic side of their nature), they set out on horseback journeys in which they cover incredible distances. The nights are spent in the open, the head supported by the picturesque sheepskin-covered gaucho saddle (el recado), and the body, wrapped in the poncho, pressed close to the friendly earth. And apropos of these horses, the wonderful ride between Buenos Aires and New York with only two of them a short time ago by A. F. Tschiffely, will not be forgotten.

CHAPTER XIII

Nearby Excursions

1. *La Plata*

IN MUCH the same way as our choice of Washington, the choice of site and the creation of La Plata as the capital of the most important province of the Republic may be said to represent a political compromise.

The question of determining the seat of the National government had not been definitely settled as late as 1880, yet the historic past, the geography and topography of the country, as well as political and constitutional antecedents, all pointed to Buenos Aires as the capital of the Nation; in fact, the three constitutions, of 1819, of 1826 and of 1853, so provided. The Congress took a decisive step in the matter when, in 1880, it passed a law which, counting upon the consent of the legislature of the Province of Buenos Aires, made a federal district of the municipality of Buenos Aires. A few weeks later the President of the Republic sent a message to the provincial legislature pointing out how inappropriate it was that the federal capital should continue to be equally the seat of the provincial government. To this the legislature replied patriotically accepting the force of the President's statements. But in so doing the province was left without a capital. However, this lack was supplied by the enactment and carrying into effect of a law of 1882, under the governorship of Dardo Rocha, by which a site was chosen and a name given to a seat of government. Work proceeded apace, and there came into being the fair city of La Plata, which may be said to symbolize internal peace and national unity.

This capital city lies some thirty-five miles south of Buenos Aires and about three miles from the river whose name it bears. Its population today is approximately 200,000, and it is growing rapidly in size and importance.

In going to La Plata one drives through a rather mean part of Buenos Aires, but beyond the city is a good, if rather narrow and dangerous concrete road. This highway passes by or near to many magnificent properties; one of these, "San Juan," the great Pereyra Yraola estancia, was recently bought by the Government to add to the park treasures of the nation. Next comes "City Bell," the estate of an Anglo-Argentine, whose charming wife has made there a beautiful garden which is the joy of all flower lovers. The old house of this estancia has not been tampered with further than unostentatiously to install modern comforts.

Hurdling the city of La Plata, to which we leap back in the next paragraph, lies another ancient estancia, "Luís Chico," property of the international Banker and economist, Dr. Alejandro Shaw, with some glorious old trees and a very fine box garden. The old and unspoiled house is filled with lovely furniture of its period. In contrast to this latter named property is the delightful modern (as modern as the day after tomorrow) house and estancia called "El Destino," created and being developed by two charming young folk, the sister and brother-in-law of Dr. Shaw, who are having the fun of planting their forest of trees and gardens to grow up with them.

Starting from scratch, like Washington and Canberra and the new Delhi, free from the accretions of former years, La Plata is a well laid out, spacious and modern city, with a flourishing university attended by some 9,000 students, and possessing all the concomitants of healthy municipal life. In the circumstances the visitor can hardly expect to find ancient structures, but in exchange he will see edifices reflecting an excellent standard of architectural taste, broad streets, adequate parks, and evidence of wise provision for future growth.

The conscientious traveler will visit El Paseo del Bosque, in which is located the Zoo; the cathedral, now under construction; the legislative palace; the national university and the governor's mansion, on the Plaza San Martín.

In front of the police department are superb trees; in fact, the city has much arboreal charm, the broad avenues being shaded by plane, maple, cherry, jacaranda, and Judas trees; while in the Avenida Monteverde, the principal street and promenade, are planted numerous lindens, among the very first introduced into the country; these flourish here with unusual vigor and beauty.

Two other points of interest require particular emphasis; el Jardin de la Paz (the Garden of Peace), and the Natural Science Museum. The Garden was conceived and is being carried out by a young Rotarian who is also the Director of Parks and Gardens of the City. Forty-six nations are already represented in the close by national flowers or plants, emblems of the various countries, the whole forming "a happy symbolism of international confraternity." Our own country will soon be represented by dogwood trees sent down by the James River Garden Club of Virginia. These floral tributes from all parts of the world in finding here "a local habitation and a name," may be said to further typify that world peace which is the goal of loftier natures, and the supreme aspiration of humanity.

The Museum of Natural Science is the peculiar glory of La Plata. I do not refer to the handsome building bearing this name, but to the outstanding collection of fossil remains from Patagonia which it houses, brought together in large measure through the efforts of two remarkable men, Florentino and Carlos Ameghino; "Florentino, self-made savant; Carlos, hardy and shrewd explorer." Sons of poor Italian immigrants, they performed unaided an outstanding work in revealing to Argentina and to the world the rich treasures of an ancient past which made of Patagonia a kind of catacomb for monsters of extinct races. Florentino, who started it all, was first a country school teacher. One day walking on the pampa he found some bones. Looking up the little that had been written on the subject he waxed enthusiastic and determined to devote his entire life to this study. After working a while in and around the province of Buenos Aires he became more ambitious and visited Patagonia, whose wealth in ancient bones he had probably learned of through Darwin. But one thing was lacking—money. So Florentino opened a little stationery store in La Plata, it being agreed that he would stay at home and try to earn a living while the younger brother Carlos should go and hunt for bones in the South. The latter spent some twenty years in Patagonia in these researches, and if he finally returned with shattered health, he yet had made, in the opinion of Gaylord Simpson, one of the world's great collections of fossil mammals. This scientist feels that in the unraveling of the broad outlines of Patagonian geology by Carlos, "he made known a whole new world."

It is because of the great work carried out by these two brothers, the one exploring and the other laboring to classify and to give to the public the results of his brother's work, that I urge my compatriots who have an interest in paleontology, geology, and biology to include a visit to the Natural Science Museum in their visit to La Plata.

2. Luján

Some forty-five miles northwest of Buenos Aires lies Luján, a famous shrine and pilgrim resort of Argentina. It is easily and quickly reached by train or else by motor over a first class road. On the way one may see the environs of the capital as well as of the beginnings of the endless expanse of the pampa.

Darwin, in the course of his excursion to Santa Fé, three hundred miles north of the metropolis, remarks: "On September 28 [1832] we passed the small town of Luxan, where there is a wooden bridge—a most unusual convenience in this country." The contrast between the Luján of Darwin's time and the present is striking. Today we enter a bustling little provincial market town, the whole dominated by the large cathedral in the Gothic style, which has been a number of years building and is today one of the prides of the country. Throughout the year and especially on certain saints' days, the cathedral is filled by pilgrims representing every grade of the Argentine social fabric. This movement naturally reaches its climax on May 21, when is celebrated the festival of our Lady of Luján, to whom the cathedral is dedicated. Her miraculous image is enshrined in the cathedral above the high altar under a vast cupola, and nearby is a kind of tribune from whence the faithful pilgrims may venerate the sacred object—a relatively small figure in wax, elaborately dressed and covered with rich jewels.

While visiting one of the chapels I fell into conversation with a canon of the cathedral, and heard the story of the miraculous image: during the colonial period a community of monks desired to send a figure of the Virgin to a branch of their order in Peru. When the wagon bearing the image reached Luján it came to a stop, and despite the addition of other and fresh oxen and the

La Nación

A Pilgrimage to Luján

The estancia "San Juan"

Boating on the Tigre

persuasions of whip and barb, it remained immovable. In this delicate situation the pious priest concluded that the Virgin desired to remain at Luján; a cult was thus slowly perpetuated, and today the image draws thousands of pilgrims from all parts of Argentina.

After visiting the cathedral one may walk the short distance between it and the historical Museum. This is housed in a building of the colonial period—a sort of Cabildo—seat of justice and a prison. Here General Beresford was confined in 1806 following his defeat and capture at the time of the first British invasion of Buenos Aires.

Beresford's conduct as a prisoner demonstrates the truth of Lovelace's familiar lines, for from his cell he carried on an active propaganda against the Spanish authorities, or as an Argentine historian, Doctor Ricardo Levene, has expressed it, he "began to disseminate revolutionary ideas," ideas which found a rich soil in the minds of those who in neighboring years were beginning to dream of emancipation from the Spanish yoke. For a prisoner to be able, following a humiliating defeat, to engage actively in propaganda sounds unbelievable, but so it was, and Saturnino Rodriguez Peña, and perhaps other patriots, visited Beresford at Luján. When this became known to the authorities they gave orders for his internment at Catamarca, far up in the northwest. The prisoner, under military escort, was actually on the way when Rodriguez Peña and his friends managed to effect his escape. He was brought back to Buenos Aires, hidden in the city for three days and finally smuggled on board a British man-of-war lying off Ensenada, now the port of La Plata.

The Museum itself is to me the most interesting in Argentina. It has an intimate, a kind of family atmosphere, and the quantity and character of the relics displayed, chiefly relating to the struggle for independence and "The Tyranny," are calculated to stir every heart.

Crossing a charming bit of old garden we enter a large building where are many objects giving reality to the everyday life of bygone days. Among these are wagons of various types of the time of Rosas, painted deep crimson to signify their owners' allegiance to the Tyrant; there are also early types of mills; and great ox-carts of a form made familiar to us by the drawings of Vidal.

3. TIGRE—"Green Heaven"

If the reader will examine a map of the fluvial region in the neighborhood of Buenos Aires, he will observe that the River Paraná shortly before linking with the Uruguay to form the estuary of La Plata has already separated into two parts; one of these, the Paraná Guazu, in turn divides, so that before these waters of the great Paraná actually mingle with the Uruguay at the beginning of the estuary, there are no less than four Paranás springing from it! These are: the Paraná Guazu itself, meaning the big Paraná, the Paraná Bravo, meaning the rough Paraná, the Paraná Mini, or little Paraná, and the Paraná de las Palmas, from the number of palms which formerly grew on its shores.

On the banks of a narrow stream lying to the south of the last named river is found the little village of Tigre, a name with which the visitor to Buenos Aires is sure to grow familiar, as applied to a zone of the great delta of the Paraná, and embracing roughly a hundred square miles. It is a region of amazing beauty, which in its luxuriant vegetation, its myriad water ways, its charming summer homes, and its yacht and boat clubs, is a kind of rural Venice. It has been aptly called by an English friend, whose helpful notes on this region I am using, "Green Heaven," in contradistinction to the epithet of "Green Hell" applied to certain regions of the Chaco.

The name "Tigre" calls up savage beasts, impenetrable jungles, and dense tropical forests. Yet none of these is manifest in this fluvial playground; quite the contrary, for if its nature is varied, none of it is terrifying; though a careful search might disclose a deer or a jaguar in the very depths of the delta. Even the forests are in some measure artificial, various trees being cultivated for commercial purposes.

The word "Tigre" as applied to this part of the delta dates back many years, certainly prior to the great southeasterly wind and extraordinary freshet of August, 1820, which destroyed the port and town known as Las Conchas (not to be confused with the town of that name existing today). The force and violence of that storm were such as to convert the incipient stream then known as the Tigre into a considerable volume of water, much wider and deeper than it had been before. Under a decree of November 16, 1821, Las Conchas was closed to navigation and the formation of a port on the site of the present Tigre was authorized. Although the decree of closure of the port of Las Conchas was subsequently annulled, that part relating to Tigre continued, and it became an active commercial center, gradually attaining its present important economic situation as the point of concentration for the sale of products from the Delta.

For the origin of the name of the river and town we must fall back on oral tradition, and this has been set down as recently as 1907 in a work published at Buenos Aires in that year entitled *Breve Reseña Histórica del Partido de las Conchas,* as arising from the fact that "a certain spot in the Tigre was the lair of a man-eating tiger which caused much ravage among cattle—for which reason the neighborhood folk gave it the name of Tigre and continued to call it so even after the beast was killed." This would explain the use of the name in the singular in a region where tigers abounded.

But perhaps one good tradition deserves another and here is what "I have heard tell": The great water of the Paraná, when in flood, literally gouges out of the banks large sections of earth bearing trees and heavy vegetation; these, in the form of green islets, are hurried down to the estuary by the swift current. Upon them wild animals of various kinds take refuge, to be borne, willy nilly, they know not where. On some occasion in the past, inhabitants of the region saw a tiger or tigers on one of these verdant rafts, which they had no difficulty in despatching by rifle fire, and then by one of those processes with which we are all familiar "the place where the tiger (or tigre) was seen" wore down with the years to "Tigre" and came to be applied to a zone or section.

Driving out from Buenos Aires over an excellent road one covers the twenty-five miles separating the center of the capital from the little village of Tigre in about forty minutes. As one draws near the river, flags fluttering from numbers of handsome boat houses are seen up and down the stream; one has glimpses too of charming summer homes. These agreeable impressions are increased on reaching the water's edge, near which lie innumerable small craft: row boats, canoes, racing shells, punts, launches of all sizes and qualities, sail boats, graceful racing and comfortable cruising yachts, as well as serious-minded barges and tugs.

Among the numerous edifices to be seen is the delightfully hospitable Tigre Boat Club, now in its fiftieth year of healthy life. Its membership embraces some eight hundred British and Americans who meet at this pleasant headquarters especially on week-ends and utilize its many pleasure craft.

However, for the visitor who must economize on his time, it is suggested that he engage one of the numerous launches for hire at moderate prices and view the landscape in this manner; he will be richly rewarded.

The natural and artificial canals over which one passes are bordered by small properties, by orchards, or by plantations of poplars and willows, commercially exploited. Charming villas, Swiss chalets, English cottages, Chinese pagodas, even Gothic cloisters, are to be seen, representing every architectural vagary one can imagine. Each property has its little landing stage where there is usually a bathing cabin, and often a sort of belvedere in which to sit and watch passers-by in the various river craft.

It is difficult to imagine a scene of greater tranquillity. The forest seems virgin, and of an overwhelming exuberance. Here a great mass of honeysuckle threatens to break down an archway; there masses of bougainvillaeas and jasmine cascade over tiny habitations perched on piles to guarantee them against inundations. In a number of gardens hydrangeas, of a size and beauty I have never seen surpassed, balance gracefully over the banks of the river.

One is in no danger of going hungry in the Tigre region; little restaurants, known as "recreos" abound, where simple, good food can be obtained and even rustic accommodations for the night.

While of course the Tigre is a haunt for the pleasure seeker from Buenos Aires, especially on week-ends, it has, too, fixed inhabitants, simple folk who earn a bare living, yet who love this untrammeled life.

A further glance at the map in conjunction with what I have said will demonstrate to everyone interested in boats that this region is a marvelous field for two types of sports: for the yachtsman, there is the great expanse of the estuary of the River Plate in which to sail, while for those who believe in the truth of the childhood rhyme, that "Vessels large may venture more, But little boats should keep near shore," have spread out for their pleasure the hundred square miles of the delta. The navigators of the smaller streams are derisively called by their brethren, who dare the outside waters, "ditch-crawlers."

The yachtsman, on the other hand, may clear from any one of the several yacht clubs located between Buenos Aires and Tigre early in the morning, profiting by a regular and favorable wind, which will carry him far out into the Plata. By five o'clock in the afternoon this will have veered to the southeast, and will bring him gently back to his moorings. (Mr. Grumpy here whispers in my ear that this is what *usually* happens; that no guarantee should go with any statement concerning wind).

As suggested, rowing, canoeing and scurrying around in motor launches, are the favorite pursuits of habitués of the inner Tigre region. At regular intervals regattas are held on the river near the town. The banks are then lined with spectators, the relatively broad stream is filled with tiny craft, and club landings are crowded. The noise of bands or of radios, the enthusiasm of the crowd, the cheers of partisans of respective shells, combine to give to the spectacle the impression of a kind of Henley.

CHAPTER XIV

Mar Del Plata

Newport of Argentina

MAR DEL PLATA, the Newport, Trouville, Brighton, San Sebastian, or what you will, of Argentina, lies on the Atlantic Ocean some two hundred and fifty miles southeast of Buenos Aires. It is reached by railway in about six hours, and by motor in approximately the same time.

The visitor today will learn with surprise that within the memory of living men the flourishing port before him consisted of only a few huts, two or three primitive stores, and a rude stockade peopled by a small detachment of soldiers; its only visitors being gauchos or occasional groups of seal fishers. But so it was. And Cunningham Grahame (the "Don Roberto" of Tschiffely's spirited story) who died only some two years ago, used to relate that when he was a young man he, with two companions, put up for the night à l'Hôtel de la Belle Etoile, the Southern Cross blazing overhead. Sometime in the night (their ears, being close to the ground, and trained to pick up significant sounds) they heard the trampling of many hoofs. Indians, on horseback! Hastily fitting bridles on three of their horses, not delaying for saddles, and abandoning all their belongings, they made a dash for the nearest military post. The Indians pursued them to the very doors of the stockade. It was only when the small piece of cannon in the enclosure was fired that the enemy sullenly drew off. And this was the Mar del Plata of not very long ago!

Modern Mar del Plata began as a real estate adventure in 1874, and contains today about 80,000 people, a figure which reaches 200,000 or more during the summer season—mid-December to Easter week. Out of the season its population is made up of representatives of great commercial houses engaged in the exportation of wheat, potatoes, and oats; of shopkeepers, of caretakers of smart houses and hotels and clubs, and of fisher folk, the latter supplying the Buenos Aires market with sea food. Also, apart from its seasonal social activities, and its year round bustle in the suggested task of helping to fill the huge maw of a great capital, Mar del Plata is an important Argentine naval port, with a ceaseless to and fro movement of men of war; in addition it is the entrance to and outlet of a rich hinterland, and the market town for many small villages and great estancias which lie near it.

In addition to marking an agreeable change in summer temperature from the capital, the city possesses limited stretches of sandy beach, bathed by the limpid but rather chilly waters of the Atlantic, which offer in color a marked contrast to the tawny flood of the Plata in the neighborhood of Buenos Aires.

The economic birth and growth of the city corresponded with the economic upswing of the entire country in a time when French influence in dress, literature, and architecture was at its peak, which is most evident physically in the architecture.

The site of Mar del Plata was well chosen. Hills which slope gently toward a wide bay are crowned by substantial mansions, villas and cottages, often with extensive and charming gardens. A French writer of only 25 years ago speaks of "the extreme violence of the wind called the pampero and of the winds from the sea, which combine to prevent trees from growing on the slopes.

The Chapadmalal Mansion

Mar del Plata

IGUAZÚ FALLS

IGUAZÚ FALLS

There is no shelter on these hills so rudely swept, no beautiful promenades in the flat and dreary country behind them."

One may smile today at these statements, for, as if a magician's wand had been waved over the land, everywhere in the city one sees trees offering both protection and beauty, while in the nearby country certain of the properties embrace veritable forests covering the former bare pampa, planted in several cases by present owners who have thus lived to enjoy the beauty of their patriotic and esthetic creations, the alchemy of soil and air effecting this precocious development.

A landmark of the city is the church of Stella Maris which lifts a graceful spire to heaven at the highest point in the town and is, like St. Philip's in Charleston, a guiding mark for seamen.

The arrangement of the well-paved streets is the familiar checkerboard pattern, and extensive public parks are to be found especially as one approaches the sea. A highway leads to the height on which the imposing golf club is built, and this with the well laid out and well maintained golf course, overlooks a part of the lower town, the beaches and the sea. A lower road takes one in a few minutes to the Playa Grande, the principal bathing center for smart folk, in contradistinction to more popular beaches. From the heights gorgeous sunsets of a vividness rather milder than those to be seen on our Pacific Coast, offer a spectacle which toward evening draws thousands of Argentines, as a magnet, to view its loveliness.

The principal hotel at the moment is the Bristol whose age almost equals that of the town itself, but possessing more or less modern dependencies, with a good cuisine, a good orchestra, a good dancing floor, and an adjoining Casino; in the latter roulette, baccarat and trente et quarante are indulged in by the large crowds which assemble there in the late afternoon and after dinner. In no other casino, not even in Monte Carlo, are there as many roulette tables. And from roulette profits a gift of 400,000 pesos is given yearly to the Province, for charity.

A defect of Mar del Plata in the opinion of many is that in its social manifestations it is an extension or a continuation of the life of Buenos Aires and therefore, apart from bathing and gambling, offers few distractions in the true sense of the word from what one has known during the preceding nine months of the year; one meets exactly the same people with the same gregarious instincts, and the diversions, save as noted, repeat those of the capital.

The outstanding days at Mar del Plata are those of Carnival when the town is swamped, overwhelmed, deluged, by visitors from the capital. Rooms in hotels are then practically unobtainable and the railway companies frequently utilize their sleeping cars for lodgings during the three days of festivities. Young folk are seen everywhere at this time in Carnival costume and often masked. But a general air of propriety reigns and the characteristic good humour of the Latin crowd keeps the prevailing informality from degenerating into anything like rough play. However, a disagreeable feature pointed out by visitors a quarter of a century ago still prevails, something as annoying and disagreeable as the pranks which characterize All Hallow's Eve in the United States and equally frowned upon by many folk; I refer to the peculiar Carnival custom of reciprocal drenching with water, alleged to be perfumed, expelled from water-guns. I wore my raincoat during this period, despite the brilliant sunshine; I recall too that when the cinema was ended a serried rank of small boys awaited the public and with all the pitiless barbarity of youth proceeded to empty the contents of their water-guns on many lovely dresses.

Apart from the excellent golf offered either over the courses lying above the beaches or at Parque Camet, the real charm and beauty of Mar del Plata for me lies in its suburbs, where are lovely villas, set in huge gardens, and in the nearby estates, such as "Chapadmalal," described below; "El Boquerón," where Enrique Anchorena gives visible proof of his knowledge of silviculture; "La Armonía," where Señora de Cobo dispenses an exquisite hospitality; "Haras Ojo de Agua," belonging to the Victorica Roca family and possessing a magnificent stud farm, etc. In domains such as these Argentine country life, which is referred to more specifically in a subsequent chapter, is seen at its best. I have personally known the hospitality of the princely estates named, and can testify to the wholehearted cordiality and gracious thought for the guest to be found in them.

I recall a day spent at La Armonía, when as a characteristically charming attention, each of the flotilla of tiny craft anchored in the lake fronting the ample house bore our country's flag, while the colors of the flowers on the luncheon table equally recalled my allegiance.

Fourteen kilometres from Mar del Plata lies what is perhaps the most spectacular estate in Argentina—certainly one of the most beautiful and impressive—"Chapadmalal."

This glorious property, originally embracing nearly 40,000 acres, has been in the family since 1854 but it was laid out by the father of the present owners, and the stately house, the forests, the gardens, the golf course, the tennis court, the polo field, the riding school, the stallion boxes, the yearling stables, the ample stables themselves, the bull boxes, the hospital boxes, represent the fulfillment of his vision.

"Craganour," "Amsterdam," "Chili II," "Pipiolo," "Botafogo," "Picacero," "Parwiz," "Sir Berkeley," "Air Raid," "Parlanchin," are names of magnificent racing sires, equine aristocrats who have brought glory to these stables.

Every visitor to Argentina of international importance has tasted the hospitality of Chapadmalal, whose recent castellan with his charming wife are as well known in exclusive circles in England and France as in his native country. It was he who drove the coach from London to Brighton in the same season in which one of our millionaires was doing something similar. But, as my host remarked to me with a smile, there was a difference: "I bred the horses which I drove; Mr. V. purchased his."

No cattle are raised at Chapadmalal for marketing; it is essentially a breeding farm and its equines including race horses, polo ponies and draft animals, its sheep, and its Shorthorn and other types of bulls, are prize winners in every rural exhibition, while the horses win many important races.

It is an interesting sight to enter one of the stables and watch the huge young bulls arrive to be fed. They are driven close to a sort of raised platform which is already occupied by a corresponding number of cows with udders heavy with milk. From these the young bulls drink deep draughts, and fairly stagger out, surfeited and content. But this is not all—for this baby-food diet is supplemented by balanced rations prepared in special kitchens! Thus are these gentle, placid monsters made ready for the cattle shows.

The owners of Chapadmalal have made it possible for the general visitor to Mar del Plata to see this property and some of its activities, and daily during the season motor 'buses go from the town in twenty minutes and tour the grounds and gardens and work-dependencies.

CHAPTER XV

River Trips

Iguazú — Asunción — Concordia

The River Paraná — Mississippi of Argentina

I CONFESS to feeling a little sorry for folk from home who having made the long voyage to Argentina, fail to make the trip up the great watercourse called the Paraná, to the Falls of Iguazú, (The Big Water) and to Asunción, capital of Paraguay. Three weeks are required to make this journey in proper unhurried style. This period would permit of a full day at Posadas, with opportunity to visit the nearby ruins of former Jesuit missions, three days at the Falls, and five days at Asunción. However a marked saving in time may be effected by proceeding by railway to Posadas (see the map), thence by steamer to the Falls, returning by the same means, and going again by railway in about thirteen hours across the little Republic of Paraguay, to Asunción. So much for the time consumed. As regards the season; the six months from April to October are most agreeable; during the remainder of the year it is apt to be warm in the north, and insects are then more abundant and voracious.

The great moving highway, as Pascal would call it, over which one travels on this northern pilgrimage is the fourth river in the world, coming after the Amazon, the Congo, and our Mississippi-Missouri, in the extent of area drained—in the case of the Paraná being estimated by scientists to be over three million square miles

—or about the area of the continental United States! The vast waterway has its hydra-headed beginning far up in Brazil, and in a final burst of splendor joins with the Uruguay to form the vast estuary miscalled el *Rio* de la Plata. Nearly four thousand miles of its surface can be traversed, practically all of it in a fair measure of comfort.

Since the purpose of this chapter is to prepare the traveler for what he is to see on the voyage north, perhaps I cannot do better than to quote from my travel diary of a short time ago. My pilgrimage was made at the end of April and beginning of May. My wife and I were accompanied by two charming friends, my Military Attaché Captain (now Major) Sharp and his wife. The former figures in these travel notes as the "Cap'n." Here are some of my unembellished remarks:

April 29:

We reached ROSARIO, our first stop since Buenos Aires, about 12:30, an hour and a half late, and did not get away until one, and then went immediately to luncheon.

Darwin visited Rosario at the end of September, *1833*, and speaks of it as "a large town built on a dead level plain, which forms a cliff about sixty feet high over the Paraná." He continues: "The river here is very broad, with many islands, which are low and wooded, as is the opposite shore . . . The cliffs are the most picturesque part; sometimes they are absolutely perpendicular, and of a red color; at other times in large broken masses, covered with cacti and mimosa trees. The real grandeur, however, of an immense river like this, is derived from reflecting how important a means of communication and commerce it forms between one nation and another; to what a distance it travels; and from how vast a territory it drains the great body of fresh water which flows past your feet."

We are due in PARANÁ at eight o'clock; this port is on the east side of the river going up; on the other side is the city of SANTA FÉ, capital of the Province of the same name.

Darwin describes the SANTA FÉ of his day (1832) as a quiet little town. "The Governor . . . . . has been seventeen years in power. The stability of the Government is due to his tyrannical habits; for tyranny seems as yet better adapted to these countries than republicanism. . . . The Governor's favorite occupation is hunting Indians; a short time since he slaughtered forty-eight, and sold the children at the rate of three or four pounds apiece."

The sunset was glorious, and the moonrise equally thrilling; delicate shades of mauve and nile green and pink, through which the moon came swimming up.

We made a brief stop at a tiny port called DIAMANTE about 7:30; too dark to see much; the town seemed to be built high up on a rocky bluff; and the scattered houses appeared cheerfully illuminated.

Monday, April 30:

Another lovely day begins; the air much softer, the sun a tiny bit stronger. At half-past eight we tied up for a few moments at a little port called La Paz. Wretched oxen drawing huge carts met the steamer; men in bombachas and bright colored shirts were strolling around; various Indian types were to be seen, and there was a greater feeling of remoteness from the Capital than we have thus far experienced.

The manner of making the landing at La Paz calls perhaps for a little comment as the same procedure is followed at many other ports:

The current of the river being very strong, the head of the vessel is turned a little inward and the bow anchor dropped; the current throws the stern around toward the landing stage, a bow line is thrown out and made fast; the outside paddle wheel is then made to turn, the donkey engine pulls on the cable, thus bringing the bow in, when another line, followed by the cable, makes the bow and stern fast. On leaving, the stern line is cast off, then the bow hawser; the pull is then on the anchor, which brings the head a bit out, pointing upstream, the inside paddle wheel revolves, and up the river we go again.

The river retains its tawny color, just like the old James at Richmond and below, whose limpid waters are churned up by the red clay coming from the Rivanna and Fluvanna in a time of freshet; the Master tells me that it is the Bermego which henna-dyes the Paraná.

The river has broadened out into wide reaches; we go from shore to shore following the channel, and sometimes are within a musket shot of the shore. The average width of the stream I should guess to be a mile.

Tuesday, May 1:

Another lovely morning, bright sunshine, balmy air, an added something of a sub-tropical clime to be remarked in the vegetation. The former low-lying banks begin to give way to bluffs, some of them as high as sixty feet, with lovely colors in the various strata; the water has washed the bases and the middle of these into fantastic shapes—turrets, spires, altars, pinnacles.

About seven-thirty we came alongside another floating wharf, EMPEDRADO; a few straggling villagers and loungers met the steamer to watch the mail and tiny bit of cargo being landed and to have a vague touch with the faraway metropolis.

We chugged along at about fourteen miles per hour (the current is approximately three miles), and about eleven o'clock swung along the wharf at CORRIENTES.

Here we will leave our present steamer, which continues to Asunción, for one which will bear us to Posadas, on our way to Iguazú.

We drove through the little town to la Iglesia de la Santísima Cruz de los Milagros. This was built about 1810; its principal glory is a rude wooden cross of quebracho, which, the legend tells us, the Indians made repeated attempts to burn at the time they attacked the town in the late sixteenth century, and failing in this, attributed to it the superhuman power which aided the Spaniards, and accepted the true faith. The town itself is, of course, ancient, and was founded by an expedition which came down from Paraguay and established a military post in 1588.

We are now in the Alto Paraná, and there is a marked difference in the color of the water, it being a dull amber, compared to the muddy streams we have known before. Also there is a much more marked tropical atmosphere; in the morning we saw a crocodile sunning himself on a sloping bank; this afternoon palms have been frequent, orange trees are everywhere and the forests suggest a jungle. The banks are much higher than downstream, and everywhere we see outcroppings of lava rock of a dark red color, which would seem to make acceptable building material. But all the habitations along the bank are of adobe, some palm-thatched and others with the accursed corrugated iron for roofs. At several spots bright mounds of gold interspersed with green proved to be oranges piled high, evidently awaiting a steamer.

We are due at Itati about eleven o'clock. Darkness has come. Dinner is over and bed beckons.

Wednesday, May 2:

Everything is a stage nearer the primitive on this stream; the one or two landing places we have touched at are rude and bare structures, constructed of quebracho. At two points today we have stopped in midstream while small boats have put out from shore to take off passengers.

The crews of both boats were Indians; roughly made leather leggings protected their legs; their feet were bare, and spurs were buckled to their heels!

The bamboo is now seen everywhere; also a beautiful tree with leaves growing in clusters, bright green on one side and light grey on the other, suggesting a large bouquet of magnolia blossoms; as far as I can determine it is the *ambay* (*Cecropia palmata*). Around the little scattered huts are seen patches of sugar cane which the "Cap'n" says may be utilized to make a type of home-brew known as "caña," of deadly potency.

The afternoon has been without incident, but the sunset has been one of such unusual beauty as will linger long in memory; for some distance our course was almost due east, with the sun setting directly over the stern. We therefore had the full effect of the rays when we looked forward and the splendor of the sun itself when we faced aft. The afterglow was as lovely as what preceded it.

> *For note, when evening shuts, a certain moment*
> *Cuts the deed off, calls the glory from the gray;*
> *A whisper from the west shoots "Add this to the rest"*
> *Take it and try its worth, here dies another day.*

After all this poetry it is anti-climax to speak of food and beds, but a word of praise must be said concerning the two vital things, not alone on this little craft, but on the larger steamer which brought us from Buenos Aires to Corrientes. Food is good, and beds are comfortable; as the water is continuously muddy, not much can be said about the baths, but hot water is always available, and cleanliness is attainable by the energetic!

The night has settled down with a cloud bank in the west and north and some lightning; as we got under way from Corrientes several hours behind the usual schedule, and as the moon is not yet up, we are feeling our way along and the lead is being cast.

Thursday, May 3:

"The dawn came in with sandals grey," also accompanied by heavy rain squalls. These latter continued intermittently but did not interfere with our coming abreast of Posadas about two p.m.

This little town of some thirty thousand folk is the capital of the ancient region which, together with parts of Paraguay, was ruled over by the Jesuits under one of the most interesting experiments of modern times in the way of a theocracy—or communism, if you will. The district is now embraced in the Territory of Misiones.

Having nothing better to do, we rose early, and found we were made fast to a trim little motor vessel called the Guayra, one of the neatest, most comfortable craft of its kind one could find in a day's voyaging, on which we continued our way.

About two o'clock we were abreast of a yerba plantation, San Ignacio, where there was a quantity of cargo to be unloaded.

Because of frequent and sudden changes in the river level, piers cannot be built; only a floating wharf would serve, and these are generally too expensive to be practical, having in mind the volume of freight. It is therefore necessary, here and elsewhere, to bring the vessel as close to shore as possible, then by means of cords to fix a heavy and rudely constructed rowboat between the ship and the shore line, place planks from the vessel to the boat and from the boat to the shore; the men passing over this to carry the cargo; in this case flour, and sacks for the yerba harvest. We were detained here until 4:45. At one or two other points goods would be loaded in the row-boat and taken to the shore; an example of shore-door delivery!

On every hand now we have evidence of the premier industry of Misiones—yerba growing and preparing of the leaf for the market. Regularly laid out plantations are to be seen from time to time and the large barnlike structures in which the leaves are prepared and classified. Most of these establishments have a sort of inclined way or chute running down from the high bank to the river's edge, to facilitate loading.

A gap occurs here in my diary. It marks in part the period when we were happily marooned at Puerto Bemberg whence we departed by speed boat for Puerto Aguirre, the little port for the falls. Thence we went by motor in forty minutes to the Falls Hôtel and immediately began our visit.

Monday, May 7:

Off we tramped, preceded by a stolid Indian wearing a collarless shirt with a handkerchief tied around the neck, blue cotton trousers, and alpargatas (rough canvas shoes with a sole made of rope, and much worn by the poorer folk in the Argentine).

Even from the hotel we had a glorious panorama of the Falls; now we were to study them in detail and much nearer.

We first had a view of La Garganta del Diablo and glimpses of other awe inspiring beauties. We continued through lovely woodland paths, known as "picadas," admirably laid out, and leading us successively to "Los Tres Mosqueteros," "El Salto de San Martín," "Bozzetti," and others, ending up with "El Salto Lanusse" or "Las Dos Hermanas." These imposing twin falls are named after the daughters of a former Governor of Misiones, Juan José Lanusse, who took them with him on one of the first trips to Iguazú in modern times; this was in August, 1898.

An American visitor on seeing these marvelous cataracts is apt to attempt to compare them with Niagara; the difference, however, is startling. In the case of Niagara, (as I recall it on my second honeymoon in times now so long past), shops and factories and houses and other works of man surround it; at Iguazú the great encircling rush of water leaps out of the jungle and is again received into its green, impenetrable depths. It is all so fresh, so green, so virginal; easily we could imagine that "We were the first That ever burst, Into that inland sea." High over La Garganta hangs a cloud of vapor, ever there, recalling that luminous sign that guided the children of Israel in the desert. The roar of the falls is continuous; again I fall back on poetry to voice my emotion; this time Francis Thompson: "That voice is round me like a bursting sea;" and again, the inspired language of the Apocalypse—"His voice was the sound of many waters."

Here I am tempted to recall a possibly apocryphal story of Mrs. Theodore Roosevelt, who, as a widow, visited Iguazú. On the eve of her departure the visitor's book was brought to her by the hotel proprietor in order that she might inscribe the conventional banalties; seizing the pen she wrote three words, followed by her signature; the delighted proprietor adjusted his glasses and read the tribute: "My poor Niagara."

I must not omit here a reference to the myriads of butterflies to be seen in the park surrounding the falls—all the colors of Joseph's coat appearing as these dainty diaphanous creatures flutter over one's head in the warm sunshine.

Again I interrupt my diary since it is hardly necessary to describe the return trip from Puerto Aguirre to Posadas. Arriving there the evening of May 8th we spent the night comfortably on board our steamer which was alongside the wharf.

Wednesday, May 9:

Again we are blessed with lovely weather, and a dash of coolness in the air. About 7:45 word came to the "Cap'n" that the Governor would call for us at nine for a trip to the ruins of the Jesuit Mission of San Ignacio, perhaps the most important of these establishments—called Doctrinas or Reducciones, meaning a village of Indians converted to Christianity.

We left the steamer in a launch to make a trip of about fifty yards to where two motors were waiting. Our trip was without incident. On the way we passed many yerbales, and some rather extensive stretches of plain on which cattle were grazing. The country rolls prettily and the hills are evidently the knees of nearby mountains. We crossed a fairly long bridge which was the Governor's pride; it was something that had been talked about for a quarter of a century, but he, the first Misionero to be Governor, brought it into being. The road, except in one of two spots and for short distances is entirely passable, but it is very rough and would be considered a poor thoroughfare in the United States. We left Posadas at 10:15 and reached San Ignacio, a tiny little village, at 12:15. We went immediately to the ruins which adjoin the village and are now become a public monument.

Of course, to fully enjoy the mission, one should know something of its history.

The planting of villages of Christian Indians in the large territory known as Misiones was begun in 1608, a year *after* the establishment of the first permanent English settlement in the New World, at Jamestown, and twelve years *before* the landing of the colonists at Plymouth. The order issued from the Governor of Asunción, and the missionaries of La Compañía de Jesus were instructed to go to Paraná Guayre and los Guaycurús to initiate the work by converting the Guaraní Indians. All would have gone well with the missions but for the incursions from San Pablo (Sao Paulo) in Brazil of bands known as mamelucos, supported and encouraged by the Portugese Government, who carried off the inhabitants to make slaves of them. Some sixty thousand were thus placed in bondage in three years. In the face of this continuing persecution the Jesuit Fathers determined to migrate with a number of the faithful in order to save the undertaking from extermination. The trip down the Alto Paraná on rafts and in canoes, of 12,000 Indians, led by a handful of priests, was an odyssey; half of the canoes or rafts were lost in El Salto Grande of the Paraná and much of the journey was made on foot, across streams, through forests, over mountains. This was in 1631-32. In the latter years San Ignacio was founded. In 1647 it had 1700 inhabitants; in 1767, some 3,300.

For more than one hundred and fifty years the Jesuits carried on in Misiones and near thereto an enterprise communal in character, in that the Indians under their jurisdiction worked for the respective reducciones; the product of their labors went to Holy Mother Church, and in return they received clothing and food and lodging, medical care and religious instruction. It is true that each mission had its town council and its mayor, all Indians, but the priests exercised a dominion and authority absolute in character, the officials named being their agents. No stranger was permitted to visit the villages, lest he contaminate the Indians, and there was no commerce since the priests sold the produce of the farms for the common benefit. If this communal system appeared harsh to its prejudiced critics, it represented an enormous advance over what the Indians had known before under the system of *encomiendas* which prevailed here, in Mexico, and perhaps in other Spanish possessions in America, under which the Indian was *commended* to various Spanish masters. The laws governing the latter system were well drawn but hideously applied, as is any law which is above the moral tone or spiritual level of the community in which it is to take effect. Against these abuses the priests, and Jesuits in particular, labored unceasingly.

The withdrawal from exploitation of so large a territory and so many of the original inhabitants naturally excited the cupidity of the colonists, while the intransigent attitude of the Jesuits provoked the hostility of many bishops of their own communion and others. In Europe, and especially at the Spanish Court, ugly reports were being constantly received and circulated, and when

Voltaire in "Candide" lashed with his satire the conduct of the priests toward the natives he was probably but giving voice to a generally accepted, if erroneous, belief concerning this ecclesiastical-communistic territory. In any event, in 1767, King Carlos III decreed the expulsion of the Jesuits from Spanish dominions, and this order was quickly and effectively carried out as far as Misiones was concerned. The number of priests in this district at the time was about fifty, ruling over probably as many thousands of natives, whom they dominated by sheer force of intellect and leadership.

The ruins of San Ignacio are a melancholy and impressive sight. There are remains of impressive portals, elaborately carved wide windows, massively built walls, all rapidly crumbling and disappearing under the green hand of the jungle. Nature is the deadliest enemy of these relics of a vanished dream of a spiritual-material empire. The wild fig tree has been a particularly destructive force, wrenching huge stones from their place, or holding others in a close embrace; in one or two instances large stone columns have been completely enveloped and hidden in the heart of a tree.

There is a huge literature in existence concerning these misiones, and in his "Apuntes Históricos sobre Misiones," Raimundo Fernandez Ramos gives a valuable bibliography.

Saturday, May 12:

The steward had us up in time to meet the sun, and we had dressed in leisurely fashion and breakfasted, very lightly, when we came abreast the landing place at ASUNCIÓN; this was about 7:05. The harbor is rather pleasing, viewed from the river; its entrance is a narrow throat, which, we learn from the amphibious "Cap'n," is sometimes difficult of passage when the river is low. Along the river bank, just below the city, is the arsenal and there are also hangars for hydroplanes; others appeared to be in construction. The skyline of Asunción shows a tower, square and capped with arrows at each corner—the capital; a rather imposing looking cathedral of nondescript architecture, but a dome suggestive of the one at Florence, in very pale copy; and another dome, with scaffolding, this latter belonging to a building said to have been begun about the time of López, or immediately thereafter, and still unfinished. On the pier was our Minister, Meredith Nicholson, whose personality is as charming as his novels would lead one to expect, the delightful Butlers, of the Legation staff, and representatives of the Government.

We drove immediately to the Legation, over streets paved with cobblestones, and which would have been unbearable but for the fact that the chauffeur followed the street-car tracks very skillfully.

The Legation is a pleasing two-story structure, in brick and stucco, set in a large garden in which many varieties of tropical plants were in full leaf or fruitage or flower.

We sat down again to breakfast, this time a real one of ham— such ham—and eggs, biscuit and excellent coffee. This over we continued the good talk which had begun from the moment we all met, and finally about noon gathered at the hotel—El Gran Hotel del Paraguay—set in a huge garden, with orange trees in full bearing, as well as papaya, mandarins, etc.; also hibiscus in full flower and many other plants. The house itself is sprawled all over the place, like a young girl who holds herself badly, yet presenting some pleasing curves; there are also pavilions containing bathrooms. The general effect is pleasingly tropical and different, far different, from what one is accustomed to in Buenos Aires.

Tuesday, May 15:

We had decided last night that provided it were clear today we would make an excursion to a nearby village called YAGUERON, where, we understood, were interesting ruins.

The road is flanked almost the entire distance by heavy undergrowth and a variety of sub-tropical trees; the manioc seemed to be almost the only cultivated thing, although cotton was being laid out seemingly to dry; however, we saw but one cotton field.

YAGUERON is a tiny village of perhaps twenty houses, built around a square, the outstanding feature of which is the ancient church. The place itself is overshadowed by a cone of rock, rising several hundred feet, similar to other hills to be seen from Asunción.

The church, a Franciscan foundation, of 1600, it is said, is a large structure of brick and stucco, the walls being nearly six feet thick; in the center rises framework of heavy timber which carries the gable roof, which is tiled; this projects well beyond the walls, and finds its support on brick and stucco columns which thus form a cloister around the entire church. The doors are heavy and simply carved; inside the woodwork is also carved in simple patterns, and every surface has been painted. The effect inside is of strength and lightness. On either side of the chancel are small chapels, with rococo altars and figures of saints. The sanctuary itself has a barrel roof, much like the one in the Church of La Compañía at Córdoba.

The high altar is really magnificent, although in florid style, and the carving, probably the work of Indian converts, is marked by vigor and sincerity.

Following this country excursion we spent another day in Asunción, dining with President Ayala and his lovely and cultured French wife, and leaving the morning of May 17, and reaching Buenos Aires three days later.

A further word before closing this chapter:

The traveler who is pressed for time but who yet would like to gain an idea of the river scenery of Argentina, may take one of the comfortable vessels plying between Buenos Aires and Concordia, the flourishing and pleasant little capital of the Province of Entre Rios. This latter political division, as its name implies, lies between two great rivers, the Paraná and the Uruguay, and is sometimes called by those who remember their school and Bible days, Mesopotamia. Much fruit is grown in this province and is a principal article of exportation. The river scenery is strikingly suggestive of the Paraná in its lower reaches; however the wharves and landing stages are of far more substantial construction.

The trip to Concordia is made in about 24 hours and the round trip, including a brief sojourn in this agreeable provincial capital, consumes about three days. It is a tranquil and agreeable inland voyage and is to be recommended.

The traveler returning from Iguazú could, if he arranged his schedules neatly, debark at Posadas and come down in one night by train to Concordia, catching a steamer for Buenos Aires the next morning.

CHAPTER XVI

Southern Argentina

Region of Lakes and Mountains

THE HEADING of this chapter is misleading! For even after one has proceeded almost due south for six hundred miles, has reached the little town of Viedma, and begun traveling in a westerly direction toward the lake port of San Carlos de Bariloche, starting point for visits to the mountains and lakes of the National Park of Nahuel Huapí, he is still more than a thousand miles in an airline from Cape Horn, and has only touched the northern fringes of the vaguely defined region called Patagonia. (There is no political division by this latter name, but the term is generally applied to that part of South America lying below the fortieth parallel of latitude.)

Patagonia means "Big Footed" and this epithet appears to have been given to the original inhabitants, now nearly extinct, by early adventurers, who also recorded their unusual height. By way of aside, I might confess to the reader that my stature is six-feet three and that my young private secretary, Stewart Bryan, who accompanied me to Argentina out-tops me with his six-feet seven. This young man, known in Argentina social circles as "Le Péri-scope de l'Ambassadeur," was with me when I first arrived at Rio, and to a newspaper man who expressed surprise at our height, I remarked, with what was intended to be lightsome pleasantry, that in our own country we were looked on as dwarfs. I rather regretted my premature hilarity when the next morning a local paper carried a photograph of Bryan and myself, with the caption "Two North American Dwarfs!"

In my first chapter I rather counseled the traveler by the west coast who wishes to visit the Nahuel Huapí District to proceed to a point in Chile, such as Osorno, and to go thence by motor and launch through the beautiful region between there and the lake regions of Argentina, taking the train at San Carlos de Bariloche for Buenos Aires, some thirty-eight hours distant. My advice still holds true, for by choosing this route the dusty trip between Buenos Aires and the Lakes will be made but a single time. Supposing, however, that the trip begins at Buenos Aires, one usually leaves the capital at night and has a fairly bearable train journey until the next afternoon, from which time, until the arrival at Bariloche a little before noon, the next morning, the dust is most disagreeable. The total distance traversed is about 1100 miles. It is predicted that in a relatively short time there will be swifter trains with air-conditioned coaches to mitigate the disagreeable features of this excursion, and in a year or so a regular service of aircraft. The trains are usually clean, except from outside dust, and the food served in the dining cars, wholesome and adequate. The traveler should make a point of visiting the Oficina de Informes de la Dirección de Parques Nacionales in Buenos Aires for full information before beginning his trip. Sometimes the trip in question is made by motor. But for the moment this is not recommended except for those who have the temperament which makes them support a measure of discomfort by calling it adventure.

There is little of interest to be seen between Buenos Aires and Bariloche beyond a characteristically monotonous portion of the pampa. But the first sight of Lake Nahuel Huapí (Tiger Island) near the end of which is the little town of San Carlos de Bariloche, with the huge bulk of "El Tronador" and an encircling group of other snow-clad mountains as a background, is an inspiring sight.

The territory embraced in the Nahuel Huapí national park which one enters here is close to 800,000 hectares and within these generous limits are to be found the most beautiful and varied manifestations of an unspoiled nature—mountains, torrents, cascades, glaciers, lakes, pools, rivers, and forests which preserve their primeval savage originality and beauty, presenting an infinity of landscapes not unlike the fiords of Sweden and Norway or the Scottish lochs; panoramas such as one finds in Italy and Switzerland; mountains continuously covered with snow; and with constant similarities to our own national parks.

The virgin forests which are composed of varied species of trees and with many centuries of existence contain rare examples of the original flora; they extend throughout the borders of the Lakes up to the snow-line. In these wonderful forests, trees two thousand years old are not an exception, and these venerable and venerated living things reach a height of from 150 to 200 feet. A prodigal profusion of flowers and many varieties of fruits are also to be found throughout the extent of the region.

On the west the Park is bounded by the snowy range of the Andes, majestic, severe, over whose high peaks set like a challenge to man, towers the snowy height of "Tronador," nearly 12,000 feet high, and from whose head and shoulders vast avalanches are constantly crashing down with a report heard long distances away, giving to the mountain its name of "The Thunderer."

Within the Park the administrative group, made up of young men of capacity and vision, who give of their time freely, has created a lengthening chain of roads over which it will soon be possible to go to almost any part by motor car, thus supplementing the service of launches already available. Furthermore, there is communication by wireless telephone between all important points, so that the tired business man who has come here "to get away from it all" may relax in the knowledge that in an emergency he can communicate with his office.

But more than this, the administration has recently completed and opened to the public one of the most delightful hotels of its kind to be found in the western hemisphere. I refer to the Hotel Llao-Llao,* constructed in wood and stone from nearby forests and hills. The ash, the oak, the walnut, the lignum vitae, the quebracho (perhaps hardest of woods), the viveró, the petiribí, trees local and from far away, have all been utilized in the construction of the attractive structure or in its furnishings. I was told while at Llao-Llao that the choice of this dramatic site on a neck of land between Lakes Nahuel Huapí and Moreno, was made by a compatriot, Bailey Willis, twenty-five years ago. This scientist in pointing out that the outstanding feature of what is now the National Park System is Lake Nahuel Huapí, remarks further that in his judgment it is comparable in beauty and majesty to the most famous lakes in the world. In extent, it suggests the Lake of Geneva; in its innumerable arms and straits, Lake Lucerne. This great sheet of water with its pendant smaller sisters, each with a peculiar beauty or characteristic (often indicated by its name)— Lago Espejo (Mirror Lake), Lago Frías (Cold Water Lake), etc., mark the line of contact between the Patagonian table land and the folds of the Andes. These bodies of water are not of glacial origin but have been dammed up by remote lava flow and have beds deepened by glacial action.

But I want to go back to the hotel Llao-Llao not alone to tell of the comfort which it offers, but to speak of the golf-links nearby.

---

*Since the above was written, it is reported that this hotel was damaged or destroyed by fire in October, 1939.

HOTEL LLAO-LLAO, NAHUEL HUAPÍ NATIONAL PARK

LAKE NAHUEL HUAPÍ FROM THE LLAO-LLAO HOTEL

LAKE GUTIERREZ, NAHUEL HUAPÍ NATIONAL PARK

LAKE NAHUEL HUAPÍ

The hotel itself is an altogether charming construction, containing every comfort. The beauty and picturesqueness of its situation has been already hinted, and certainly the architect and his associates have given a real stamp of originality and charm to the edifice. It is under the immediate direction of one of the big and successful hotels of Buenos Aires and the traveler may be sure of luxurious care.

A short walk from the hotel brings one to the golf links, which, though recently created and as yet possessing only nine holes, promise to be among the best in the Republic. Already in sublimity of setting it may be said to stand first. All that is needed is to complete the promised remaining nine holes, and allow the hand of time to add a little mellowness and maturity to the greens. Already the fairways are good, and there is a nasty bit of water to be cleared with an iron from the seventh tee—but why in the midst of this panegyric do I want to bring up something disagreeable!

Because of its relative remoteness it is difficult to imagine Nahuel Huapí ever becoming as popular as our centrally located national parks, but the enthusiastic and capable group who are charged with its destinies have this problem well in mind, and already steps have been taken to facilitate the use of the Park by visitors of moderate means. Once the difficult question of transportation costs is solved, this should be effected, for the whole Park offers ideal sites for camping at a moderate expense during a number of months in the year.

There is much to divert the visitor to Nahuel Huapí. Every year roads are becoming better, making motoring an increasingly agreeable pastime. On the lakes themselves are launches which go to such beauty spots as Puerto Blest, Correntoso, Cascada, and Isla Victoria. (The latter island is a nursery for trees and to anyone interested in silviculture and the flora of the region a visit to it is rich with interest). For the alpinist the heights to be seen in all directions are a continual challenge. Furthermore, for riding and hiking there are endless paths and trails; for anyone seeking thrills the boar may be hunted; to the student and scientist investigation of the fauna, flora, geology and ethnic elements beckon; to the artist, everywhere are landscapes and colors; for the fresh air fiend, camping sites exist in all directions. Skiing is practised in the winter months while fishing for trout and landlocked salmon is a favorite sport in the appropriate season.

This latter sport in its varied aspects is discussed in Chapter XIX. But it is permissible to recall here that the fish hatchery, situated near Lake Moreno, about nine miles from Bariloche, was created with eggs and fish from various countries including our own in 1910, when the centenary of Argentine independence was celebrated. A famous fishing resort which is also referred to in Chapter XIX is on Lake Traful. In going there one travels over much of the distance the route leading to San Martín de los Andes, which traverses a valley of striking beauty known as El Valle Encantado.

To all that has been said of the beauty and charm of this national park must be added a brief word concerning the delightful rural life led there by prominent Argentine families who possess properties within or near its limits. Naturally it is only the lucky few who are privileged to see these homes; lovely as they are, they become more so through the hospitality practised within their gates. The names of "Huemul," "Cumelen" and "Peninsula Quetrihué" come to my mind, with their respective owners, the Ortiz Basualdo, the Bustillo, and the Lynch families, in writing these words. Each calls up its special and pleasing memory. And there is a nook for which I have special fondness known as "Tuahe Mua," with a breath-taking view over the lake and of the snow-capped mountains beyond, where we once spent a happy fortnight. The name of this place is a little bit of spoofing practiced on the public by its charming owners, Leon Fourvelle Rigolleau and Jorge Bunge, who, taking the simple intimate phrase "toi et moi," give a spelling suggestive of an ancient Indian origin!

The Northern Central Region

1. Santa Fé

THE AIRLINE DISTANCE from Buenos Aires to the northernmost point on its frontier—the little hill town of La Quiaca—is 1,000 miles. The traveler who proceeds to the latter-named village by railway (he could do it with "dule and teen" by motor) would traverse the provinces named in the head of this chapter, passing from pampas swept by breezes having a tang of salt in them, through the foot hills of Córdoba, on through the gradually rising spaces of Santiago del Estero, Tucumán and Salta, until he reached the foot of the lofty puna, the upland of Bolivia.

If one is not pressed for time at least a week should be given to this journey, the first and natural stop in which is at Córdoba, capital of the aristocratic province of the same name. To this city one may fly in the magnificent planes of the Panagra Company in two hours.

In the past, the rail journey from Buenos Aires to this city has been usually made at night, but with the introduction of an excellent air-conditioned train which covers the distance in nine and a half hours, the day trip may appeal to those who wish to study the country, although the endless plain traversed is of a monotonous character. An alternative journey may be made by motor over excellent roads. The distance by this highway is 475 miles, and since this is a rather longish drive for one day it is easier to break the journey at Rosario, which is just under half way.

Rosario is a modern town as Argentine cities go, having been founded in 1730. And it was still a small village up to the middle of the nineteenth century. Darwin makes a bald reference to it and then turns his attention to "the Noble River, the Paraná," flowing before it, which he had seen shortly before for the first time. In 1854 the town assumed some political importance since Urquiza, at that time at the head of the Argentine Confederation, made it the port of the ten inland provinces then at war with Buenos Aires.

Rosario of today, with a population of approximately 515,000, is the second city of the Republic in size and trade. It is accessible to ocean steamers drawing twenty-six feet, and immense quantities of wheat pass through it on the way to world markets. The city began its forward leap in population and importance soon after the great immigration movement, especially of Italians, which started around 1870. As a natural result the cachet of the city was and is largely Italian (although there are British and German colonies of importance), and the names of citizens are in general indicative of this Peninsular origin.

The city is pleasingly laid out in a regular manner and there are some good buildings, but in general there is little to appeal to the tourist.

That Rosario should become an important city was inevitable. Standing on the eastern margin of the great pampean plain, accessible by land and by sea, peopled by a race thrifty, astute, and accustomed to hard work, the natural outlet for one of the most fertile regions of the Republic, its growth was assured. World products for northern Argentina, for Paraguay and even for

Bolivia, are brought here in large quantities, while it is the outlet for sugar from Tucumán and Salta, quebracho extracts and wood from Santa Fé and the north, and above all, as suggested, cereals from the three great provinces of Santa Fé, northern Buenos Aires and Córdoba, and to an extent, Entre Rios.

2. *Córdoba*

Córdoba, a city of age and tradition, lies inland from Rosario some five hours by train or motor. There are ample railway facilities and an excellent highway links the two centers.

The relatively low range of beautiful hills, known as the Sierras of Córdoba, runs like a spinal column from beyond the northern borders of the Province to a point more than half way toward the southern limits. Within the Province are many minerals of value, while its wealth in live stock and agricultural products makes it one of the most important sections of the Republic. But it is as a popular playground of the nation that I wish to speak of it. Blest with an incomparable climate throughout the year, and with innumerable resorts each with special charm and appeal, it is a haven for the invalid, for the nature lover or for the merely jaded. Natural phenomena of interest are the great saline depressions lying to the northwest, and the salt lake known as Mar Chiquita, (small sea) which is much resorted to by invalids. Works of man which are proving of great value to the country are the Rio Tercero and San Roque Dams, the former the most important in all South America, whose accumulations make possible the irrigation of hundreds of thousands of acres!

The railway over which we ride to the capital of the Province is due to the initiative of an American, William Wheelwright, who in 1863 obtained a final concession for a railway from Rosario to Córdoba; this he finally constructed with the aid of British capital. The first section, which now forms part of the Central Argentine system, was opened in 1864; the first railway of the Republic goes back to 1857. The broad street on which is located the station at which we arrive in Córdoba, bears as its true name, "La Avenida Wheelwright," but as it is as difficult for an Argentine to hurdle an "h" after a "w" as it is impossible for a Cockney to avoid one before a vowel, the generality of folk in Córdoba simply balked before "Wheelright" and compromised by referring to the thoroughfare as "La Avenida del Gringo," the latter word in popular parlance meaning stranger, although a French traveler declares it has special application to the French; Italians, he points out, are called "Bachichas," without doubt on account of the frequency with which the "chi" is heard in their tongue!

The traveler who does not feel the charm of Córdoba is dull indeed. Eyes tired by an over-long contemplation of the monotonous pampa (although this, too, has its peculiar appeal) and the uniformity of many of the smaller towns, experience a happy surprise in viewing a city of rather varied aspect, in which exists an obvious cult of the past. One lifts one's eyes to the low hills, sensing the heights beyond, and there are seen streets which actually climb! The fever and the rush of Buenos Aires are behind and one is aware in vague indefined and indefinable ways of an impulse, a tug from the high Andes. This latter is natural when one recalls the foundation of the city and the fact that for more than two centuries allegiance was due under the Spanish crown to the far off Viceroyalty of Peru.

Córdoba, as was the case of other important cities of Argentina, such as Tucumán, Salta, La Rioja, Jujuy, Santa Fé, and Buenos Aires itself in its second avatar, was founded from up country. This took place in 1573, when Jerónimo Luis de Cabrera, the then Governor of Tucumán, acting with the passsive consent if not under instructions from the Viceroy of Peru, sent an expedition to establish the city which is today the third in size and importance of the Republic.

Cabrera is described as "a person noble, affable, with other good qualities of a gentleman," a characterization in which the modern Córdoba, with its three hundred thousand inhabitants, may take pride.

Forty years from its founding were to pass before the little frontier town was to receive that necessary cultural institution, a university. Founded by the Jesuits in 1613, its existence made the city the intellectual and theological center of the entire River Plate region. In addition to its faculties for sacred and other studies, there were in the university chairs of various Indian tongues which fitted missionaries to go into the vast mountain and forest regions on their proselyting errands.

Although Bryce did not visit Córdoba, he was fully aware of the part played by its citizens in the life of the nation, and refers to it as possessing "an ancient university and a society of cultivated men." In another illuminating comment he notes that Buenos Aires "has continued to maintain its supremacy by constantly drawing from the country." And alluding to the University at Buenos Aires and the one at Córdoba, he characterizes the latter as "more ecclesiastically colored," although, as a matter of fact, the faculty of theology disappeared under the presidency of Roca in the early 80's. Another British traveler, Andrews, who visited Córdoba about 1827, states that at that time the influence of the church was stronger there than in any place in South America. And even today Córdoba has the reputation of being, with Mendoza, the city where the religious spirit is strongest; "Ville de moines et d'églises," is the characterization of Córdoba by a French traveler of a few years ago. Obvious evidence of this ecclesiastical influence, certainly of the past, is to be seen today by the interested traveler, in the many religious edifices.

The Cordobeses are proud of their churches, and justly so. The Cathedral was built by the Jesuits; commenced about 1680, it was not finally completed until nearly a century later. It is one of the oldest monuments in Argentina, of composite style, and possessing much dignity. Within is shown a tabernacle of large dimensions in the form of a temple in massive gold and silver; also to be seen are paintings representing the legend of Our Lady of the Snows; and, in the sacristy magnificent copes and other vestments of the period of the last Viceroy and earlier.

Córdoba, as may be gathered, was for a long time the center of the activities of the Jesuits in the entire Plata basin. The university, of course, was theirs, since they had created it, as well as the Church of the Company (de la Compañía), which is not far from the Cathedral. This church is of severely plain exterior with a small forecourt, and quite without decoration. However, the interior is pleasing because of the judicious use of gilding and color. It contains a domestic chapel of great beauty, and especially worthy of attention is the barrel roof, like the hull of an inverted ship. It is said to have been constructed by a sailor and in its original construction to have been put together with wooden pegs and rawhide thongs.

Other churches of interest in the city are the Basílica of Santo Domingo, La Capilla San Roque, and la Iglesia de Nuestra Señora de la Merced. In the latter is preserved the bâton of Belgrano, given by him to the image of the Virgin after his victory of September 24, 1812, at Tucumán, referred to elsewhere.

In the Santo Domingo church, is an image of the Virgin said to date from 1592. It was found on the shores of the Pacific in 1602 near Callao, the box containing it being addressed to the

Dominicans of Córdoba. It is not known how this particular chest alone escaped in the shipwreck of the vessel which bore it.

Of historical and architectural interest and value is la casa del Virrey Sobremonte, the last of the Spanish grandees to hold that office. The house is now a colonial museum, and a visit to it should be surely made.

The ancient university is today housed in part in buildings of the early period, and has faculties of law, medicine and science. There is also in the city, in a picturesque situation, the National Observatory.

This reference to the National Observatory inevitably brings up the name of a very remarkable man, who was its first director, Benjamin Apthorp Gould (1824-1896). After preliminary studies in the United States and Europe, Gould was in charge of the longitude department of the United States Coast Survey, a service which he organized and developed. He was one of the first to determine longitudes by telegraphic means and employed the Atlantic cable, in 1866, to establish longitude relations between Europe and America. In 1868 he undertook on behalf of the Argentine Government to organize the National Observatory, beginning his observations in 1870 with four assistants. In 1874 he had completed his monumental Uranometria Argentina, following this with a zone catalog of over 73,000 stars, and other valuable astronomical works.

In his scientific activities Gould was sympathetically aided by President Sarmiento, whom he had met while the latter was Minister at Washington, and Sarmiento, then become President, attended the inauguration of the Observatory, together with Avellaneda, on October 24, 1871.

This observatory is the most important of its character below the equator, and possesses a telescope not equaled by any in the southern countries of the globe. From Gould's time until quite recently all the directors have been from the United States. However, the present director is an Argentine, assisted by a chief astronomer who is from our country.

In addition to these internal interests and advantages Córdoba is the natural tourist center for visits to a variety of charming places which spread out fan-like from it in all directions. To visit these with a maximum of pleasure and profit the wise traveler will discuss his trip in advance with El Córdoba Turismo Argentino, which has offices both in Buenos Aires and in Córdoba.

But speaking from that personal experience which in daily life generally diminishes in value in transmission I may point out that I have spent happy days in La Cumbre and nearby spots, and in Ascochinga. The former is a pleasant little mountain town containing the charming houses of all-year or summer or winter residents, and one of the best golf courses in the Province. From here motor trips can be made in various directions, notably through the lovely winding road in the direction of Los Cocos. In a dramatic situation, on a high bluff, overlooking the valley, and with towering hills behind it, is the exquisite modern chapel dedicated to La Santa Teresa del Niño Jesús. The missal in this little chapel was a tribute of admiration from an alleged "heretic" diplomatic representative of our Government and his wife, who resided in Argentina during the first and second administrations of President Franklin Roosevelt!

But my final choice, if not my first love, as a site for an agreeable sojourn in the neighborhood of Córdoba is Ascochinga. This is reached from the capital of the Province by motor over a splendid highway in an hour's time.

The road winds over a slightly inclined plain, rising from 1200 feet at Córdoba to 2300 feet at Ascochinga. Several tiny villages, unknown to history, are passed on the way, hardly worthy the attention of the motorist; but every tree-lover will slow down, if not linger a moment to examine and admire a group of seven superb walnuts, flanking the road in front of a police station, some forty minutes from Córdoba.

The hills surrounding and sheltering Ascochinga are of unusual loveliness. And to them in a measure may be applied Thackeray's eulogism of the hills of Attica:

"Around this . . . . plain," he says, "there ascends, as it were, a sort of chorus of the most beautiful mountains . . . not at all lofty or terrible, but superbly rich and aristocratic." Later, he tells us how these "hills rise in perfect harmony, and fall in the most exquisite cadences."

Ascochinga and the nearby region once formed part of a huge Jesuit mission to Indians, a *reducción,* of which the church of Santa Catalina, referred to later, was a spiritual center. With the departure of the Jesuits, the vast area, approximating 500,000 acres, was sold, and fell into the hands of various owners.

On the site of the present hotel was a typical estancia dwelling of brick and stucco, low, spacious and tile-covered, with an encircling terrace whose roof was borne by round columns. The hotel owners have had the wisdom and taste to preserve this older portion and to make additions in harmony with the original rustic architecture. The present structure rambles over a low hill top, its floor plan resembling nothing so much as an unfinished game of dominos, the branches being linked up by tile-covered colonnades which afford protection on those rare days when it rains.

In the remote distance, below a hillside, is a sanatorium for the treatment of tuberculosis, whose victims in this dry healthful air are given every facility in their fight against this dread disease. The presence on the sanatorium staff of some of the best qualified physicians in the Republic is a kind of insurance and gives an added sense of security to hotel guests.

The hills to which I have referred each invite one to exercise on foot or on horseback, or else to drive through them by motor over the rapidly expanding network of roads to be found in the province.

Of course there is golf, else this particular paragraph would not have been written, and while the course as yet possesses only ten holes, they are good and sporting ones, and the setting is among the loveliest in all Argentina. The immediate proximity of the course gives time for a game in the morning, leaving other less valuable time for visits to points of beauty and interest not far away. Among these latter should be mentioned the little Jesuit church of Santa Catalina which with its dependencies is now, I understand, a sort of communal property of the de la Torre-Diaz family, but since this is a numerous clan, it is probable that the individual interest of any one member is limited to something like half a brick. However, the church is open to all who care to enter.

Within ten minutes of Ascochinga is the noble estate of the Rocas, a family which directly or indirectly has given much to the nation—a President, a Vice-President, ambassadors, cabinet ministers, etc. This estate bears (and merits) the name of "La Paz." It was inherited by an ancestor (on the distaff side) of the present owner. It originally formed part of the huge estate of the Jesuits. Following their expulsion in the eighteenth century, their properties here, as elsewhere, were sold. One of the family of Diaz then bought in the vast tract of land now embraced in the Santa Catalina, Ascochinga and La Paz estates; the latter was in turn bought by a Funes, and the lovely Clara Funes married Julio A. Roca, General and President, whose son now owns it. The long low house is vine-covered, with a broad colonnade affording generous shade, and faces a beautiful sheet of water on which many aquatic fowl are to be seen; beyond sing the woods, and back of them are silhouetted the mountains. Some of the shade trees are lovely in foliage and symmetry, especially some century-old walnuts. I recall a happy afternoon at "La Paz" when one of the guests recited the sonorous verses of "Martín Fierro" and our host's sister related legends of the countryside, in which local Robin Hoods figured largely.

Easily reached by motor from Ascochinga is the lovely property of the Cárcano family. The present head of the house may be described as the Grand Old Man of Argentina. He recently retired as Ambassador to Brazil. I asked one of his secretaries his age. He replied that he did not know, but judging by his activity, mental and physical, one would deduce that he was in the early forties. The brilliant son of this great father is now his country's Ambassador to France and will be further heard from in the political life of the nation.

3. Tucumán

The traveler to Tucumán and other provinces to the north must resign himself to enduring something very disagreeable—the dust. It enters through crevices in doors and windows of the railway carriage and in such quantities that one's neighbor is seen as through a fine veil. This is at its worst as one traverses a section of the province of Santiago del Estero; but it is left behind as one approaches the frontiers of Tucumán, where there is more verdure, and cattle are fatter and more frequent. From time to time a pleasing white farmhouse meets the eye with columns and balustrades, somewhat after the Italian manner. Fields are separated by barriers of huge cacti whose broad leaves carry ferocious points. At last, a little tired, more than a little dusty and thirsty, one reaches the capital. But first a word about the province of Tucumán.

With an area of a little more than ten thousand square miles it might be almost called the Rhode Island of Argentina—even if more than eight times the size of our diminutive state. The country is in large measure very fertile and the most densely populated of the Argentine provinces. Although rich in minerals, which have been as yet but imperfectly exploited, it is the production of cane and the manufacture of sugar which constitute the chief occupation and industry. At present approximately a million acres of irrigated land are given over to the raising of the cane which is crushed in some thirty mills. Over 72 percent of Argentine sugar production is from this region which yields an annual average of 369,000 tons of sugar as well as 17,000,000 litres of alcohol, the latter produced from the residue of the cane.

San Miguel de Tucumán is the sonorous name of the capital of the province and since the traveler is now seven hundred and eighty miles north of Buenos Aires, in about the latitude of Palm Beach, the temperature, even in midwinter, is high. The town is one of some charm, and still retains many old characteristically low buildings, enclosing large courts (patios) with huge rooms, thick walls, and tiled roofs. May the man who endeavors to impose galvanized iron roofs on these innocent folk be escorted to the edge of town astride a narrow rail, and warned never to return.

As previously indicated, Tucumán was founded by elements from the northern jurisdiction—by order of the then governor of Santiago del Estero—in 1564, at a point near the site of the existing city. Frequent inundation however led to its removal to its present site about twenty years later. Ere a century had passed it had supplanted Santiago del Estero as the capital of the territory but still continued under the jurisdiction of the Spanish Viceroy at Lima. With the creation of the Viceroyalty of La Plata in the year that saw our Declaration of Independence Tucumán was transferred to this jurisdiction. Forty years later, from "a humble house of sun-dried brick" in this city, the United Provinces of La Plata gave to the world on July 9, 1816, the solemn declaration of their independence.

As an Argentine author, Doctor Ernesto Nelson, has pointed out, the revolutionary cry resounded in South America in 1810, when Europe was beginning to put behind her the adventure upon which France had embarked in 1789; furthermore, the actions of democracy were then rather scorned in continental political circles, dominated as they were by a skepticism against which the relative success of Saxon America in putting into practice democratic ideas and ideals had but little effect. Again, in North America, in the beginning at least, the desire to set up a government of their own took precedence in the minds of the English colonists over the wish for entire independence. In the Plata region it was the desire for independence which came first, and the form of government thereafter. The dream of liberty in France dissolved in a military imperialism, and the short lived Republic discredited by the memory of the crimes under the Terror, Democracy had no special attraction for the promoters of the revolution, at least for the most practical spirits. Furthermore the adoption of this form of government by the representatives of the United Provinces meant accepting perils, the most serious of which was without doubt that of not obtaining in Europe the attempted recognition of independence.

If these are historical reasons, and therefore accidental, others, deeper, and of a social order, as Doctor Nelson further points out, made the procedure different in the two extremes of America, and as regards South America, more dramatic and more painful than in the north. The Spanish Government had established a colonial régime founded in oppression and selfishness, whose program permitted not even the least local initiative. In many former colonies of Spain the political evolution has been understood at most as a step from autocratic despotism to benevolent paternalism. Even today the student can discover in the legislation of certain Spanish-American countries a certain superior assumption that the people are the passive subject of the social activity exercised by the state, from whom all initiative should be awaited.

The "humble house of sun-dried brick" stands today, but happily within a handsome structure which insures its preservation. Around the walls of this protecting edifice are bas-reliefs recalling that historic date of July, 1816, and against a principal wall is commemorated in bronze the deed, meriting and finding in the hearts of this people a monument more lasting than brass. The spot is one enshrining noblest memories for Argentines and a visit there should provoke deep emotions in every lover of liberty.

Another glorious deed in the history of Tucumán occurred on September 24, 1812, "el Día de la Virgen de la Merced," when Belgrano, turning a deaf ear to orders from superiors to retire to Córdoba, defeated there a royalist army with the support of gaucho horsemen and poorly armed citizens of Tucumán. It was following this occasion that Belgrano placed his bâton of command at the feet of the image of the Virgin which was carried through the streets of the little provincial town.

An interesting character is this Argentine hero, possessing that quality of valor allied to fervent faith which we associate with a St. Louis, a Bayard, a Jackson or a Lee. Just prior to the victory reported above, Belgrano had taken over the command of a recently defeated army, and immediately addressed himself to the task of improving the discipline of this dispirited soldiery. Daily in the midst of his troops he would kneel and recite the rosary, and on the second anniversary of the revolution, May 25, 1812, he reinforced his previous appeals to their traditional racial and religious feelings, as well as to their newly born patriotism, by displaying for the Church's blessing the banner of white and blue which was to become the national flag. Less than four months later the fruit of his efforts was made manifest.

4. Rosario de la Frontera

And now may we travel a bit more!

Leaving Tucumán in the morning we reach Rosario de la Frontera in a few hours. In doing so we cross frontiers and find ourselves in the Province of Salta. The road has slowly climbed upward and is now three thousand feet above sea level. But even in the course of a mid-winter day the temperature is summer-like.

Our objective is the "Hotel Balneario de las Termas" set in a fold of hills a few minutes by motor from the village of Rosario de la Frontera. Here is the oldest spa in the country, and one of the best known in South America. The simple but comfortable hotel has a northern exposure, with hills protecting it on the other three sides. The special characteristic of Rosario is the extraordinary quality and variety of its mineral waters, which gush forth from neighboring hillsides at various temperatures, and are efficacious in the treatment of a number of ailments.

By a kind of snobbery not unknown in our own country, these waters are not patronized by Argentines to the extent they merit. But with the passage of time and with improved transportation and hotel accommodations a change may occur.

There is little to do at Rosario besides taking the cure, beyond riding in the neighborhood hills, or playing golf over the little six-hole golf course. At night one may go into the tiny casino in the hotel itself and lose money in the orthodox ways; also there is an orchestra for dancing. And it's a grand place for meditation and reading!

5. Salta

Some six hours by train from Rosario de la Frontera is Salta, capital of the province of the same name.

The city stands in an open plain, and is dominated by high hills. There have been in the past two sites each of which in turn was the capital of the region; the first, established by a thoroughly qualified scoundrel named Abreu, was called San Clemente de Nueva Sevilla. It is to the discredit of this individual that he caused the chivalrous Cabrera, founder of Córdoba, to be beheaded, succeeding to his office after this atrocious deed. But in turn we learn with satisfaction that Abreu was himself beheaded by Hernando de Lerma, who was no improvement on his predecessor morally, being characterized by an even possibly partial historian as "a rapacious and sanguinary tyrant." Lerma established in the beautiful valley a settlement which he called San Felipe de Lerma, but during the course of the seventeenth century the name Salta came to be applied to this, the change possibly arising out of a desire of the town folk to forget the name of their oppressor.

The territory is rich, very rich, in natural resources, and the prophecy of an observant traveler of thirty years ago that "the province of Salta one day can hardly fail to be of great importance," is being rapidly fulfilled. Its wealth is in agriculture, in mineral deposits, and in forests. In the former, sugar is an outstanding crop, but rapidly increasing in economic importance are the wonderful oil deposits now being exploited by both the Government and by private companies.

The dominating element in Salta remains of Spanish origin, and the town-folk rather pride themselves on preserving its colonial tradition; in fact there is just the tiniest bit of disdain to be observed in their attitude toward the inhabitants of the southern cities nearest to them. But this may be reciprocal! And I can imagine a Cordobes or a Tucumano as he strolls around the plaza of his native town softly hissing to himself the poet's consoling lines:

> *Scorn'd, to be scorn'd by one that I scorn,*
> *Is that a matter to make me fret?*

I managed to have several good talks with the Governor of Salta and with members of his official family. In these conversations I was interested and impressed to observe with what a sense of nearness in time they discussed men and events connected with the War of Independence, a conflict in which Salteños had played so heroic a part. The names of men long ago dead, San Martín, Belgrano, Dorrego, not to mention those of "favorite sons," fell from their lips as if they were but just departed. Again I had the sensation of ties of blood and sentiment with the upland, not unlike those invisible links which I have sometimes felt united folk of "the Port" to Europe.

And, of course, there was much talk of a railway to be built some day from Salta to a railhead in Chile, which would thus place this far-inland town in contact with the Pacific and open an additional door to the rest of the world. But I gathered that the question in its larger aspects was both economic and political, and having this latter in mind, I speak hesitantly of it.

The history of Salta in the colonial period is perhaps not very different from that of its nearby, sister cities. Like them, and owing in large measure to jurisdictional ties, it maintained a closer contact with the hills than with the lower country. The presence of savage Indian tribes in the territory was a Damoclean sword over their heads; in fact, in 1735 these sleepless enemies dashed through the streets of the town scattering death and destruction.

It is in the period of the wars of independence that the history of Salta shines with brightest luster. Following his victory at Tucumán, Belgrano advanced northward. Reaching the river Pasaje, he swore allegiance in a dramatic ceremony to the flag, the blue and white flag of La Patria, which a short time before had been solemnly blessed in Tucumán.

In this gesture he was followed by all his troops; the river has ever since borne the name of El Juramento (the oath).

Near Salta in February, 1813, Belgrano again gave battle to the royal forces, and although almost prostrated by illness he inflicted on them a severe defeat. Seeking refuge in the city, the King's representative capitulated a few days later with his troops, obtaining what many have criticized as too favorable terms. But Belgrano, inspired by a true spirit of conciliation, allied to deep political wisdom, realized that in permitting the departure of this defeated foe with his army the seeds of disaffection would be sown in all Upper Peru, native soil of most of the soldiers.

In the highly confusing movements of armies in northern Argentina in this period two Salteños contributed greatly to the success of the rebel cause; the first of these, Martín Güemes, a devil-may-care horseman, adored by the wild gauchos under his command, was later fatally wounded in the suburbs of the city which he so dearly loved. His equestrian statue stands today on a hillside over-looking the town. He is shown "bearded like a pard," and astride a hardy caballo criollo. The second of these worthies, a Salteño "by adoption through marriage" was Arenales; a reserved, dignified soldier, he might be said to reincarnate the Spanish hidalgo of a preceding century. One of his victories was at La Florída, in what is now Bolivia, on May 25, 1814. An important residential street of the capital bears his name, while the affectionate remembrance in which he is held by Salteños, is recalled by his monument which stands in the central plaza of the provincial capital.

In a preceding paragraph bald mention was made of the importance of sugar as a source of wealth to the province, even though in actual production Salta is still well behind Tucumán. However, one of the most up-to-date sugar plantations and mills in the entire republic is situated within the province of Salta, at Tabacal, and we were fortunate in being invited to visit this. Its presiding genius is Dr. Robustiano Patrón Costa, Vice President of the Argentine Senate and an outstanding figure in the political and financial and social life of the Republic; he may be fairly described as the Duke of Salta.

The Ingenio in question is located in the northern part of the province on a branch of the railway line which reaches the Bolivian frontier on the east at Yacuiba. Here, in a vast plain in which cane is cultivated, there has arisen a modern village, centering around the huge sugar mill, with a school, a chapel, (the latter a gem of its kind), and a modern, well-equipped hospital, all fitted to minister respectively to the cultural, spiritual and physical needs of the villagers and built by the owners of the property. The product of the extensive area under cane is brought to the mill in special cars over a net-work of décauville railway lines. These cars at a given moment tip their burden into a huge chute; through this it is borne onward to where steel rollers crush the rich juice from the stalks and send it in a tawny flood toward the containers; in these latter it will undergo its first change in its eventual transformation into the snowy white product which comes in on the breakfast tray.

I think I am not exaggerating when I say that at the time of our visit the number of employees in the mill, working in three shifts, was approximately 15,000. I was naturally interested in learning how an aspect of the labor problem was solved, having in mind that the harvesting of the cane and its grinding are seasonal occupations. I was told in reply to my questions that every effort is made by the able administrators of Tabacal to meet the situation thus created by nature. In the first place, it was pointed out that cane cutting is done by Indians from the mountains or from the regions washed by the Bermejo. These arrive with the opening of the season from their upland or fluvial homes and to these they return when the harvest is finished. However, much work must be done between crops, and an effort is made to employ as many of the mill hands as possible in order to avoid a heavy lay-off, with a corresponding demoralizing result.

To visit the mill itself at this, the height of the season, is like entering a bee-hive. From one direction is heard a hissing sound, as the succulent stalks are pressed to give up their sweetness, from another the gurgling of the fresh juice, as it flows through open channels to the vats; from still another the groan of the mechanical carriers bearing the completed product, packed in sacks, to the storage warehouse. The laboratory, staffed by a qualified group of chemists is an interesting place. Here elaborate reports relating to the progress of the work in all its branches, including figures setting forth the rate of cane arrivals, the quantity of juice being produced, the quality of the combustion of the fuel under the boilers, the percentage of carbon black in the smoke, etc., are made up hourly, and submitted to the scrutiny of eyes trained to interpret these, to a layman, cryptic figures.

I have refrained thus far from making other than casual mention of what is now a chief source of wealth, not alone to the province of Salta, but in a measure to the entire Republic. I refer to the valuable deposits of petroleum. These oil fields have been developed in a comparatively short space of time. The first mining claim in this region looking to the exploitation of oil, was only made, I am reliably informed, some thirty years ago. Naturally, a prime desire as we turned our backs with sincere regret on the hospitable little capital of Salta, was to see the work being carried on by our own countrymen in exploiting this source of wealth in a far-away land. And everything that we saw of their activities was calculated to make us extremely proud.

It has been the fashion for too many years past, especially among the ignorant and among a certain type of politician, to say harsh things of those who labor "that the earth may bring forth her increase" in the form of petroleum. But an experience and contact extending over many years and in various countries warrants me in declaring that whatever such companies may have taken out in the way of wealth, they have done it in a way not below the commercial standards of the time and usually above them, and have at the same time contributed greatly to the economic advance of the countries in which their enterprise has been manifest.

Leaving the train at Manuela Pedraza, not far from the Bolivian frontier, we drove the few hundred yards which separated us from the headquarters of the American oil company known as Tartagal. The investments of this company here and in other parts of Argentina amount to many millions of dollars, but I sometimes wonder if it is realized what a large percentage of those millions have been spent in prospecting, in research and in other activities, or how positively, if unobtrusively, the efforts of their geologists and engineers have contributed to the general exploitation of those sources of wealth throughout the country.

The administrative offices and residences at Tartagal occupy a pleasing situation on a hillside. A delightful park has been created out of the forest; attractive houses, outbuildings, offices, etc., are to be seen, and at the highest point is located a modern hospital, excellently equipped with qualified doctors and nurses. No selfish policy dictates the conduct of this institution, for, while primarily designed for company employees, its wards are open to others living in the neighborhood.

After inspecting various buildings at Tartagal we went by motor for an hour or so over an excellent road, another gift of the company to the Province, to San Pedro, where the oil wells are located, and whence the product is brought by pipe and truck to the railway.

The remainder of our visit to this northern province is soon told. A brief glimpse of Jujuy, founded in 1593, one of the original outpost towns founded in the course of the prehensile southward movement of the Viceroys of Peru, made us regret that engagements in Buenos Aires obliged us to hurry homeward.

On our southward journey from Jujuy we visited one of the great fruit properties of the Province—for it must not be forgotten that oil and sugar are not the only sources of wealth of this region, and grapefruit, alligator pears, and mangoes here reach great perfection. We spent the night at "Calilegua" with a group of delightful and hospitable bachelors in charge of this development. They inhabit a charming eighteenth century estancia house, set in the midst of orchards and groves which would have made California or Florida envious.

CHAPTER XVIII

Mendoza—An Inland California

THE TRAVELER who has elected the western gateway, from Santiago, for his entry into Argentina, would do well to linger for a while in the charming city of Mendoza, which is the capital of the province of the same name, and the leading city of the section of Argentina known as Cuyo, which latter embraces the provinces of San Juan, San Luis, and Mendoza. (Or from Buenos Aires he may go by train or air, perhaps including Córdoba in the plane trip).

The city of Mendoza, which with various independent municipalities, tucked closely under its wings, forms an aggregate of about 150,000 people, is an altogether delightful provincial town, nestling just under the foothills of the Andes whose peaks crowned with eternal snow look down in really benign fashion over the country below, providing it with an abundance of water for irrigation purposes and protecting it from devastating winds. Its height of approximately 2300 feet gives to the air a peculiar tang—dry, fresh, vivifying.

The capital is a relatively ancient city, having been founded by direction of Mendoza, then governor of Chile, in 1559, who chose to give the town his name. It was made the capital of the old province of Cuyo, and actually belonged to the Viceroyal domain of Chile until 1776, when the Spanish crown, having created a new viceroyalty under the name of La Plata, with its

seat at Buenos Aires, transferred the whole territory to that jurisdiction.

The city and surrounding territory is absolutely arid, save where
the inflow of water through irrigation ditches has laid an emerald
carpet over otherwise brown fields. One of the principal irrigation sources is a channel from the Mendoza river, some fifteen
miles away, which, according to a tradition, confirmed to me as
an historical fact by the youthful and capable governor Don
Rodolfo Corominas Segura, was originally the work of an Indian
chief, head of the sedentary tribe which occupied the territory
at the time of the Spanish conquest.

The charming, smiling city, which is laid out in a regular
manner, with broad well-paved streets, and numerous squares, is
traversed by several artificial streams, and on both sides of the
principal streets water flows constantly, wetting the feet of the
poplars and cottonwood trees which everywhere abound, with
branches uniting overhead to form long cool avenues of green.

Mendoza derives undoubted importance because of its position
on the main route uniting Chile and Argentina, and because of
its excellent railway connections with various cities of the Republic. Furthermore, within the next twelve months it will probably
be feasible to go from there by a first-class motor road to Neuquén,
Rio Negro, and the Lake regions of the south, which are more
specifically referred to in another chapter.

The Province of Mendoza, especially in the neighborhood of
the capital, is blessed with fertile valleys, made so by vivifying
waters from the hills, so that the resulting harvest may be said
to be a gift of the mountains to the plains. While vegetables,
cereals, and alfalfa are produced, the vineyard industry comes
first and large quantities of wine are made; and grapes with
other superb fruits are finding their way not alone to the Buenos

Aires market some six hundred miles away but also, after being chilled in a local refrigerating plant, to the port to be placed in the cool rooms of vessels bound for the United States or Europe.

The contrast of seasons between the two continents favors Mendoza in making possible entry into the New York market of apples, peaches, pears and grapes in our winter season.

Some time ago, in inaugurating a new school, the young superintendent opened his remarks by declaring to his pupils and their parents: "The tradition of this school shall be as follows:" and proceeded then to lay down an ideal to be attained. The remarks of this pedagogue come to mind in recalling the festival celebrating the completion of the vine harvest which for several years has taken place in Mendoza around the first of April. This is surely an occasion destined with the passage of time to become an increasingly delightful tradition, swelling the local heart with pride and provoking interest in the visitor by its general charm, the simplicity and good taste of the various local costumes of the chief participants, the originality of the floats on which they ride, and their own Maude Muller-like beauty. Allied to this is the spontaneous gaiety and good humor of the onlookers, so peculiarly Latin in its quality. Why do we northern folk when in large crowds often want to hit the head that is nearest to us?

From what I have just said it will be gathered that Las Fiestas de la Vendimia as celebrated in Mendoza are of very recent origin. It was my happy privilege to witness the celebration of 1938 as the guest of the Governor, and the whole occasion remains one of my happiest experiences in Argentina.

The festivities this year reached their culmination on April 2. That morning enormous crowds assembled in the city park where a temporary theatre in the Greek style had been built. On the stage of this stood the venerable and apostolic figure of the Bishop of Cuyo with a group of priests behind him. At the foot of the steps leading to the stage, men of the vineyards in new smocks and dark trousers, stood in line each with a basket of luscious grapes on his shoulder. In the center of the stage was a gigantic bowl of fruits of all kind, symbolizing the harvest. And over this the Bishop murmured his blessing. With the closing of the episcopal benediction several thousand pigeons painted in many colors were released and fluttered over the huge crowd, some of them rising high in the air until they appeared as glittering motes in the blue sky.

Later from a high stand the Governor and his guests and members of his Government, witnessed a parade of floats representing each of the seventeen districts of the Province in which grapes are grown. The loveliest young girls of the respective districts were borne on these floats, and as the procession wound its way through the dense crowds the fresh and lovely young faces and the charming reactions which they registered to the applause of the multitude were a delight to see. As outriders to the floats were slim-bodied young cavaliers from the various districts, dressed in the picturesque gaucho costume, and with a profusion of silver adorning their sleeves and shoulders and belts, and even the trappings of their horses.

At night we again assembled in front of the Greek theatre and saw the queens of the various grape producing districts of the Province each with her twelve ladies in waiting arrive and stand before the judges who would select the queen of the Vendimia. I suggested to the Governor that it would be good politics to appoint political enemies to the Jury of Award; he smilingly agreed, and said he would keep the idea in mind for next year. The crowd of perhaps 50,000 people were not backward in making their choice known to the judges, and I must confess there were several good claques at work. But with "unperturbèd pace, Deliberate speed, majestic instancy" the jurors moved on toward their verdict. At last it was announced, the choice falling on a charmingly-dressed little girl from the vineyards, a skin bronzed by sun and wind, sparkling eyes, red lips, seemingly yet virgin to a lipstick, who for the next twenty-four hours was to be the first citizen of Mendoza.

But the evening was not over; there were balls in various centers, regattas on the lake, fireworks; in a word, everything to make it a glorious holiday. And the next day was Sunday.

No sojourn in Mendoza is complete without a visit to the various *bodegas* or plants whither the grapes are brought for pressing and the resulting wine prepared for the market. Also in these bodegas are underground storehouses where thousands upon thousands of bunches of grapes of all varieties, exquisite in their perfection and formidable size, are hung up in the cool depths of "the deep delved earth" until, after further chilling in the frigorífico, they are started on their long journey to the capital or on the still longer voyage to the United States or Europe. While bodegas are usually open to visitors previous enquiry at the Oficina de Turismo of the Province, located in Buenos Aires or in Mendoza itself, will facilitate a tour.

Slight earthquake tremors felt from time to time in Mendoza are a displeasing feature of life there. Hence, as a precaution, practically all the houses are of one story. There are a few folk still to be met who were alive at the time of the terrible earthquake, followed by fire, of 1861. In this catastrophe not a single building was left standing and the loss of life has been estimated as high as 12,000. By one of the ironies of fate the French geologist, Bravard, who had predicted that an earthquake was menacing the city, was one of the victims of this cataclysm.

The traveler to Mendoza will doubtless wish to visit the thermal springs of Cacheuta, reached over a good road in about an hour. Here are waters possessing medicinal qualities of high value, baths which may be taken in comfort in a high, dry climate. Not the least interesting feature of this excursion is the opportunity it gives of examining the effects of a downrush of water in 1934, let loose through the breaking of a natural dam formed over a long period of years by a glacier, high up in the mountains. The water rose nearly ninety feet in the narrow gorge in which the hotel is situated, and reinforced concrete structures were simply effaced by it. A steel curtain weighing one hundred and twenty tons used in connection with a power line was borne off by the raging torrent and has never been found! Within less than ten hours the flood had passed and the sun was shining down upon a scene of desolation. However, persons living along the valley had been warned in time and the losses were chiefly material.

Within the city one should linger in the lovely park, inspect the cactus garden, have tea at the restaurant overlooking the artificial lake, attend a performance at the little "Teatro de los Niños" and perhaps dine at the Balneario at the end of the lake. An impressive site is the vast monument to General José de San Martín, the Washington of Argentina, which crowns the Cerro de la Gloria (Glory Hill). This memorial erected some twenty-five years ago is a marvel of vigor, realism and movement, and probably the happiest monument in artistic conception and execution in all the Republic. Around its base are reliefs representing San Martín preparing for his victorious march over the Andes.

It was in Mendoza, it will be recalled, that San Martín, El Santo de la Espada (The Saint of the Sword), organized and launched his Expeditionary Force of 5,200 men, first against Chile and then against Peru, to free Argentina from the government of Spain.

And the memory of this great figure remains a vivid one in the region.

The French under Napoleon, the Carthaginians under Hannibal, crossed the Alps in a spirit of conquest. But under the leadership of San Martín, the Argentines, aiming at ends which were more than national, crossed the Andes and took a generous part in a movement for liberty beyond their own borders which was to deprive Spain of a vast empire in the New World.

The strategy of San Martín made this possible. He had a character apt for war—severe in discipline, honorable, austere, and disinterested. Political conditions of the National Government depriving him of material assistance, he made his own logistics, devising from the beginning, or obtaining from the faithful Cuyanos, his uniforms, commissaries, munitions and transport—everything needful for the passage of an invading army through desert mountain passes of more than Alpine height.

His strategy was to reinforce his army with the Chilean soldiers who streamed over the Andine passes into Cuyo after the Chilean Republic had been temporarily overthrown by the Royalist invasion from Peru in October, 1814, to cross the Andes and end the anarchy there, and then with additional reinforcements to proceed by sea to take Lima, the headquarters at that time of the Spanish Viceroyalty in South America.

His plan succeeded. In January, 1817, the height of summer— for the Andine passes cannot be traversed in winter—he crossed the Andes in two columns through the passes of Uspallata and Los Patos, each 12,000 feet above sea level, and with a united force defeated the Royalists at Chacabuco on February 12, 1817, and entered Santiago, the capital of Chile.

In August 1820, after two years delay due to efforts to end war through diplomacy, San Martín's little army set sail northwards from Valparaiso, and disembarked at Pisco one hundred and sixty miles south of Lima. His total strength was 4,400 while the Royalists numbered 23,000.

Again sound strategy played its part, for San Martín's main object was to arouse and support revolution in Peru. This was accomplished. In July, 1821, the Royalists evacuated Lima and San Martín entered the agitated capital, proclaiming the independence of Peru, and assuming the direction of the Government with the title: Protector of Peru.

Thus Argentina made her contribution to the continental war, which, by freeing her neighbors, gave security to her own independence. The fifty Spanish flags which adorn the walls of the National Historical Museum in Buenos Aires offer the best commentary on the course and issue of that war.

Big Game Hunting, Shooting, Fishing

ᗣᗢᗣᗢᗣᗢᗣᗢᗣᗢᗣᗢᗣᗢᗣᗢᗣᗢᗣᗢᗣᗢᗣᗢᗣᗢᗣᗢᗣ

1. *Big Game Hunting*

WHILE ARGENTINA is not a big game country in the same measure as India and Africa, nevertheless there still exist good specimens, and a not too exacting hunter can find some interesting sport. However, there is at present no organized hunting and shooting; nor are there any offices providing information to the hunter, nor are professional guides available. Yet there is to be found in the country an unbounded hospitality, inborn in the Argentines of the old stock, which is extended in lavish measure to hunters bearing adequate letters. When a guest has been invited to some properly situated estancia, the proprietor in person or his foreman, if he is away, will do his best to appease the sporting appetites of his guest.

Before discussing the game to be found and its location, a word of counsel should be given concerning the inescapable obligation of completing with Argentine authorities in the United States (or in England if the voyage begins there), the formalities necessary to obtain permits for the introduction of rifles and cartridges. Otherwise, as with us, difficulty may be encountered with the customs authorities. While the attitude of the Government in the past has been liberal in the matter of the entry of weapons the property of bona fide tourist-hunters, yet recent regulations tend to prevent the introduction of rifled arms above .22 caliber. And

[216]

since rules and regulations are changing from time to time, it is essential that permits be in order before embarking. In any event, strictly military rifles should not be brought.

The best type of rifle to use, legal restrictions having been overcome where these exist, is any piece from the 30-30 class up. Prior to the enactment of existing regulations the most popular rifle in general use throughout South America was the old 44-40, and authorities tell me that the larger percentage of jaguar pelts shipped from South America are from animals killed with this "Old Reliable." Of course there are many of them remaining in the hands of original owners, but cartridges are increasingly difficult to obtain and are costly.

On the plains and in the mountains long shots may be required, game being generally scarce and wary; therefore, especially in the South and West, a rifle possessing a flatter trajectory than a 30-30 is preferable. In the northern woods however almost any of this type of firearm will suffice—even the old Black powder rifles of a generation ago. A combination gun—shotgun and rifle—will be found useful, as small game—partridges, wood grouse, and often ducks—abound in the same country in which big game may be found.

With regard to the season: keeping in mind that these are reversed, it should be pointed out that shooting in Argentina is mostly done in their winter, except in the West and South, where autumn is the favorite time, since in winter snow blankets the ground. In the autumn, in the regions indicated, cold-weather shooting togs are worn; these need not be conspicuous as with us, as one is hardly in danger from other hunters unless they are subject to homicidal mania!

Even winter days in the northern provinces are more than warm, but night temperatures are below freezing. Also to be remembered is that in this sub-tropical region nearly every forest plant is barbed, some thorns being short, some long, some straight, some curved like a hook, but all ferociously sharp, and offering a constant danger to clothing as well as to foot-wear. An experienced local hunter will wear over his usual clothing a cap, a coat (often sleeveless) and trousers, all of sailcloth, which resists the thorns.

It should be stated that in the whole of the central belt, which includes the wheat provinces, there is no big game today. On the other hand, wooded stretches in the Northwest and Southwest and some of the mountain and plain country in the West and South, still contain "objects of venery," to use the ancient phrase.

The principal big game animals of Argentina are among the deer family: to begin with, the swamp deer, which is found in the marshy regions of the provinces of Entre Rios and Corrientes; the camp deer, formerly common all over the republic and now only in some of the wildest spots (both these deer are about the size of a white-tail, and do not grow very imposing horns); and the "huemul," a mountain deer, found sporadically along the entire Andes chain from North to South, a type which, in the opinion of a qualified hunting friend "wears a pretty good head." Unfortunately its numbers have been sadly reduced in recent years. Also, in the forests of the northern provinces and territories there still roam—and in places they are quite plentiful—a small number of the cervidae family known as "the spike deer," so-called because it carries only a pair of small spikes.

European red deer liberated in recent years on certain estates near Lake Nahuel Huapí are reported to have flourished. However, shooting of these is restricted to owners and friends.

Writing over a century ago, Darwin refers to the camp deer, mentioned above, as being "exceedingly abundant throughout the countries bordering the Plata and in northern Patagonia" and relates that he once shot on foot three out of the same herd. He adds that, conversely, if approached on horseback they are exceedingly shy, and points out that since in the country nobody goes on foot the deer recognizes man as his enemy only when he is mounted!

In several of the northern provinces wild boar, known locally as "jabalí," are plentiful. This beast is also to be found in the National Park of Nahuel Huapí; where, as an exception to the strict general rule, he (as well as the puma) may be hunted. These latter named and larger species descend from European wild boar (Sus scrofa) introduced some years ago by a well known Argentine, Sr. Aaron Anchorena. They have a reputation for fierceness and are said to be especially dangerous if wounded. In the case of the northern domestic variety this may be exaggerated; perhaps he is no more vicious than the patient animal told of in the familiar rhyme:

> *Cet animal est bien méchant,*
> *Quand on l'attaque il se défend.*

In some parts of Formosa, in the Chaco territory, in Misiones, and possibly in the northern part of Corrientes, near the big rivers, the ungainly tapir, the only South American pachyderm, may be found. However, his true realm is really farther north, in Paraguay and Brazil.

The same territorial reference may be said to apply to the South American tiger, known as the jaguar, whose numbers have been enormously reduced over the years. A smaller brother of this latter, the puma, or mountain lion, may be frequently encountered even now in the northern as in the far southern territories. A number of smaller "cats" also roam the depths of primeval forests, although they are seldom seen. But less rare, even to be seen occasionally in the central territories, is the plains cat—the gato pajero—a grayish cat of the size of our domestic Tom.

In a spirited page of Sarmiento's great philosophic-historical work, Facundo, that "portrait of Argentina in the epoch of Rosas," the author relates in thrilling fashion the story of how his hero was treed by a man-eating jaguar (called *cebado,* because of this unnatural appetite), and how for more than two hours he clung in the branches of a small tree just out of reach of the blood-thirsty animal, his place of refuge swaying under him, anticipating from moment to moment that with the gradual decline in his forces he would finally relax for a moment and fall into the jaws and claws awaiting him. For the fortune, good or bad, of his country, two comrades galloped up and quickly lassoed the beast, into whose body, in a blind fury, the caudillo plunged his knife, over and over again. "Then I knew what it was to be afraid," Facundo remarked in relating his experience in after years to a group of his officers. It was perhaps the only time in his life he knew this emotion.

Darwin refers during the course of his visit up the Paraná, to the fear which the jaguar provoked and relates that they had killed many wood-cutters and even entered vessels by night. They become especially dangerous when rising floods drive them from the little islands which abound in the great Paraná waters.

All over the plains of Argentina roams the rhea, or South American ostrich, known as the "ñandú;" in the central belt, however, he is so near to being tamed that an attempt on his life would be like shooting fish in a barrel; it simply offers no sport. Furthermore, its inferior plumes and feathers are only good for making cheap brushes. A compatriot tells me the flesh tastes somewhat like low grade rubber.

In the southern and western provinces the guanaco is still found. They were plentiful a century ago; in fact Darwin relates that he saw a herd of not less than five hundred. But today this animal is being unmercifully persecuted in order to obtain the pelts of its young, and unless measures are taken for its protection it is not difficult to foresee a time when it will have completely disappeared.

In the northern woods is sometimes encountered an extremely rare animal, the aguará-guazú, a sort of maned wolf, which is really not a wolf but a type of wild dog.

Northward from the delta of the Rio de Plata, near to the big streams, and in the swamps, may be found the carpincho, or water-hog, which becomes more plentiful as civilization is left behind. There are many in Corrientes and Entre Rios, and a few years ago they were common south of San Pedro, but owing to the ravages of the professional hunter they are now almost unknown there.

Passengers on river steamers plying northern waters frequently see large numbers of the yacaré, the South American caiman, or crocodile, and indulgent captains sometimes permit travelers to shoot at them. This is an innocuous form of sport; it diverts the man behind the gun and usually does not disturb the beast, for they are not at all easy to hit, being extremely wary. Even when struck they seem to possess the ability to carry away a large amount of lead. They abound in the swamps of Entre Rios, Corrientes and Misiones, and, as suggested, along the water courses. Since no industrial use has yet been made of them, the nature lover may hope to see them for a long time to come.

In hunting guanacos (and occasionally deer), drives are usual, but in general still hunting is the prevailing method. Veteran camp folk often hunt on horseback, slipping off their steeds when near enough, and shooting from the ground.

2. *Shooting*

To the man or woman who thrills to the prospect of a good day of shooting, who loves the feel of a shot-gun in hand and arm,

Argentina offers many attractions. Of course, one who reads books of travel of a decade or so ago and learns of vast quantities of fowl simply waiting for the hunter to shoot them down will be disappointed. For, as in the case of older countries, and especially sections near large cities, the sportsman must go farther and farther afield for his game.

But since, as has been made clear in many pages, Argentina is still divided in liberal fashion and the vast estate is the rule and not the exception, the estanciero who is fond of shooting may create his own game preserve, the task being a relatively simple and inexpensive one. And happy the visitor to one of these.

The feathered game to be found within the province of Buenos Aires, not to mention many other regions, are duck; snipe; "the small bird" or partridge, the local name for which is perdiz; and the martineta, or so-called double-partridge. The latter has tan markings similar to our prairie chicken, and its flesh is of peculiarly delicate and agreeable flavor. It is a poor flier, and lives in the tall grass of the open country.

Another large bird of tasty flavor somewhat resembling our sage hen, is the copetona. Ducks are found in considerable quantities, and at certain seasons that great voyager, the plover.

In past years, when game birds abounded, there was no need for restrictive laws. Today, in view of the declining number of birds, necessary legislation has been enacted, which it is hoped, in view of its great importance, will be strictly enforced.

When one is invited to an estate where game is preserved, the trip out will usually be made by motor, over dirt roads. And a wise driver will carry his chains in order to combat the mud in the event of rain. Argentina is at present engaged in an extensive road-building program which is destined to have a marked effect on the social and economic life of the country; but it is a slow and expensive task owing to the lack of road-building material, with resulting heavy construction costs. And furthermore, since the pampa is a vast natural landing field, only needing a "sausage" and three or four flags to mark limits in order to create a landing ground, numbers of Argentines are beginning to use their own planes to facilitate accessibility to properties which although sometimes only a few miles from the capital are yet for all practical purposes quite remote in the rainy season.

Shooting generally commences in the morning, and if one is after perdiz or field birds there is no need to rise early; in fact, one may start out after breakfast for that part of the estate recommended for shooting. These favorite spots are usually well-sprinkled with tufts of pampa grass and coarse cover. As a rule one is assured of good shooting, and within a few minutes of leaving the car or other vehicle the dog is pointing. You know the rest of the story: with head well in the air, the animal goes forward slowly, his tail projecting like a ramrod; suddenly the air seems rent by a roar of wings, and a huge bird, a martineta, rises almost vertically into the air to straighten out into swift flight. You aim and fire and hope for the best. And a few minutes later the performance is repeated.

After shooting over one section of the property, the faithful peon who has been put at your disposition suggests a change. And just here I shall let an enthusiastic compatriot who has furnished me with the preceding helpful details concerning big game hunting and shooting in Argentina continue the story:

"Bueno, Señor, vamos al arroyo," says Juan, suggesting that we try our luck along the stream for ducks. We return to the car and drive across the fields to a small stream with deepish banks that twists and turns through the dense grass camps. We stop and out we get to decide on one of us circling up stream to approach the bank, hoping to surprise some feeding ducks. Soon a couple of shots ring out, the flock swings upstream, straight towards you, coming like an express train. Well, take your brace, you have marked up another milestone of life. You will cherish the memory and, out of season by your fire side, you will recall to memory the fleeting picture with its colorful setting. If you made a clean miss with both barrels, you will still see the birds as they wove together with curve of wing and rocket-like speed, gone almost before they came. You will still recall the scene and still wish them well. You will remember the blue or green these teal carried on their wings, the black soil, the wonderful grass, the unlimited expanse of the big estancias, the fine cattle in the fields, the big fine horses, the kindly sun, the vast distances, the colorful sunsets, the genuine Argentine hospitality of your host, the fine types among these estancias, the dignity of the Argentine gauchos, the comeliness of the women at the "puestos." You must know these places and men to understand them and, knowing them, you will like them. These are the men who ride the camps, brand the cattle, sort and bring them to the rail head. Many know Paris, Rome, London, New York, better than you do. They are big-minded, generous Americans of South America. They are the last of the Argentine cattle barons.

3. *Fishing*

Fishing as a sport has begun to manifest in Argentina and already there are great numbers of amateurs.

However, in general the sports-fisherman yet observed is still unfamiliar with the technique of the gentle art. But every day that passes sees an advance. Fishing clubs are being formed throughout the country, supplementing veteran organizations already existing, and the sport now has its first magazine and organ "Carnada" (Bait). Following the examples of this latter, newspapers of the capital are commencing to publish sections devoted to fishing, while reviews whose complexion is rather of a social nature are waking up to the importance of supplying their readers with information concerning the many localities where the angler's efforts will be rewarded.

Fishing is now pursued most actively in the appropriate seasons in the northern reaches of the Paraná, in the estuary of the Río de la Plata, at Mar del Plata and in nearby waters, in the national Park of Nahuel Huapí, and in many semi-private localities such as Tornquist in the Province of Buenos Aires.

The following observations concerning the sport in these various waters will, it is hoped, be of interest to anglers.

FISHING IN THE NATIONAL PARK OF NAHUEL HUAPÍ

To many folk, despite the breath-taking physical beauty of Nahuel Huapí, the beauty of outlook and comfort of the hotel Llao-Llao, the excellent golf to be found nearby, the excursions by motor or on horseback or in launches, over spectacular roads, by mountain trails, and on crystal lakes, the real attraction of this region is in its fishing.

Although this absorbing sport only commenced in the Argentine lakes a few years ago, the region is already attracting the attention of many outstanding foreign devotees, and annually there come to the territory fishermen from the United States and Europe. The fish most often found in these waters are salmon, and brook and rainbow trout.

During November of last year a skilled and enthusiastic fisherman spent several weeks casting his spoon or fly in the various waters in and near the National Park, and his revealing notes of this are given as Appendix VII. Fishing in Lake Traful takes place at the point where its waters flow into the Traful River, which in turn is received by the larger Limay, draining Lake Nahuel Huapí. A spoon or fly may be cast down the first named stream and on its upper reaches by those having the fishing privileges of the Club which now owns the rights. Below these points the former holder of the upper rights is prepared to take care of a limited number of anglers. Of course anyone proposing to fish in these waters will put himself in touch with the Park authorities, at Bariloche if he enters from Chile, or with the administrative offices in Buenos Aires if he begins his journey to the Lakes there.

The initiative in the introduction of salmon in these waters is said to have come from one of our countrymen, Mr. Walter Titcomb, who in 1904 was attached to the Argentine Ministry of Agriculture. As a result of his efforts a special division of Fishery and Fish Culture was established in the Ministry named, and under the direction of another compatriot, Mr. E. A. Tulian, who personally took charge of the planting of salmon eggs in the Andes lake district. During the course of five years, from 1904 to 1909, over four million eggs including several varieties of salmon as well as brook, lake, rainbow, steel-head, and European brown-trout were brought from Europe and the United States and over three and a half million planted. These were left to propagate, but their existence may be said to have been overlooked or forgotten until in quite recent years an experienced fisherman who is still an enthusiast, rather accidentally casting a fly in the neighborhood of Traful landed a salmon—and initiated a sport!

FISHING AT MAR DEL PLATA

A fisherman who visits Mar del Plata, whose worldly charms are set out in Chapter XII, will do well to walk along the rocky water front somewhere in between the public beaches in front of the Rambla and the Playa Grande; there he will see a number of folk, young and old, lining the water's edge, and either with hand lines, or with rods, trying their luck. He will also see there or on one of the piers a certain number fishing for sharks with stout rods and huge reels. I was nearby when one of these shark, after a suitable bit of fighting, was being brought in. This weighed something over three hundred pounds; the line used was the ninety-pound variety. In general sharks are numerous near Mar del Plata but rather small in size.

The principal edible fish sought in the waters of Mar del Plata are the pejerrey, most popular of Argentine fish, at least on the table; the Corvina negra, running up to thirty pounds and more; and the Pescadilla, a small fish of the hake family. As an aside, and whispered in the ear of the gourmet and not the fisherman, may be mentioned that enormous quantities of prawns are taken locally for the Buenos Aires market. A type of net called "medio mundo" (in French demi-monde!) is employed for this purpose.

In June of one year I spent a day fishing at Mar del Plata with the then President Justo. We went out in the presidential yacht to a point some twenty miles from land, where the water shallowed, with a resulting swell which gave to our craft a rather sickening roll. We fished for several hours; and it was really fishing de luxe. My hand line was baited with five hooks and at the end of fifteen minutes of steady hauling in I experienced a pang of disappointment, considering my efforts wasted, if less than five fish attached themselves to these hooks before the line reached the bottom. And to cap it all, the modest sybarite who records this had a man standing by to remove the fish and rebait the hooks. How Hotspur would have snorted at this daintiness!

At the end of an hour, when the gentle roll, the damnable swell, was beginning to do its work, when salt water and a sharp line were combining to amputate fingers, I turned to my host and said: "Mr. President, these fish appear to still have an appetite but I am physically unable to haul them in any longer," and walked quickly to the side of the vessel to conceal my emotion.

Our mixed bag of the day contained over five hundred fish, and these by a characteristically thoughtful gesture of the President were sent to the hospitals and orphan asylums in Mar del Plata. In Buenos Aires itself there are flourishing fishing clubs, the favorite catch being pejerrey. These institutions are doing much to stimulate interest in fishing as a sport. And the acute observer will notice all along the shore of the river in front of the city fishermen of every class from the small boy with the bent pin to the well-equipped angler.

Dorado Fishing in the Upper Paraná

My enthusiasm for the unspoilt beauty of the Upper Paraná is made evident in Chapter XIII. I said nothing in that chapter, however, of the joys of dorado fishing. And for the identical reason set forth by Dr. Johnson to a woman who inquired why he had been guilty of a certain obvious error in his great lexicon: "Ignorance, Madam, ignorance." However, a veteran fisherman, who knows these waters well, has placed in my hands valuable notes relating to this branch of fishing which, as suggested, is enjoyed in its perfection in the reaches of the Upper Paraná; and these helpful notes are included an Appendix VIII.

CHAPTER XX

Birds, Flowers, Trees

1. *Birds*

SINCE ARGENTINA occupies a north and south length far exceeding the United States there are found in the more temperate portions of the Republic many birds similar to those we know and love at home. But because of this very extension, from the sub-tropical forests of the north to the bleak plains of lower Patagonia, the variety of feathered inhabitants is far greater than with us.

However, writing as I do, as a complete tyro, I must content myself with endeavoring to indicate a few of those birds which for one reason or another—in form or plumage or flight or habits —are apt to impress the observant visitor traveling from north to south or east to west in this country as somewhat different from those he has known at home.

We offspring of a northern race have been greatly favored in having an Audubon to spur us on to know more of the birds of our native land. In this respect, however, Argentines are not a whit behind us, having had Hudson (whose parents, by the way, were two "down-east" Yankees), to write of their bird and animal life in pages glowing with the essential poetry of the man, although he lacked the brush of Audubon to portray graphically what he speaks of with such charm. And there was a young English scientist, too, referred to elsewhere, and frequently, named

Darwin, who, visiting South America when only twenty-three years old, seemed to have an eye for everything and a gift for recording what he saw with a technical accuracy which gives value today to what he wrote more than a century ago.

Suppose we begin near home in our chat on birds. We might go first to the nearby golf links of Palermo, in Buenos Aires, which is also my outdoor aviary. These pleasing links lie in the center of the huge park called "3 de Febrero," and as the city is flowing rapidly around the whole area, many varieties of birds recognize it as a kind of sanctuary, and linger there to build their nests.

When I played my first round of golf at Palermo I noticed in the branches of a low tree a mass of mud and straw, in shape like an oven or a bee-hive flattened down. This I was told had been built by an hornero, an oven bird (gen. *Furnarius*), which is la Casera, or housemaker, of the Spaniards. Not far away some brute had knocked down a similar nest, and I was able to see that it had a large, arched opening with a partition directly behind this, reaching nearly to the roof, thus forming an outer room, and giving privacy to the real nest behind—a sort of two-room apartment, with southern exposure and plenty of air. In another walk I actually met the tenant of one of these elaborate bird-dwellings, who slowly fluttered away at my approach.

An amusing little bird is the teru-tero (*Vanellus cayanus*), which sometimes wakes me at night. I met one of these little fellows also at Palermo while hunting for a golf ball which had gone into the rough (my wife spoke, and made me slice that shot). He appeared to be wounded, and screamed harshly as if in pain. He was able, however, to flutter along the ground toward the fairway and I followed, the ball having been recovered. I paused for a moment, and he came quite close to me; but as I stooped toward him, he again fluttered away. Once more I followed, prepared, before addressing my ball, to render first aid to this wounded brother, as St. Francis might have called him, when turning suddenly he mounted in the air in strong, rapid flight. I realized then that I had walked near his nest, it being the breeding season, and that, like our peewits, he had feigned being wounded to draw me away from this dangerous proximity.

In the neighborhood of Buenos Aires and elsewhere one sees a well-formed bird of graceful flight strongly suggestive of the swallow's. It is known locally as the Tijereta (*Tyrannus Savana*), or scissor-tail. Darwin points out that it has the power of turning very quickly on the wing; in doing so it opens its tail feathers exactly like a pair of scissors.

Frequently, relatively far inland in the province of Buenos Aires, I have remarked sea gulls, driven in by a storm or perhaps coming inland to vary their sea diet. It pleases me to pick out one of these and to try to follow his flight; and I like to suppose that despite his inland voyage he feels a nostalgia for the sea. He is a bird I greatly admire; for his intelligence, for his courage, for his powers of endurance, for his efforts not to lose "his heritage, the sea." While not an artist in song, the gull is one in flight.

Flamingoes abound in marshes not very far from Buenos Aires, and they are continually offered for sale on the streets of the capital; beautiful, yet wretched and bedraggled, they seem to implore the passer-by to rescue them. My wife and I succumbed to this silent appeal one day and installed two of these lovely splashes of color in our garden. A short time after we began to notice that flowers and plants of which we were rather proud were being attacked by some enemy—leaves and petals missing and buds cut off as if with a knife. "Ants," said the gardener, and he planned to be up early to catch them at work and destroy them. But his matutinal efforts proved fruitless in establishing the identity of the enemy. One day, however, my wife glancing from a window saw—tragedy—our garden ornaments gorging themselves on a particularly handsome plant! We "sold them down the river" that very day, but to a friend whose ample estancia and love for birds insure their leading a peaceful and happy life with her.

The South American ostrich (*Rhea Americana*), which is scattered over a large stretch of country in Argentina, I have only observed through a wire fence! The male of this feathered family, one famous throughout the world for erroneous views concerning invisibility, is popularly believed to hatch out the eggs laid by his spouse, and to also accompany the young for some time after they leave their shell. Darwin accepts the correctness of this singular belief.

The South American bird is rather a poor relation of those inhabiting Arabia and Africa, being considerably smaller, lacking their fine plumes, and with feathers of a generally dirty brownish white. These latter are hardly of a beauty or quality warranting their use to adorn women's hats, but they make excellent dusters! And the ostrich often performs yeoman's service in northern Argentina in destroying locusts.

An unattractive bird present in large numbers in the province of Buenos Aires is the Chajá—a species of large wild turkey, nonedible, however; the creature seems aware of this fact which perhaps explains his indifference to and lack of fear of man.

Silver-winged storks with necks suggesting a Venetian glass bottle, are to be observed in many parts of the country where there is water or a marshy expanse.

It was at lovely "Miraflores," described in Chapter XII, that I saw great numbers of small green parrots, with grey breasts—doubtless the species (*Conurus murinus*) which Darwin observed on the lower reaches of the Paraná. When not in flight they alight in tall trees, and in some of these I saw what appeared to be their nests. Flying about in large flocks these parrots do great damage to fields of grain, comparable to the raids of our old enemy the crow. But as "Miraflores" appears to be almost like a sanctuary, to judge from the variety of bird life there, their large numbers suggest that they are not molested.

Von Humboldt, encamped on the slopes of Chimborazo, relates that he saw a condor in strong, level flight at a height of more than 23,000 feet! These immense birds, which average four feet in length and nine feet between wing tips, would thus seem to be the feathered creature rising highest in the ether: "Par delà les brouillards hantés des aigles noirs." In fact their favorite haunts are from ten to sixteen thousand feet above sea level. My learned friend, the Encyclopedia Britannica, informs me that the condor is "almost the largest of existing birds of flight," but without telling me what species is larger, which is tantalizing. Perhaps the E.B. has in mind the albatross, whose wing-spread is often, if not usually, greater than that of the condor, reaching seventeen feet, although the body is smaller.

The young Darwin seems to have been fascinated by these birds, and to have spent much time staring at them overhead, admiring their graceful flight. He records that except when rising from the ground they appear never to flap their wings, and relates that on one occasion he kept his eyes fixed for more than thirty minutes on several condors flying close together without seeing one of them give a single flap. He further describes a method of trapping condors practiced in Chile, which is to place a carcass on a level piece of ground within an enclosure of stakes, with an opening. When the birds have gorged themselves the trappers gallop up on horseback and close the entrance; "for when this bird has not space to run, it cannot give its body sufficient momentum to rise from the ground." I am reminded in this connection of the departure of our planes from the airport at La Paz, 13,500 feet above sea level, and with air correspondingly thin. Unlike the condor, the pilot is careful not to gorge his plane with too much weight, and even then he must utilize every inch of the runway in order to leave the ground!

I have said nothing thus far of the song-birds of Argentina, who merit special mention; among these are the dove, and the mocking bird (*Mimus orpheus*), called locally the Calandria. This latter, in the opinion of qualified judges, possesses a song superior to that of any other bird in the country. The calandria's song is low, and like that of the sedge warbler of England, but far more beautiful. Other birds besides these and the hornero, are the cardinal, the mirlo (our black bird), and the jilguero (our linnet).

The fact that I, an average city dweller, with occasional excursions to the country, have not heard a greater number of song birds in Argentina, is explained in part by a fact to which Hudson calls attention; that while nearly all British song birds (and this may be said to be true in a measure of those found in the United States) are semi-domesticated and sing in gardens and orchards, songsters of South America in general "certainly do not, like those of Europe, mass themselves about the habitations of men, as if sweet voices were given them solely for the delectation of human listeners; they are pre-eminently birds of the wild forests, marsh, and savannah."

The traveler must visit, at least once, the rich Zoological Garden of Buenos Aires. He will see there perhaps for the first time in feather and flesh, birds and animals made familiar to his eye by studies in natural history. The aviaries, with their collection of rare birds, many of fantastic form or color, invite closer study.

2. *Flowers*

"God Almighty Himself," as Bacon reminds us, "first made a garden." Coming down the centuries it is Bulwer Lytton who later assures us that where flowers and birds are seen around a house we may be sure the occupants are wiser or better than their neighbors.

It will be recalled that medieval gardens had both a practical and an esthetic side. For in them many plants were grown which had or were supposed to have—often the same thing—a medicinal, curative or gustatory value. Something of this eminently utilitarian side doubtless lingered and was manifest in early gardens in Argentina. And every estancia possessed its garden, mostly of the practical type. But with the passage of the years very beautiful ones of purely esthetic value have been developed. In this connection I have in mind the pleasances of Chapadmalal, with their English flavor, the lovely riot of color in "Azucena's" beautiful natural rock gardens, "Acelain's" stately Spanish garden, and the flower-bordered walks at "Miraflores" and "Armonía." I am mindful, too, of lovely old gardens surrounding villas on the barranca (the river bluff) beyond the northern suburbs of Buenos Aires, to which in the old days before Mar del Plata and other resorts became popular the elegant folk of Buenos Aires resorted for the summer.

The stimulus given by the former and present Directors of the Botanical Garden in the creation and promotion of the many public gardens in and about the capital has been a strong one. And the Horticultural Society, which with the Buenos Aires Garden Club promotes enthusiastically the efforts of amateur gardeners, is something for which every flower-lover must be grateful.

As in the case of trees, I shall only make mention here of certain flowers which, because of being new to a visitor from my country, or because of a richer local development, are likely to attract the garden-lover's attention. For after all, the flowers found in the United States and England flourish here—and how! Dahlias grow to twice the size of those seen at home; tulips and chrysanthemums, in violation of Nature's labor laws, blossom twice yearly, being shown in florists' windows in both spring and autumn; while the poinsettia, our Christmas "potted plant," is even more luxuriant here than those to be found in Mexico or in the Highlands of Burma. The Argentine name for this latter is *estrella federal*. The plants in the Embassy garden attain a height of ten feet or more, with blossoms frequently eight inches in diameter!

Garden-lovers who are also interested in the origin of the names of flowers will here recall that at the first exhibition of the Pennsylvania Horticultural Society held in June, 1829, in Philadelphia, an example of the poinsettia was exhibited by the proprietor of the Bartram Botanic Garden, Colonel Robert Carr. This plant had been sent to the Garden by the Honorable Joel Roberts Poinsett, who from 1825 to 1829 was our Minister to Mexico.

Following this gift, a specimen of the plant was sent to Professor Robert Graham of the Royal Botanical Garden at Edinburgh, who suggested for it the name of the original donor; it was accordingly exhibited later on as *Euphorbia poinsetti,* and finally as *Poinsettia pulcherrima.* (A justification for dragging in by the heels this informative paragraph is found in the fact that Poinsett, some years before beginning his stormy diplomatic career in Mexico, had served as "Agent for seamen and commerce" and later as Consul General of our Government, in Buenos Aires, where he may first have seen and admired this striking flower.)

The estrelitza, known to us as the bird-of-paradise, also flourishes locally. This beautiful and strange flower of the banana family, which, as a garden-lover once remarked, is exotic-looking even in its own home, "with an air of some wild creature caught," here has a relation, and not a poor relation either, which grows in large and luxurious fashion indicative of its plantain kinship, bearing enormous blossoms which glisten like different tones of mother-of-pearl.

Argentina has her orchids as well as Brazil, and these are found especially in the far northern woods. But unlike the more delicate blossoms of Brazil, certain varieties can be hung under or in the trees with safety in a Buenos Aires garden, where frost is almost as rare as in Avalon and where they can bloom without benefit of glass, producing sprays of yellow butterfly blossoms of varying size and pattern.

Roses are absolutely at home in Buenos Aires, and, in fact, in large sections of the Republic. In the huge park opposite the Embassy is one of the most beautiful rosedales to be found in the world. Our own garden is not far behind this in beauty, and great pink roses in rich profusion clamber over the walls, invade the wrought-iron fence and monumental grill over the gateway and cascade down from this to form a beautiful archway. These flowers were at their best when President Roosevelt on November 30, 1936, passed through these gates on his arrival on his mission of peace.

The fox-glove, the digitalis of medicine, shows its stately spires in wild and magnificent profusion in the southern lake region, literally in great carpets of gorgeous color, constituting, however, a menace to cattle.

Also to be noted around the southern lakes is a shrub known as the "notro," bearing a brilliant red flower, with which during a Christmas season spent in that neighborhood we made gorgeous garlands for the festal day.

La Liana de agua, of the bignonia family, a flame-colored trumpet vine clambers up the trees along the highways near Nahuel Huapí, and the tilco, or fuchsia, grows as bushes in the same neighborhood, with blazing pendant blossoms. The fuchsia, it will be recalled, is named after Leonard Fuchs, a flower-lover of long ago, who thus attains a verdant immortality!

One further reference to our Embassy garden. Before leaving the United States in 1933 I ventured, as an ex-member of the Board of Visitors of Mount Vernon, to solicit the gift of a mint plant from George Washington's own mint bed. While Argentina has a species of mint found widely here, yet I like to think—patriotic motives triumphing over scientific doubts—that the plant I transported with so much difficulty has a more delicate aroma and certainly is of more distinguished birth than the lowly native product. In any event my Mount Vernon specimen has flourished in my garden, possibly under the fiction of extraterritoriality, and its descendants are utilized as gifts to friends or for sale into happy servitude by the local garden club. These gifts and sales are accompanied by a famous recipe, and it requires no effort of the imagination to realize it is not one for preparing mint sauce!

The love of flowers, which is as innate in Argentines as a love for music, is demonstrated by the countless number of flower shops, which seem to vie with each other in the magnificence of the blossoms exhibited and the taste of their arrangement. Of the various flower markets, I know two, one supplying dealers (entry is by special permit), the other, an open air market in the center of the Calle Basavilbaso between Leandro Alem and Juncal. Both markets merit a visit, and of course must be seen early in the day.

In the botanical gardens of Buenos Aires under the direction of Charles Thays, who succeeded his father as Director General de Paseos Públicos y Director del Jardín Botánico, will be found examples of rare plants, indigenous and exotic, of a character to provoke pleasure and interest. Bryce visited this garden and speaks of it as "extremely well arranged, and of the highest interest to the naturalist." Another traveler, Huret, after paying tribute to the Thays of his day, declares that this garden "is without doubt the most valuable and the most complete of the botanical gardens of the world." I dare to add after this distinguished testimony my own happy impression of this "perfumed paradise," and urge my compatriots to visit it, and often.

3. *Trees*

In the same merely suggestive manner in which I have spoken of the birds and flowers to be seen by the visitor to Argentina, I want to say something concerning certain of the trees likely to attract his attention.

Trees are one of the peculiar glories of Buenos Aires, and in fact of the entire country. Owing, however, to the immensity of the pampa and to its special and picturesque product, the gaucho, both of which early captured the imagination of the foreigner, the general picture has become blurred and Argentina's rich forest treasures are less manifest—except perhaps to those having a special commercial interest in their exploitation.

Owing to its being the title of one of Hudson's most popular works, and to the further fact that it is the subject of a poem learnt by every Argentine schoolboy, El Ombú is perhaps the best known of Argentine trees. In the rhymed composition referred to, after being informed of a striking characteristic of Brazil, Peru and Uruguay, the reader learns in the concluding lines that the beautiful country of Buenos Aires boasts the pampa, and that the pampa nourishes the ombú:

Buenos Aires, patria hermosa,
Tiene la pampa grandiosa,
La pampa tiene el ombú.

It seems appropriate, therefore, to begin these simple observations on the forest wealth of Argentina with something concerning this interesting tree.

El Ombú would be described by someone fresh from his study as of the family of the phytolaccaceae, to be more exact, Phytolacca dioica. With this as a background we have no great difficulty in tracing a relationship between it and the humble pokeweed of our childhood.

The ombú is one of the loveliest and most impressive trees in all Argentina. Its trunk assumes colossal proportions and rises to a height of from forty to fifty feet. Its magnificent arms are spread in all directions and there are huge knees and exposed roots extending well beyond the trunk and making the wide extension of the branches possible. Its leaves are dark green in color and a long oval in shape. Its flowerings hang in a cylindrical form, masculine and feminine and of a snowy white, surrounded by leaves of a whitish green. Set in the vast expanses of the pampa, the ombú is often the only tree, the solitary examples providing the sole shade for cattle.

The ombú is essentially decorative, having been much used in former years in the formation of avenues; but it is quite without commercial value. Country folk extract a purgative from its bark as well as from the leaves and the tiny fruit. But it is its lovely and venerable form and the poetic associations which surround it that make the ombú the best known tree in Argentina. In Palermo park are magnificent specimens as well as in La Plaza Intendente

LAKE MASCARDI, NAHUEL HUAPÍ NATIONAL PARK

Coppola

PALO BORRACHO, THE "DRUNKEN POPLAR"

Alvear, while La Avenida de los Ombúes presents some superb varieties.

Another tree of unusual beauty, to be found more especially in the north, is the jacarandá (*J. mimosaefolia*) of the bignonia family. Besides possessing commercial value in its wood, this tree is one of the most decorative to be found in the country. It reaches a height of from 25 to 40 feet, with trunk and branches of symmetrical form, bearing magnificent foliage, and in the flowering season clusters of blue bell-shaped flowers so closely blooming that the tree is like a huge bouquet of violets. At this time a walk along the Avenida Alvear from Calle Agüero to where this thoroughfare begins its graceful turn toward the Recoleta Cemetery, offers a rich reward.

A great Virginian and a great scientist, Matthew Fontaine Maury, just before his death is said to have asked that his body be carried to its last home through beautiful Rockfish Gap when the rhododendron was in bloom. I can imagine a patriotic Argentine, a porteño, asking that his remains pass down this lovely bit of avenue on their way to the Argentine Pantheon.

One of my illustrations is of the tree known as el palo borracho (*Chorisia insignis*). Translated literally, the name means the drunken stick, and is said to be derived from the fact that from the center a small quantity of water may be extracted by perforating the trunk; it is thus a kind of traveler's tree, save that in the case of the latter the water collects in one of the large, long-stalked leaves. Both in name and appearance the palo borracho is a grotesque thing; a bulbous, green body, formed like a badly blown bottle, and with trunk and limbs protected by savage thorns. In the warm north it attains a height of from thirty to forty feet. It bears lovely, creamy-white or pink blossoms growing like orchids on the branches. I recall once seeing in the upper Paraná River a canoe made from the hollowed-out trunk of this tree, and I am told that the Indians use it, because of its relative lightness, in the making of rafts. These trees are to be seen in Buenos Aires, notably one recently transplanted to the Plaza 9 de Julio. There are also one or two, male and female, in the Parque 3 de Febrero, and a good example in the garden of the Embassy. A standing prize of 100 pesos which I offered some time ago to the person who without artificial aid climbs this low-branched tree, has not been contended for up to this writing, and is still open.

Along the shores of many rivers to the north of Buenos Aires is to be admired the superb ceibo (*Erythrina fulgens*), bearing a velvety, crimson blossom, "whose hue, angry and brave" gives a relieving note to the too uniform color of the willows and sarandíes of the streams. The ceibo sometimes attains a height of 90 feet, but those seen in the neighborhood of Buenos Aires (*Erythrina Crista Galli*), are much lower. The flowers hang from the branches in long clusters like bunches of grapes. Although the wood is too light and fibrous for use in carpentry, its bark is utilized in tanning leather. It is therefore of value commercially, although essentially ornamental.

Some of these trees may be seen in the Parque 3 de Febrero and there are four lovely specimens in the Embassy garden; these remained in flower up to Christmas night in 1936, and the blossoms decorated our Christmas table at our farewell dinner to Secretary Hull and our delegates to the memorable Buenos Aires Peace Conference.

That same day the Secretary had planted in the lower garden a jacarandá tree of the type described in a previous paragraph, called locally "tarco." This followed the example of President Roosevelt, who, on December 1, set out a promising specimen of the tree known locally as a gomero (*Ficus subtriplinervia Mart.*), choosing for this an exposed spot just below the dining room windows, where some day it will offer a grateful shade. A few weeks later, on December 28, the President of Argentina, General Agustín P. Justo, following an informal luncheon, planted a similar tree and in a corresponding position below the ballroom windows. Both Presidents and plants are thriving at this writing, but in time the exuberant growth of the latter will have to be curbed.

The type of the tree planted by the two Chief Magistrates is as suggested of the genus ficus (of which, the learned ones tell us there are over 800 varieties). Its best known member, apart from the variety which yields the well-known figs of commerce, is the banyan (*Ficus indica*), which is often of vast extent, since the parent tree continues to throw out aerial roots as long as the earth continues her sustenance. World travelers will here recall the centuries old banyan in the Royal Botanic Gardens in Calcutta, which has circumference of over 900 feet!

Magnificent specimens of local gomeros are to be seen in various parks in Buenos Aires. I have especially in mind those in the Parque Intendente Alvear, which are of great age, and the extension of their branches and the deep shade provoke the admiration of every observant passerby.

La Tipa (*Tipuana speciosa*) is at its best in the provinces of Salta, Tucumán, and Jujuy, where some of the largest examples grow over 150 feet tall, with trunks measuring nearly 40 feet in circumference. It is a shade and ornamental tree of exceptional value, and is seen everywhere in the capital. It bears a feathery, yellow flower, suggestive of the acacia. In Avenida Alvear may be easily studied this lovely shade tree of which there are some good examples immediately in front of the Embassy.

A famous tree of Argentina is the sarandí (*Cephalantus glabiratus*) of the Rubiaceoe family, one which has given its name to many towns, rivers and streams. It is only 6 to 10 feet in height with widely extended branches and is apparently most at home near the rivers and streams which converge in the formation of the Rio de la Plata. The traveler who makes one of the river trips which I have recommended will see this tree to his heart's content.

There should be mentioned here in passing the names of some of the trees not native to the country, but which have flourished in their new setting and have been of the greatest service in the creation of artificial forests and in providing shelter for animals on country estates. For example, poplars, planted with the idea of a ready exploitation; these include the familiar cottonwood (*Populus angilata*), the Lombardy poplar (*Populus pyramidalis*), the white poplar (*Populus alba*), and the Carolina or necklace poplar (*Populus monilifera*); also willows (*Salix babylonica*), which were planted literally by millions in the wide, moist spaces of the Paraná and La Plata; and also, the Paraiso (*Melia Azedarach*), which has the advantage of being able to resist the attacks of locusts; and the acacia, in several varieties. Finally, and for me presenting greater charm and possessing certain advantages over any of those named, I would mention the different varieties of eucalyptus (*E. globulus, E. resinifera, E. amygdalina, and E. viminalis*), which were imported in immense numbers in the early '60's and which have given and give a rapid vegetation and a healthful shade.

Before proceeding to refer further in this casual fashion to some of the Argentine trees which flourish best in tropical or

A Gomero tree

Eucalyptus trees in Palermo Park, Buenos Aires

La Prensa

PRESIDENT JUSTO RECEIVES PRESIDENT ROOSEVELT AND THE AMERICAN
AMBASSADOR IN THE CASA ROSADA, BUENOS AIRES, NOVEMBER 1936

sub-tropical surroundings, let us salute in passing an historic tree which flourished or used to flourish in the little town of San Lorenzo, on the Paraná, north of Rosario. Here, 125 years ago, in February 1813, to be exact, San Martín, that Chevalier *sans peur et sans reproche,* at the head of his famous grenadiers, ambushed and routed a landing party of three times his number from the Spanish river squadron, a success of enormous strategic importance since it opened up river communications with Buenos Aires. The combat took place between the river and the monastery of San Lorenzo. Following the engagement San Martín spent some moments with the Franciscan fathers, resting under the shade of the venerable pine, which even at that time was of magnificent growth. In pursuing the fleeing Spaniards in this engagement, San Martín's horse had fallen, pinning one of his legs to the earth. An enemy turned and was about to stab him when the patriot Sergeant Juan Bautista Cabral interposed; he thus saved San Martín, and with him, as has been aptly said, the liberty of half a continent. A street in Buenos Aires recalls the Sergeant's name.

Besides the tipa, already mentioned, the algarrobo (*Prosopis alba*); the red willow (*Salix humboldtiana*); the lapacho (*Tabebuya flavescens*), with white, rose, copper colored or scarlet flowers, forming huge bouquets, are especially common in the north; and the traveler who visits the ruins of the Jesuit missions of San Ignacio, a journey described (and prescribed) in another chapter, will see the ivapohy (*Ficus ivapohys*) carrying on a work of destruction in these ruins which is simply diabolical in its effectiveness. In Córdoba and San Luis are forests of Algarrobos, mentioned above, whose wood of medium density is employed in large quantities for street paving.

But from the standpoint of commercial value it is the famous quebracho colorado (*Schinopsis lorentzii*), which is outstanding among Argentine trees. This is found in forests which have been considered, and quite falsely, as inexhaustible. The name of this tree means literally break-axe, a title which it has won on account of the extreme density and resulting hardness of the wood. It contains a large proportion of tannin, and therefore is of particular value in commerce. Railway folk rise up and call it blessed for its wonderful adaptation as a railroad tie, while its resistance to the action of water makes it of equal utility in the construction of wharves. A fantastic story, probably apocryphal, is told of a stranger who, never having been in the country, yet invested a huge sum in the purchase of a forest of Quebracho trees remote from a railroad but located on a river by which, as he told folk, he expected to get his timber to market. The joker in this case, it is hardly necessary to point out, is that Quebracho is as buoyant as lead!

The far South also has forest wealth, and here magnificent specimens of oaks and beeches are to be found; cypresses; magnolias; the gigantic *Fitzroya patagonica* (named after the Commander of Darwin's "Beagle"); the superb coihué (*Nothofagus Dombeyi Mirb*), (especially to be observed in the neighborhood of the hotel at Llao-Llao); the palo santo (*Flotowia diacanthoides Less.*), and the many varieties of the sauce, or willow.

Before closing this chapter reference should be made to a shrub, which might by courtesy be called a tree, growing in Argentina, Paraguay and Brazil—a species of holly known as maté (*Ilex paraguariensis*). The dried leaves of this plant are used to make a non-alcoholic infusion which might be called the national drink. Like tea and coffee it contains caffeine, but in less quantity.

Especially in the camp, will the traveler be invited to partake of this beverage. Where drunk in the orthodox manner it is served in a small gourd; the dry leaves being placed in this, and boiling water poured over them. In this gourd (often a cocoanut shell and decorated with silver), is placed a bombilla (literally a little pump) which is a tube of metal, generally of silver, from six to seven inches long, through which the tea is sucked; a bulb at the end of the bombilla in which holes have been pierced prevents the particles of the leaves being drawn up into the mouth. One gourd of maté serves for a small group, it being handed around in turn. Fastidious persons might object to this communal system, and it is not difficult to have the maté made like tea, filtered, and then drunk from a cup, with the addition of sugar and milk; this is called maté cocido. In the camp in former days meat and maté formed the staple diet of the gaucho; the latter supplying the dietary lack of vegetables and bread.

Jesuit fathers were the first to attempt to cultivate the shrub, hence the name of Jesuit's tea, or Mission tea, sometimes given the infusion.

Maté is a valuable article of commerce, and Argentina today is not alone a heavy consumer of it, but also an active producer. In recent years it has been necessary to import a certain quantity of the leaves from Paraguay and Brazil to supplement domestic production; it is estimated, however, that in a few years the country will be self-sustaining.

The traveler who thinks seriously of studying the variety and extent of the forest wealth of Argentina would do well, as a preparatory step, to discuss the matter with the Department of Agriculture of the Argentine Government and with the Director of the Botanical Garden in Buenos Aires.

CHAPTER XXI

By Way of Background

As a background to what has been said in preceding pages are added the following paragraphs in which are set forth in the baldest and briefest terms the antecedents, the birth and the growing pains of this great Nation called on to play such an important rôle in the forward progress of the world.

With the expulsion of the Moors from the Iberian peninsula, contemporaneously with the discovery of America, Spain was prepared to begin its great prehensile movement toward the west, which was to give it mastery of southern North America, of Central and of South America, and of the Philippines. Later, through union with Portugal, Spain was also to have vast possessions in the Orient; so that to her, in greater measure than to Venice, might be applied the poet's lines:

> Once did she hold the gorgeous East in fee,
> And was the safeguard of the West.

An important part of what we now know as Argentina was first brought to the notice of Europe by the voyage of de Solis in 1515, when he penetrated the estuary of La Plata. Some ten years later Sebastian Cabot explored the river; and as the century wore on the Plata region was visited and opened to settlement through the labours of a group of hardy explorers. But the river was not the only approach to this rich territory; expeditions came from

Peru, others from Chile, and still others from the vaguely defined region known as Cuyo. The cities then founded dominated the early history of the various regions; Asunción, Buenos Aires, Santa Fé, Tucumán, Salta, Córdoba, the latter the site of a University founded in 1613, which exists today as a center of beneficent culture.

It was not until 1776 that Buenos Aires became a viceroyalty. But this distinction marked only a slight mitigation of the restrictions on trade imposed on all her overseas dominions by Spain, and discontent in commercial circles was but one of many influences at work to stimulate the hunger for independence. The principal restrictions on commerce were in favor of Spanish monopolies, coupled with heavy tax burdens; the exclusion of colonists from high offices wounded local pride, and this conspired with other grievances to breed discontent. "But more than this, than these, than all" was the powerful repercussion throughout Spanish America of the revolution in the British Colonies in North America. This latter was not, as will be remembered, a revolution against a social order, such as has characterized many modern movements, but one seeking freedom; allied to this was the influence of France. Leaders of Argentine thought in that day were, as at present, profoundly affected by French political philosophy. "Le Contrat Social" was as widely discussed in intellectual circles in Buenos Aires as perhaps in the French Capital, and the ferment of intellectual thought in Paris was equally heavy in South America.

An immediate cause of the movement for independence observable in all South America was the chaotic condition of Spanish affairs produced by Napoleon's invasion of the Peninsula. The proclamation by the Emperor of the accession to the Spanish throne of Joseph Bonaparte was bitterly resented in all of Spain's colonies. In Seville, as you will recall, existed a Junta which represented the legitimate monarch; this Junta having fallen, the authority of the viceroys and captains general disappeared with it. In these circumstances revolts broke out almost simultaneously in Venezuela, New Grenada, Buenos Aires, and Chile, the royal officers in each case being deposed and local juntas established whose avowed purpose was to hold the countries for Ferdinand VII. Here we may observe a process of thought not dissimilar from that prevailing in the Colonies at the very beginning of our struggle for independence; a greater measure of liberty, or an equality of liberty, under constituted authority, was the first step or aim.

But despite movements of capital importance in Buenos Aires (in 1810) and elsewhere, it was only on July 9, 1816, a full forty years after our great charter of freedom was penned, that from a humble structure of sun-dried brick in the city of Tucumán the delegates of the United Provinces of La Plata gave to the world the solemn declaration of their independence.

I have just referred to this movement towards independence in other South American countries. But it must be carefully borne in mind that it is quite impossible to study South America from *any* standpoint *en bloc!* And if we see in the various countries many common grievances, if in the final struggle for independence San Martín, the Argentine, fought far beyond the borders of the former Viceroyalty, and Bolívar, the Venezuelan, led victorious troops to regions remote from the land of his birth, all in the common struggle for freedom, yet local forces were constantly at work advancing or retarding the forward movement. I have in my possession a rare volume which recounts the British invasion and occupation of Buenos Aires in 1806. The author mistaking what proved to be a temporary stay, followed by a humiliating departure, as a permanent conquest, set forth in glowing terms the advantages of the country as a site of future colonization by Great Britain.

I mention this in passing because the effect of this invasion was to consolidate varying political opinions, while the cowardly conduct of the then viceroy facilitated the plans of the Argentine group which deposed him. The climax came on May 25, 1810, when a large assembly composed of the Council of the city of Buenos Aires, a gathering to which the more prominent citizens had been invited, met in the Cabildo, or Town Hall, of which a portion still remains, and proceeded to organize a provisional government. Small towns within the former territorial jurisdiction of the viceroyalty of the river Plata were then invited to elect representatives to a national congress to determine the *form* of national government. Following this there were several constitutional conventions, in each of which representation was on the basis of the town.

And here it should be said that the history of the several provinces of the Argentine Republic is so closely bound up with the history of the various towns that it is impossible to separate them. The provinces themselves were born of *intendencias* which existed under the viceroyalty, whose seats were the chief cities. Finally, as I have already noted, the declaration of independence came in July 1816, followed as with us, but over a larger period, by the conflict by which that freedom was finally won.

In this struggle local prejudices and sentiments contributed to the growth of various disruptive forces, and the United Provinces, despite the implications of the name, were sadly torn asunder. In various sections of the country lack of communications facilitated the rise of local politico-military leaders, known as *caudillos,* who were almost supreme in their districts, despite efforts at real union of the various groups, especially under Rivadavia. The varying governing juntas gave way under the stress of circumstances to a Triumvirate which in turn was displaced by a Supreme Director.

Finally in 1829 there appears on the stage of Argentine history a sanguinary figure—Juan Manuel de Rosas. He was a man of much natural mental vigor, of undaunted physical courage and capable of almost incredible feats of horsemanship. He established an extraordinary ascendancy over the group of irregular cavalry made up of "gauchos" which he brought together. Becoming governor of Buenos Aires, he inaugurated a period of personal rule known in Argentine history as "The Tyranny," which lasted until 1852, when, following the defeat of his army, by Urquiza, at Caseros, near Buenos Aires, on February 3, he fled to England, never to return.

In Buenos Aires, Rosas achieved a certain harmony by the ruthless expulsion or execution of his political enemies. The press was muzzled, commerce was restricted, justice was a matter of the dictator's caprice. In all his proclamations and in the conclusions of his letters Rosas denounced the so-called *Unitarios*, as savages who sought, he alleged, to bring about the creation of a strong central rather than a federal union. But paradoxically, the effect of his tyranny was to foster the very result which he denounced. With some of the outlying provinces he was able to form a loose alliance, and these in charge of his henchmen insured his domination, although nominally he was only governor of Buenos Aires.

The great purging work of Urquiza in ridding the country of Rosas once accomplished, the gigantic task facing him and his collaborators was nothing less than the substitution of a national system for a confederation quite as loose and feeble as that which prevailed at the end of our struggle for independence; and equally in a country as yet lacking a constitution, and with provinces and sections ruled by caudillos; added to this was the jealousy of the dwellers in Buenos Aires of the remaining sections. But a constitution was adopted under Urquiza early in 1853, although it was not until 1859 that, with certain modifications, it was accepted by the nation. During this interim there was much internal unrest provoked by rival leaders which made Urquiza's position a difficult one. But by 1861 Urquiza was no longer in the field as a national political influence, and in 1862 Bartolomé Mitre entered upon his 6-year term as the first constitutional president of Argentina. Before further reference to this truly great national figure a word should be said of the genesis of the Argentine Constitution. Looking backward, with the wisdom so easily acquired after events, it appears inevitable that Argentina should eventually have adopted a federal system of government. The forces of a common tongue, allied to common sacrifices in the cause of liberty, all tended to weld the scattered provinces and peoples into a union. But disjunctive forces also prevailed. For many years the provinces had enjoyed practical independence of one another, and of a common superior. They were loath to sacrifice local interests to the general welfare of a nation only coming into being. Federalism was then the natural compromise, and in accepting this principle Argentine leaders turned to the Constitution of the United States for a solution of their problems. Furthermore, although Rosas' departure had left the country free to determine its form of government, there were serious differences between Buenos Aires and the rest of Argentina, and between the partisans of Unitarian and Federalist viewpoints, differences which were not fully settled for many years.

In 1853, the year following the flight of Rosas, therefore, there met in the city of Santa Fé a group of outstanding men charged with the duty of drafting a constitution. These delegates were not representatives of united states or provinces, but of the Argentine nation—"We, the representatives of the people of the Argentine nation" reads the preamble. It is noteworthy that these men desired to secure the blessings of liberty not only to themselves and their posterity, but again to quote the language of the preamble, "to all men in the world who may desire to inhabit the Argentine soil." This was a prompt recognition of the necessity of encouraging immigration to a country whose population at the time numbered a bare million souls. Since then every appropriate inducement has been given Europeans to forsake their native countries for this promised land of the new world. Besides the stress on the necessity for immigration, as shown in the Preamble, an article of the Constitution specifically imposes upon Congress the duty of fostering immigration, while other articles are framed to guard the foreigner against injustice, and to induce him to accept the duties and responsibilities of citizenship.

Returning now to a brief consideration of the character and achievements of the first President under the Constitution:

In the opinion of qualified historians President Mitre is of the stature of the great ones of the past in his native country, of men like Moreno, Belgrano and Rivadavia and San Martín, but perhaps of greater versatility than any of these. And in considering his capacities and gifts he suggests one of those many sided geniuses with which the history of the Renaissance makes us familiar. For he was at once statesman, soldier, bibliophile, and humanist, while as organizer and pacifier of the nation and of democracy he led and educated the popular conscience. As translator of Dante he showed himself a master not alone of the idiom of the great Florentine but of the technique of harmonious and flexible verse. In his "History of Belgrano" and of "Argentine Independence" and of "San Martín and South American Emancipation" he has traced in broad and significant lines the history of a great epoch. His accumulation of a valuable library and documents relating to Argentine independence which are now in the museum bearing his name, referred to elsewhere, is a source of inestimable value to all historians of South American and Argentine history. His continuing influence is seen in the contribution to democratic thought being made daily throughout the republic and elsewhere by the great newspaper—La Nación—which he founded.

The National Congress in solemn session fittingly declared that Bartolomé Mitre merited well of his country.

Mitre was followed in the Presidency by Domingo Faustino Sarmiento. The Administration of Sarmiento is marked by two great contributions to the national life: effective steps to wipe out the caudillo and second, but far greater in its implications, the development of public instruction.

As firmly as Thomas Jefferson believed in the ultimate wisdom of the people did Sarmiento hold the faith in matters of public instruction as the means for settling political and moral problems and as a lever to raise the level of general culture. It is gratifying to recall here that in his task of popular education Sarmiento had in mind the public school system of our country and brought from there to Argentina a number of school teachers, the happy choice of whom is being constantly testified to by those who came within the orbit of these gentlewomen. The last of these teachers recruited by Sarmiento died within the past year or so, lamented by a devoted circle of Argentine friends.

In the score of years from 1853, when the Constitution was adopted, to 1874 Argentina may be said to have been occupied with the vital business of working out its destiny.

In this period there was much waste—of human life and of material wealth. But its close saw the country launched on a wave of progress which has continued ever since. Naturally and inevitably there have been serious setbacks. But viewed over decades, progress has been amazing. The increase in population has been marked, the political growth of individual and of nation has been equally impressive, and Argentina, in this year of grace, 1939, may be said to have her feet firmly planted in the path of progressive reform and her face set toward the goal of increased peace, prosperity and plenty.

Appendices

Appendices

Appendix I

AIR ROUTES TO ARGENTINA

The following is a simplified itinerary of air routes to South America, showing the elapsed flying time from Newark to Miami via Eastern Air Lines, and from Miami to Buenos Aires by the four different routes of Pan American Airways System. These are:

(a) Atlantic Coast Route Miami-Rio de Janeiro-Buenos Aires.

(b) Coastal route from Miami to Rio, and thence inland via Curityba-Iguazú-Asunción (Paraguay)-Buenos Aires.

(c) Miami-Cristobal-Arequipa thence by the Diagonal route, *i.e.,* La Paz, Jujuy, Salta, Tucuman, Cordoba, Buenos Aires.

(d) Miami-Cristobal and thence along the Pacific Coast to Santiago, Chile and to Buenos Aires.

(a) Trip from Newark to Buenos Aires via East Coast

(*Through Porto Alegre*)

Lv. Tue. Newark	9:00 p.m.	
Ar. Wed. Miami	5:20 a.m.	8 hrs. 20 min.
Lv. Wed. Miami	7:30 a.m.	
Ar. Wed. San Juan	5:45 p.m.	10 hrs. 15 min.
Lv. Thu. San Juan	8:15 a.m.	
Ar. Thu. Port of Spain	3:15 p.m.	7 hrs.
Lv. Fri. Port of Spain	5:45 a.m.	
Ar. Fri. Belem, Para	5:30 p.m.	11 hrs. 45 min.
Lv. Sat. Belem, Para	6:00 a.m.	
Ar. Sat. Recife	4:25 p.m.	10 hrs. 25 min.
Lv. Sun. Recife	6:00 a.m.	
Ar. Sun. Rio de Janeiro	4:20 p.m.	10 hrs. 20 min.
Lv. Mon. Rio de Janeiro	8:00 a.m.	
Ar. Mon. Buenos Aires	3:45 p.m.	7 hrs. 45 min.

Total . . . . . . 65 hrs. 50 min.

(b) Via East Coast

(*Through Asuncion*)

Lv. Sat.	Newark	9:00 p.m.	
Ar. Sun.	Miami	5:20 a.m.	8 hrs. 20 min.
Lv. Sun.	Miami	7:30 a.m.	
Ar. Sun.	San Juan	5:45 p.m.	10 hrs. 15 min.
Lv. Mon.	San Juan	8:00 a.m.	
Ar. Mon.	Port of Spain	12:40 p.m.	4 hrs. 40 min.
Lv. Tue.	Port of Spain	5:45 a.m.	
Ar. Tue.	Belem, Para	5:00 p.m.	11 hrs.
Lv. Wed.	Belem, Para	6:00 a.m.	
Ar. Wed.	Recife	3:10 p.m.	9 hrs. 10 min.
Lv. Thu.	Recife	6:00 a.m.	
Ar. Thu.	Rio de Janeiro	3:30 p.m.	9 hrs. 30 min.
Lv. Fri.	Rio de Janeiro	6:00 a.m.	
Ar. Fri.	Buenos Aires	3:55 p.m.	9 hrs. 55 min.

Total . . . . 63 hrs. 5 min.

(c) Via West Coast

(*Through La Paz*)

Lv. Fri.	Newark	9:00 p.m.	
Ar. Sat.	Miami	5:20 a.m.	8 hrs. 20 min.
Lv. Sat.	Miami	7:15 a.m.	
Ar. Sat.	Cristobal	4:55 p.m.	9 hrs. 40 min.
Lv. Sun.	Cristobal	6:30 a.m.	
Ar. Sun.	Guayaquil	2:40 p.m.	8 hrs. 10 min.
Lv. Mon.	Guayaquil	6:00 a.m.	
Ar. Mon.	Arequipa	3:40 p.m.	9 hrs. 40 min.
Lv. Tue.	Arequipa	8:00 a.m.	
Ar. Tue.	Salta	4:25 p.m.	8 hrs. 25 min.
Lv. Wed.	Salta	7:00 a.m.	
Ar. Wed.	Buenos Aires	1:00 p.m.	8 hrs.

Total . . . . 52 hrs. 15 min.

(d) Via West Coast
(*Through Santiago de Chile*)

Lv. Mon.	Newark	9:00 p.m.	
Ar. Tue.	Miami	5:20 a.m.	8 hrs. 20 min.
Lv. Tue.	Miami	7:15 a.m.	
Ar. Tue.	Barranquilla	4:30 p.m.	9 hrs. 15 min.
Lv. Wed.	Barranquilla	5:45 a.m.	
Ar. Wed.	Guayaquil	5:15 p.m.	11 hrs. 30 min.
Lv. Thu.	Guayaquil	6:00 a.m.	
Ar. Thu.	Arica	6:25 p.m.	12 hrs. 25 min.
Lv. Fri.	Arica	8:00 a.m.	
Ar. Fri.	Santiago	2:50 p.m.	6 hrs. 50 min.
Lv. Sat.	Santiago	8:15 a.m.	
Ar. Sat.	Buenos Aires	2:45 p.m.	6 hrs. 30 min.

Total . . . . 54 hrs. 50 min.

[*N.B.*—These are the schedules in effect as of February 1940.—Ed.]

STEAMER ROUTES FROM NEW YORK AND
SAN FRANCISCO TO BUENOS AIRES

Travelers may leave New York every other Saturday throughout the year on steamers of the American Republics Line or sail on alternate Friday nights on steamers of the Furness Prince Line, proceeding down the eastern coast of the hemisphere to the Capital-Port of Argentina. The voyage usually consumes eighteen days.

Steamers of the Grace Line leave New York on Friday nights at weekly or fortnightly intervals, going through the Panama Canal to Valparaíso, Chile, a voyage consuming seventeen days.

A traveler desiring to embark at San Francisco will find occasional steamers—passenger, or freight with passenger accommodations—on which he may proceed to the Panama Canal, sailing thence on a Grace Line steamer for Valparaíso.

APPENDIX II

(*See Chapter II*)

TRAVEL AGENCIES

Thos. Cook & Son—Florida 602

Villalonga Express—R. S. Peña 560

Cordoba Turismo—San Martín 565

Mar del Plata—Maipú 470

Asociación Turismo Argentino—Cangallo 541

Exprinter—Pasaje Güemes

Dirección Provincial Turismo de Mendoza—Florida 762

Compañía Nacional de Turismo y Veraneantes—Cordoba 1758

Turismo a Tandil—Maipú 39

Bureau de Informes—Bartolomé Mitre 299

Appendix III

(*See Chapter II*)

"PERSONAL SERVICE"

"1. Shows the country intelligently by providing as hostesses and guides, women who 'belong' socially (thus having access anywhere), who know their country, the unknown places of interest as well as the known.

"2. Provides expert shoppers, knowing where to go for what and guaranteeing value and quality at the same time saving time and money. Fast service for hurried clients on deliveries.

"3. Provides competent secretaries and interpreters who are also capable of showing the city while they aid the traveler who is in Argentina on business as well as pleasure.

"4. Meets incoming travelers and provides competent care of children, as well as recommends doctors and dentists.

"5. Makes contacts for strangers and provides entertainment for the tourist without cards of introduction.

"6. Is a clearing house for apartments, houses, furniture and servants.

"7. Acts as bureau of information for the newcomer in Buenos Aires."

Also, to Americans of character, Personal Service can, by special arrangement secure cards to the American Club, where one finds an atmosphere provoking a nostalgia for home, and a restaurant where dishes "such as Mother used to make" are served at very reasonable prices. Commenting on the unique quality of the assistance rendered by this organization, the head of the leading tourist agency in Argentina stated recently, "Personal Service fills a want which it is practically impossible for the ordinary travel agency to supply, touching as it does the social side of the traveler's stay in a country."

It is therefore suggested to the new arrival who may be without letters of introduction and without friends to call Personal Service, telephone (between 10-12 and 2-6 p.m.) U.T. 33 Avenida 7541-7549); in the evening or on a holiday, U.T. 33 Avenida 5288, and put himself in the hands of this capable agency. The cable address is "PERSER."

APPENDIX IV

(*See Chapter V*)

HOTELS

Good hotels at moderate rates:

> NOGARO—Avenida Julio A. Roca 562
> SAVOY—Callao corner of Cangallo
> AVENIDA PALACE—Victoria 442
> CASTELAR—Avenida de Mayo 1152
> ROYAL—Lavalle 570
> GRAND—Florida 25

Hotels well-spoken of and with still lower rates:

> GRAN HOTEL ESPAÑA—Avenida de Mayo 964
> D'ARC HOTEL—Avenida de Mayo 984
> PHOENIX—San Martin 780

APPENDIX V

(See Chapter V)

WHERE TO LUNCH AND TEA AND DINE AND DANCE AND SUP

First of all must be mentioned the cuisine and dance facilities in some of the leading hotels:

The Plaza Hotel Grill Room (not to be confused with the regular dining room, on another floor) is probably the most popular restaurant with Buenos Aires society. It is situated below the street level in a new section of the hotel, and embraces the smart cocktail lounge, the tap-room where young bloods of the town meet, and the grill itself. Air-conditioning makes it especially comfortable in hot weather. No dish stands out above others, the menu being catholic, and the cooking of a high order. One or two wines of merit can be found in the cellar, although at high prices; however the choice is perhaps naturally below that offered by a European sommelier.

The Alvear Palace Hotel.—In winter, say from April to November, there is a restaurant night-club attached to the hotel, which is entered from Calle Posadas; last year this was known as *Le Tourbillon*. The interior which is in pleasing rococo style was designed by the architect who collaborated in drawing the plans of the delightful Llao-Llao hotel on Lago Nahuel Huapí in the far South. Here one may dine or sup to the music of a jazz band playing acceptable American music, or an Argentine tango orchestra, or a Cuban rumba band; the latter also plays Brazilian zambas and maxixe with fair success. The floor space is limited following the Paris tradition. This place is distinctly smart and elaborate dinners are given there.

In the summer *Le Tourbillon* closes, and dining and dancing are transferred to the roof of the hotel where there are broad terraces offering lovely views of the city. One or more of the winter orchestras may leave to take seasonal positions in Montevideo, Mar del Plata, or other resorts but these are adequately replaced by other bands of the same type. Incidentally, the roof is a pleasant and popular place for luncheon.

The City Hotel, previously mentioned, may be also visited, especially for those who are attracted by a good dance orchestra.

Turning now to restaurants the following may be mentioned:

El Gran Restaurant Corrientes, or "Corrientes Chicken House," as it is more familiarly known, is at No. 1772 Corrientes. (The word "chicken" as used here is to be taken in its usual and literal sense.) There are two entrances, the one nearer Callao being to the restaurant proper and the other to a large section divided into curtained booths on the order of an American Pullman car. "The Chicken House" is an old favorite of the public and while its mirrored walls and old-fashioned decorations give it an out-of-date look compared with the modern Plaza Grill, the Continental Hotel dining room, and other smart restaurants, its kitchen appears to have maintained its traditional excellence. Chicken is of course the dish of the house and is served in many ways with equal success.

Loprete, in Presidente Luis Saenz Peña No. 749, is an old-fashioned Italian restaurant, well known for its canelloni, a type of meat or chicken-liver paste, with a cream sauce. Its decorations suggest those of "The Chicken House."

Los Patitos, situated opposite the fish market at No. 263 Carabelas, is a small, simple eating house, specializing on "Vica," or milk-fed duck, and crêpes Suzette, both of which are culinary masterpieces that make the place justly celebrated among gourmets. The location and modest appearance of Los Patitos should not be allowed to discourage the visitor, for it is a quite suitable place for dining.

El Odeon, Esmeralda 355, is another old-style Buenos Aires restaurant, not much to look at from modern standards but possessing a regular clientèle that appreciates its good food. While it has no specialties like Los Patitos, its fish dishes, such as snails, shrimps, and oysters, are known for their excellence.

La Cabaña, situated at Entre Rios 436, is probably the best known "criollo," or "native," restaurant in Buenos Aires. It preserves in its decorations, which include a busy grill and spit just inside the entrance, and a part of its cellar on shelves lining the walls of its three rooms, the atmosphere of an old-time tavern, as well as this can be combined with efficient, modern service and cleanliness. While it serves food of all kinds, including oysters and snails, its great specialties are meat dishes, brought to the table on small, deliciously smoking charcoal braziers. Chilled beef, and Parrilladas, the latter a mixed grill of meat cuts, sausages, chinchulines, are the plates that have made La Cabaña famous, yet a special word must be said of the grilled boned chicken and of the steaks served, the latter of the finest quality of the finest Argentine beef, which literally melt in one's mouth. I remember protesting against the portions served me as being enough for several persons, and finding that I had eaten it all and was ready for more. The great Erasmus once in an expansive mood and on Friday gave vent to his intense dislike of fish and every variety of sea-food, remarking that while his heart was Catholic his stomach was Lutheran. In general this humanist would have found himself happy in gathering around the mahogany tree of mine host of La Cabaña. "The sauce of the House" is a combination, not too hot, of meat gravy, sliced olives, pepper seeds, and condiments of various sorts; it should not be neglected! A bottle of it will be usually found on each table; if you don't see it, ask for it! It is said that the proprietor maintains his own farm for eggs, sheep, beef, chickens, etc., which may explain in part the modest prices which are charged.

The following menus of a "criollo" dinner, which may be ordered in La Cabaña with the certainty that it will be well cooked and served, has been given me by a discriminating friend:

THREE TYPICALLY ARGENTINE MENUS

Salpicon de Ternera, Criolla	(Salmagundi of veal)
Empanadas Salteñas	(Salta meat pies)
Locro Tucumana	(Tucuman Stew)
Achuras a la Parrilla	(Grilled Tidbits)
Ensalada Mixta	(Mixed Salad)
Salsa Criolla	(Creole Sauce)
Alfajores Cordobeses	(Córdoba Pastry)
Chirimoya	(Cherimoya—tropical fruit)

Asado con cuero	(Meat barbecued in the hide)
Humita en Chala	(Mashed corn, dressed and baked in the husk)
Carbonada Criolla	(Meat Stew with Rice and Fruit)
Cordero al Asador	(Lamb roasted on a spit)
Ensalada Surtida	(Mixed Salad)
Dulce de Zapallo	(Pumpkin Jam)
Maté Cocido	(Maté Tea)

Matambre Arrolado	(Stuffed meat, baked in a hole in the earth over slow fire)
Cazuela Mendocina	(Mendoza stew cooked in earthen pan)
Choclo Asado	(Roast Corn)
Parrillada Criolla	(Grilled mixture of sausage and specially tasty bits)
Ensalada Mixta	(Mixed Salad)
Mazamorra con leche	(Boiled corn with milk and sugar)
Maté Cocido	(Maté Tea)

Some folk after dining at La Cabaña return to the Avenida de Mayo to an amusing place called *La Querencia,* which is somewhat along the lines of a family beer garden. Here gaucho dancers, from the country, are to be seen in various native dances. Families sit on one side of the dance floor and unattached men on the other—the young bloods giving the señoritas the once, twice and thrice over and being carefully but unobtrusively checked up in turn. Here you may sip your coffee or guzzle your beer and in addition to the dancing hear local songs and also recitation of folk poems.

The Comega Club, a public restaurant atop the Comega Building at the corner of Leandro Alem and Corrientes, provides a beautiful view of the river and the city. It possesses a bar and cocktail lounge and serves a simple but good luncheon in the small restaurant. The price of the fixed menu is lower than in most of the other good-class restaurants in Buenos Aires. The visitor would do well to have a meal here and also on the roof of the Alvear Palace in order to gain an idea of the situation and extent of the city.

El Cantábrico, Corrientes 1776, is highly spoken of also for its skill in preparing and serving the langosta received by the day's Panagra 'plane from Chile.

O'Mar' o Surriento, Sarmiento 651, has an attractive grill near the entrance where one may choose his cut. This is another of the many Italian restaurants making a special appeal to the enormous Italian population of Buenos Aires. Its macaroni, minestrone alla Milanesa, and gnocchi, are recommended.

London Grill Pork Pie House, Reconquista 455, is situated in a street whose name recalls to the patriotic Argentine a crushing victory over invading British troops. This is a favorite eating house for both Americans and British and is favorably known for its grills and sea food.

"Night-spots" that should be mentioned are, beside Le Tour-billon and the Alvear Roof:

The Gong, at Libertad 743, a small, over-crowded, gay boîte where the grand-duchesses of Porteña society rub shoulders with equally chic and beautiful women of less established position.

The *Embassy,* Florída 841, an ordinary type of international night-club with two and sometimes three orchestras for tangos, jazz, rumbas, and maxixe.

L'Ermitage Russe, Tucumán 576, of the same general type as the Embassy.

In none of the above three is there a floor-show. Entertainment is provided in a number of cabarets by "hostesses;" Argentine ladies do not usually go to these resorts. Two of the better-class establishments of this sort are the *Ta-ba-ris,* an old-established place, and the *Novelty,* of more recent appearance. It seems to be permissible for foreign ladies to attend these cabarets with their escorts; as a matter of fact mixed groups of tourists are a regular sight in them.

El Tropezón, an unobtrusive all-night restaurant of the old-fashioned, many-mirrored type situated at Callao 248, just above the House of Congress, is recommended for midnight supper. Its creamed-onion soup, turkey ravioli, and frog-legs are among the most delicious dishes to be found in Buenos Aires.

Other restaurants which might be visited by the persistently curious traveler are:

The Jousten Hotel, at Corrientes 300, with a fine view of the city from the summer roof-garden.

Conte's, at Victoria 420, a famous rendezvous of yore and still famous for its food. It is renowned for a dish called "chicken of seven perfumes" which is of a succulence calculated to make a modern Dives give all his substance to obtain; here also a wonderful dessert, Conte's special, is prepared before your eyes, and served; its chicken dishes are equally delicious and devastating to the figure.

The Bauernschanke, or "Farm Yard," at Tucumán 133, with a German atmosphere; and

The *Munich,* on the Costanera, or water-front drive, where one may find dining comfort in summer on its open terrace.

"Dietze's," a little remote from the center and in the leafy suburb of Belgrano, at No. 2292 Echeverría; an open air beer garden, much frequented in summer. Good music may be heard, but there is no dancing.

Tea may be enjoyed to the accompaniment of music in either of the two *Copper Kettles*—one in Florída 681 and another in Lavalle 764; at *Harrods* in Florída, where an excellent luncheon may be also eaten; and at the *Comega Club,* previously mentioned.

One other restaurant must be mentioned; it is known as *El Pescadito* and is situated in a section of Buenos Aires called La Boca (the mouth), and indicates the entrance to the Riachuelo, or Little River, which flows through a part of Buenos Aires, and has been dredged to receive ocean-going vessels. This district would correspond to the lower West Side of New York, or the dock section of London. It is inhabited by folk in humble circumstances, employees of transportation companies, of the frigoríficos, etc.

This restaurant is famous for its *criollo* (old-fashioned Argentine) cooking, as tempered by Italian culinary art. Its specialty is bouillabaisse, as tempting and as fiery when it passes the lips as anything in France. The ingredients of this lordly dish are given by Thackeray:

> *This Bouillabaisse a noble dish is—*
> *A sort of soup, or broth, or brew,*
> *Or Hotchpotch of all sorts of fishes,*
> *That Greenwich never could outdo;*
> *Green herbs, red peppers, mussels, saffron,*
> *Soles, onions, garlic, roach, and dace;*
> *All these you eat at Terré's tavern*
> *In that one dish of Bouillabaisse.*

With this latter aside, it may be said in general that Buenos Aires though a great city, has as yet been lacking in public places of entertainment, such as night clubs and restaurants; remarkable development in this direction has however been noted in recent years. For an explanation of this previous lack it would probably be necessary to go into the organization of Argentine family life, under which its womenfolk are more sheltered than in other parts of the world. Likewise, a tendency toward modernization of this viewpoint may be the reason for the recent development remarked.

Forewarned is forearmed, and a word of caution should be uttered concerning the bills presented on leaving some of the more notorious night clubs. The proprietors of these are quite as, if not more, rapacious than any to be found in New York or Paris. And David Harum's cynical advice, never to give a sucker an even break, is carefully followed out. With these last words uttered for *acquit de conscience* I bring this section to an end.

APPENDIX VI

(*See Chapter V*)

ANTIQUE SHOPS

Lopez—Juncal 1052
Pardo—Sarmiento 531
Kerteux—Libertad 1249
Galerie d'Art—Santa Fé 879
The Old Curiosity Shop—Lavalle 612
Vilanova—Paraguay 1336
El Buda—Florída 599
Ad Insigni Aldi—Talcahuano 468

OLD BOOK SHOPS

La Facultad—Florída 359
El Ateneo—Florída 336
Viau & Co.—Florída 530 (Classic Works and
    Modern Books in fine bindings. Also
    Engravings and Works of Art. Art
    Gallery)
Espiasse—Santa Fé 1058
Palacio del Libro, Hachette S. A.—Maipú 49
Librería Americana—Corrientes 1301
Librería Moro—Corrientes 1340 (Second Hand
    Bookstore)
Librería Ameghino Helmann—Talcahuano 442

Appendix VII

(*See Chapter XVI*)

NOTES ON FISHING IN NAHUEL HUAPÍ

During November I spent three weeks fishing in some of the rivers in the Neuquén territory. The results have been set out in the notes which follow, in the hope that they may be of interest.

With the exception of the salmon at Traful and half a dozen rainbow trout which were taken on a fly, all the fish were caught on a spoon.

The weights were measured on a spring balance as soon as the fish were landed.

The salmon were all in good condition. Some of the trout were flabby, it being a little early in the season.

Rio Quilquihue

This river carries about the same volume of water as the Traful. The fall is greater and hence the current much faster.

Unlike the Traful there are practically no pools suitable for salmon. The banks of the upper reaches where the river leaves Lake Lolog are too thickly wooded to enable a fly to be used in comfort. The lower waters, however, above the confluence with the Chimehuin are ideal for fly fishing.

I had two and a half days fishing in this river and took out 17 rainbow trout weighing 27 lbs. ranging in size from 1 to 3½ lbs. I only caught 1 brook trout, which weighed 3 lbs.

Any point on the river can be reached in an hour from San Martín by motor car plus a short walk.

Rio Chimehuin

Where this river leaves Lake Huecheufen it is in size equal to the Traful. Heavy rapids alternate with deep pools affording conditions suitable for large fish. The banks are precipitous and covered with trees and scrub, making it difficult or impossible to fish in some of the pools.

The reach for a league above Junin flows through "Mallin" and appears to hold a lot of fish. The banks are flat, but covered with scrub.

After it has absorbed the Quilquihue the river suggests the Limay on a small scale, but with a more rapid current. The banks are free of trees and scrub and hence there are no impediments to casting. There is a great lack of deep pools.

There is a road parallel with the river over its whole course from Lake Huecheufen to the Sollon Cura. From San Martín to the nearest point takes one hour by car. The Lake can be reached in 2½ hours.

Fishing on 3 days I landed 19 rainbow trout, totalling 40 lbs. The individual weights being from 1¼ to 4¾ lbs. Two fish of over 4 lbs. each were caught near the lake. Two brook trout of ½ lb. and 2 lbs. were also taken.

Rio Collon Cura

A fast flowing river with the characteristics of and same volume of water as the Limay. The banks are low and clear of scrub; there are no impediments to casting. The river is two hours distance from San Martín.

On one day I fished about 3 miles of water from the "balsa" down stream. I landed 11 fish, 9 brook trout of 1 lb. to 2 lbs. weight and two rainbow of the same size, total weight 18 lbs.

On another day fishing above and below the "balsa" 4 rods

took 26 fish, weighing 50 lbs., 20 brook trout 1 to 3 lbs., 6 rainbow 2 to 3½ lbs., and a large-mouthed bass (trucha criolla) of 4 lbs. weight.

Rio Caleufu

A river larger than the Traful on the Gente Grande property. The banks are clear and free for casting. Except for the upper reaches the river is from one to two hours' distance from the main "estancia" house.

In company with others I fished the middle section. The take for four rods totalled 18 fish, all brook trout, weighing 31 lbs., ranging from ½ lb. to 3 lbs.

Rio Limay

From Nahuel Huapí where it leaves the lake down to Chacabuco "estancia" the river is clear, very fast and full of large eddies. These conditions seem to be unfavorable for fish. Below Chacabuco there are long smooth reaches which appear to carry a lot of fish. This part of the river has banks that are free of obstructions.

I fished the right bank from the Traful confluence for two kilometres up stream. I landed 2 brook trout and 5 small salmon, which were put back. The trout weighed 2 lbs. and 1½ lbs. The salmon about 1½ lbs. each.

Fishing at Paso Miranda, above and below the "balsa" on one afternoon I caught 2 brook trout and 5 salmon. One salmon weighed 5 lbs., the rest were small scaling 1½ lbs., the trout were 3¼ and 3 lbs., respectively. Weather hot and still.

Paso Miranda is an hour by car from Paso Flores "estancia" house.

At Paso Flores I had two days' fishing, during which I took a salmon of 8 lbs. The rest of the bag comprised 6 small salmon of about 1½ lbs., 7 brook trout of 1 to 3¼ lbs., and 2 "trucha criolla" of 2 and 3½ lbs. The total weight of fish being 35 lbs. The river was about a metre above normal summer level and somewhat turbid.

M.F.R.

Appendix VIII

(See Chapter XIX)

NOTES ON DORADO FISHING IN THE UPPER PARANÁ

I

Dorados generally begin to appear in the Upper Paraná about the middle of September and in my opinion the best time to take the trip is at the end of October and November. Summer months are very hot and unproductive. Some fishing is still done in March and April but dorados are less abundant and river conditions very changeable.

The depth of the river is a point of great importance: It is necessary that the rocks or reefs forming rapids be uncovered, because the dorados await their prey in the pools of quiet, smooth waters that precede rapids. In these pools are found the largest dorados, their heads downstream (contrary to what occurs with Salmonidae) and the smallest are found at the end of rapids waiting for tiny fish going upstream. The depth of the water is therefore an essential factor where successful fishing is concerned and before starting on a trip it is well to find out river conditions and probabilities.

II

Besides the airway which takes six hours to Posadas there are two other means of reaching the last Argentine city in the North West. One of them is the Mihanovich River Steamer line up to Corrientes, it being necessary at this latter place to tranship to other boats which can go through the famous "Salto Apipé" between Corrientes and Posadas. This trip lasts four days and proves interesting though somewhat monotonous owing to the slowness with which the panorama is displayed. The other means of transportation is the railway which starts from Lacroze station and then crosses the beautiful provinces of Entre Rios and Corrientes in a thirty-six hour journey.

At Posadas one finds one's self in a tropical clime, the streets and gardens show that reddish colored earth typical of Misiones and of Paraguay and tiled roofs give to the houses a colonial aspect which is quite attractive.

III

In order to go up the Upper Paraná it is necessary to hire a launch or to take the river steamer plying between Posadas-Iguazú or Guayra. The best steamer is that of the Mihanovich line, but its sailings do not coincide with every train arrival and it is advisable to be informed of its departures. There are also several boats of lesser importance, also much slower and much more uncomfortable, trading along the Upper Paraná. Once Posadas is left behind, contact with the rest of the world is lost and communication is possible only through radiotelegraphic stations at El Dorado, Puerto Aguirre, and the steamer Guayra which goes by once a week. Once in the Upper Paraná it is no longer possible to depend on time-tables for one is at the mercy of freight loadings and above all of fog which sometimes envelops the river making navigation impossible.

To hire a launch is undoubtedly more costly but it is almost indispensable in order to fish successfully and it enables one to try all the interesting waters to be found on the way.

At Posadas, launches with a cabin and beds can be hired, with a pilot, for between 60 and 100 pesos per day, fuel and food supplies to be provided by the hirer. The average speed of these launches is 20 Km. per hour, or 10 and 12 Km. going against the tide.

IV

Although dorados are found all along the Upper Paraná, one must reach the places where they are very numerous, that is, in the rapids. The first place, recommended by General Harrison, is opposite Posadas where certain islands form rapids, but these are not very interesting.

At "Mineral" about one hundred kilometres from Posadas one begins to find more productive waters. Puerto Mineral belongs to the firm Yerbatera Martin & Cia. Going towards the north a few good places are to be found but one of the best regions is situated between the Paraná River and the northern part of the Caraguatay island along a stretch of about 20 Km. where many excellent rapids are found, particularly the famous shoal "Mboy-Mbossu." On the Argentine side are the estate of Messrs. Echague and Avellaneda and the residence of Engineer Carlos Benson, expert amateur, whose counsel will be very valuable. Not far from there is the Port of the Monte Carlo Colony where all necessary supplies may be obtained. Further up towards the north, rapids are found opposite the Port of El Dorado and the mouths of the Rivers Piray Guazú and Piray Mini. The island of Pareja also forms interesting rapids. A short distance from this place lies Puerto Pinares where there is a rather comfortable hotel which attends to the needs of the El Dorado Colony.

Beyond Port Delicia there is a region which is almost as good as that of Mboy-Mbossu, called Toro-Cua, and further up the shoal named Ita-Pité, the island of Paranambú and the rapids and also the mouth of the Uruguay River near Puerto Bemberg.

I am not acquainted with the river going upstream from the standpoint of fishing; however, I have seen rapids which seemed favorable and I was informed that the Guayra is a very interesting river especially beyond the rapids. Any information on this region can be obtained from the Maté Larangeira Co.

V

The river is wide and rapids are far apart, the current very strong and one cannot handle a rowboat very easily; it is advisable to get a motor-boat or carry an out-board, in which case a good supply of spare parts ought to be obtained because, when close to the rocks, the screw propeller knocks against them and something almost always gets broken. The boat must be solid and stable in order to stand the waves, because if it is dragged it may easily turn over upon bumping against a rock.

The best way to travel along the river is to tie a boat to another; greater stability is thus provided and passage through certain spots is made possible where it would be unwise with only one boat. But even so, care should be taken to avoid whirlpools which are extremely dangerous in the Upper Paraná, because they are very large and have caused the loss of numerous boats.

It is generally impossible to approach rapids and manage to pass between them with launches hired at Posadas because they are too large and it would be useless to try trolling properly with them.

VI

In October the days in the Upper Paraná are hot but the nights are usually cool and sometimes cold. During the day while fishing it is well to wear a closely woven linen coat to protect one's self from the voraciousness of mosquitoes and above all from the Mbariguí.

The Mbariguí is a very tiny insect resembling the "polvorín" whose bite causes an unbearable sensation, but after a time one seems to become more or less immune to it. Mosquitoes and Mbariguí are annoying almost exclusively when fishing near the river or when crossing damp parts of the woods. The use of veils while fishing is uncomfortable and makes one feel hotter. To protect one's self from the insects, a good remedy is to pour a few drops of citronella on a handkerchief around the neck and rub one's face and hands with Pond's cream "No-Mo." This is by no means an unfailing method and it would be well to have two good remedies at hand: Gibson's Camfofenil and Sambuck cream.

VII

The most appropriate rod for fishing dorados is the spinning rod for pike or salmon. A good reel will be necessary to make the casts as long as possible, for when a dorado thrusts at the spoon it means hard work.

Some 150 metres of yarn will be necessary to be entirely at ease, with a resistance of about 30 lbs. The average weight of dorados is generally between 20 and 25 lbs., but some are caught which weigh between 30 and 40 lbs. Waterproof or coated yarn is not recommendable because the gummy mixture melts in the heat and makes casts difficult or impossible. It is also advisable to take several additional spools for the line may easily catch in the rocks or be cut by a dorado.

The most effective spoons are the largest and the most brilliant, and white metal or nickel-plated ones are preferable to the copper colored. The Pflueger No. 7 spoon, the largest, meets these requirements and has the advantage of having a fixed hook so

To Armistead L. Bradford, Ricardo Diaz-Herrera and William W. Copeland, Esquires, for reading my manuscript and for many notes and helpful suggestions.

To Edmund B. Besselievre, Esq., for a number of the photographs which illustrate this book.

To Philip B. Massey, Esq., for notes on Hunting and Fishing.

To the members of the Staffs of the Embassy and Consulate General, for much and constant help, and

To my wife, for her patience!

Index

Index